Thomas

Mann:

Profile

and

Perspectives

Studies in

Language

and

Literature

CONSULTING EDITOR
HASKELL M. BLOCK
Brooklyn College of
The City University of New York

Thomas Mann: Profile and Perspectives

WITH TWO UNPUBLISHED LETTERS AND A
CHRONOLOGICAL LIST OF IMPORTANT EVENTS

ANDRÉ VON GRONICKA

University of Pennsylvania

RANDOM HOUSE *New York*

Acknowledgments for permission to translate and/or quote from copyrighted material are gratefully extended to the following authors, publishers, and agents.

Katharina Mann for *Thomas Mann: Gesammelte Werke in zwölf Bänden*, edited by Hans Bürgin. Copyright © 1960 by S. Fischer Verlag, Frankfurt am Main.

Katharina Mann and S. Fischer Verlag for *Thomas Mann: Gesammelte Briefe* (Vol. 1, 2, and 3), edited by Erika Mann. Copyright © 1961 by S. Fischer Verlag, Frankfurt am Main.

Alfred A. Knopf for *Death in Venice*, by Thomas Mann, translated by H. T. Lowe-Porter. Copyright © 1930 by Alfred A. Knopf, New York.

Germanic Review for "Myth plus Psychology: a Stylistic Analysis of Thomas Mann's *Death in Venice*." Copyright © 1956 by Columbia University Press. For "Thomas Mann in Russia." Copyright © 1948 by Columbia University Press. For "Thomas Mann's *Doctor Faustus*. Prolegomena to an Interpretation." Copyright © by Columbia University Press.

To
Andrea

Hier ist ein Mensch, höchst mangelhaft:
Voll gross und kleiner Leidenschaft,
Ehrgeizig, eitel, liebegierig,
Verletzlich, eifersüchtig, schwierig,
Unfriedsam, masslos, ohne Halt,
Bald überstolz und elend bald,
Naiv und fünfmal durchgesiebt,
Weltflüchtig und doch weltverliebt,
Sehnsüchtig, schwach, ein Rohr im Wind,
Halb seherisch, halb blöd und blind,
Ein Kind, ein Narr, ein Dichter schier,
Schmerzlich verstrickt in Will' und Wahn,
Doch mit dem Vorzug, dass er *Dir*
Vom ganzen Herzen zugetan!

Meinem lieben Paul Ehrenberg
München, Juni 1903

THOMAS MANN

*Here is a man most imperfect: full of great and small passions,
ambitious, vain, thirsting for love, fragile, jealous, difficult,
restless, excessive, without hold, now overbearing, now miserable,
naïve and overly refined, fleeing the world while yet in love
with it, full of longing, weak, a blade in the wind, half clairvoyant,
half dumb and blind, a child, a fool, a poet, yet painfully
entwined in will and illusion, but endowed with the one virtue
of being yours with all his heart.*

Thomas Mann in a letter to Paul Ehrenberg,
Munich, June 1903.

PREFACE

The great amount of interpretative work on Thomas Mann that is now before us can generally be divided into two categories. There are the detailed, often highly technical studies written for the specialists on the one hand and the numerous efforts to introduce the general reader to the artist and his work on the other. I attempt to steer a middle course, hoping to offer some new insights to the specialists while helping the general reader to orient himself in Thomas Mann's vast and complex world.

In keeping with this purpose of the book, I focus attention on central themes—such as "mediation," "humanism," "myth plus psychology," among others—and trace these through Mann's great novels, novellas, and essays, thus opening up important ideational "perspectives." I examine the chief devices of style used and developed by the poet—the leitmotif, parody, and montage-technique and try to establish the special character of Mann's irony, his humor, and the musical quality of his prose.

Since much biographical material is still inaccessible,* I

* Thomas Mann's diaries are sealed in accordance with his will until 1975. A significant part of his correspondence has not yet been made public.

have not attempted a biographical account, but rather have sought to render the salient features of the man and the artist, to draw his "profile." A chronological listing of important events in Mann's long and active life is provided in Appendix II.

In my efforts I was helped, first and foremost, by Mann himself. I let him speak to us from the pages of his works and letters often and at length. Thus, we can follow in intimate detail the development of Mann's thought on the social and political problems of the day. We can join the poet in his untiring probings of the enigma posed by art and the artist and can enjoy insights that could not possibly be gained without his guidance.

All references to Mann's works were made to Hans Bürgin (ed.), *Thomas Mann: Gesammelte Werke in zwölf Bänden* (Frankfurt am Main: S. Fischer Verlag, 1960). Thomas Mann's letters were quoted with their dates of writing from Erika Mann (ed.), *Thomas Mann: Gesammelte Briefe*, 3 Vols. (Frankfurt am Main: S. Fischer Verlag, 1961–1965). Two letters by Thomas Mann to the author of this study are published for the first time in Appendix 1. For quotations from *Death in Venice*, Mrs. H. T. Lowe-Porter's translation was used. All other quotations are given in my translation.

I have drawn freely on the great body of secondary sources. To acknowledge all the assistance obtained from Mann scholars individually would be a sheer impossibility. Some contributions are singled out in the text, others are listed in the bibliographies. My sincere appreciation goes out to all the industrious, ingenious, and perceptive researchers who have done so much to illumine Mann's life and work.

Special gratitude is due to the institutions that have generously supported the author's labors—to the Guggenheim and the Social Science Research Foundations, to the American Council of Learned Societies, and to the Fulbright Commission. Even though their grants over the years were not made specifically for this project, they provided the precious opportunity for travel, research, and contemplation uninterrupted by the chores and distractions of professional routine.

Grateful mention must also be made of the liberal scholarly-leave policy of the University of Pennsylvania without which this work would still be far from completed.

It is a pleasure to acknowledge the special help that my colleagues and good friends, Professors Adolf Klarmann and Heinz Moenkemeyer, rendered with their sensitive and knowledgeable reactions to portions of the manuscript. Nor could I have succeeded in my efforts without the constant encouragement, aid and comfort offered by my wife. To her my most heartfelt thanks, and thanks also to my daughter Andrea, who subjected the manuscript to a thorough critical reading and offered delightfully uninhibited comments and suggestions.

CONTENTS

Thomas

Mann:

Profile

and

Perspectives

The Artist's Enigma

Any attempt to illuminate an artist's personality, to trace what might best be called his inner biography, must, by its very nature, remain an illusive undertaking. However, in our effort we enjoy a significant advantage since we are helped by Thomas Mann himself, by the poet's penchant for autobiography, overt and covert. We accept his guidance in full awareness of his penchant for ambiguity and ambivalence.

Almost obsessively, Mann delved to the roots of his personality and tried to solve the challenging enigmas of the artist and of art. He has traced and retraced his family tree to the solid burghers of Nuremberg and Switzerland, to the Manns and the Martys on his father's side, and to the exotic land of South America, to Brazil, where his mother Julia da Silva-Bruhns was born, the daughter of a German planter-pioneer father and a Creole mother of Portuguese-Indian ancestry. To this unusual mixture of blood Mann ascribed special significance, recognizing in it an important source of his make-up as man and artist. He liked to apply Goethe's famous quatrain to himself, not without some prideful satisfaction cloaked in playful irony:

Vom Vater hab' ich die Statur
Des Lebens ernstes Führen
Vom Mütterchen die Frohnatur
Die Lust zum Fabulieren.

In his "Lebensabriss" ("A Sketch of my Life"), Mann wrote:

Whenever I search for the source of my natural bents and talents, I am reminded of Goethe's famous little verse and am led to the conclusion that I too inherited "the serious conduct of my life" from my father, and from my mother, "the happy constitution," the touch of the artist, "the joy in the spinning-out-of-tales," this term taken in its broadest possible meaning.[1]

As Thomas Mann looked back over the years, he recalled how frequently he had been made to realize that it was his father's personality which had determined the pattern of his life: "How often in my life did I literally *catch myself* realizing with a smile that, after all, it was the personality of my departed father who, as a secret exemplar and model, determined all my actions [mein Tun und Lassen]." [2] He recognized himself to be the child and grandchild of a German bourgeois culture—a typical product of the city—of the free patrician cities, Lübeck and Nuremberg. "Were not my forebears artisans of Nuremberg," he asks with an evident touch of pride, "were they not men of that particular stamp and make-up whom Germany sent to all the corners of the world, to the far reaches of the East, in sign and token of the fact that it was an urban land, a land of cities?" [3]

Provenience, upbringing, and example had unquestionably shaped and molded Mann's personality. His forebears' uprightness, their respectability, their strict sense of order and responsibility, their unwavering conscientiousness and perseverance in the performance of duties large and small—all those solid bourgeois virtues, which found their brilliant culmination in Senator Thomas Mann, the poet's father, had left their indelible imprint on the boy and had remained influential throughout his life. And so did his mother's affinity for the world of art, her imaginative, often extravagant spirit and lively temperament, sensibilities atypical of the sphere of burgher-probity into which she married. This twofold heritage accentuated, perhaps even initiated the burgher-artist conflict dominant in Mann's early life and work. And yet we need but think of the other two sons in the Mann family, Heinrich and Victor, poles apart in their sensibilities and predilections and both so different from their brother Thomas, to lose faith in parentage and tutelage as master keys to the mystery that is a poet's personality.

More light is shed upon this mystery by Mann's frequent moments of introspection, which reached below the level of parentage and early training to the enigmatical depths of being. In a revealing essay, "Süsser Schlaf" ("Sleep, Sweet Sleep"),[4] Mann confided that he had always felt in himself the spirit of India—"much of a heavy and indolent yearning after that form or rather non-form of perfection which is called Nirvana." [5] And he goes on to confess that, though an artist and therefore dedicated to flawless form, he yet had always harbored in himself the very unartistic affinity for eternity, which expressed itself as "an antipathy for articulation [Gliederung] and proportion [Mass]." [6] Mann continues this revealing self-analysis to stress that there were, at the same time, strong corrective drives in him which in their totality constitute what he has called the morality of the artist. "What is this morality of the artist?" he asks and answers, "It is the power of concentration, of an egocentric concentration, it is that strength which decides to embrace form, shape, limitation, and corporeality and to disavow a freedom that is limitless, to reject a slumbering and hovering in the infinitude of inarticulate emotions—it is, in a word, the will for creative labor [der Wille zum Werk]." [7] Here indeed we feel close to the very source of Mann's genius: his longing for Nirvana, for self-surrender to the infinite, which yet is checked and made productive by the will to work—by the artist's urge to transmute the shapeless chaos of impressions and emotions through a tensely willed mastery over self and matter into the articulation and proportion of a work of art.[8]

Thomas Mann has given artistic expression to these ambivalent drives in their interaction upon the artist's personality in his masterful novella, *Tod in Venedig* (*Death in
Venice*). Here he personified, literally bodied forth, the seemingly contradictory impulses that he had experienced in their
effect on himself. Their incarnation is the figure of Tadzio in
his influence on the poet Gustav von Aschenbach. Tadzio is
the manifestation in palpable form of the poet's "morality,"
of his "will to work" as well as of his yearning for Nirvana.
Tadzio, that paragon of Apollonian beauty, sparks the poet's
desire to form and shape, to write in his inspiring presence.
Yet Tadzio is also Aschenbach's tempter to lassitude and to
that blissful "hovering in the infinitude of inarticulate emotions." As a Hermes figure he is the poet's summoner to self-
oblivion in the bliss of Nirvana, to the land of the dead, to
"an immensity of richest expectation." [9]

Thomas Mann has subtly reinforced Tadzio's ambivalent
role in Aschenbach's life by closely associating his figure with
the motif of the sea, with that symbol of vastness, of formlessness, of the void, and of death. Repeatedly he describes
Tadzio as approaching the shore or leaving it or standing or
walking at the edge of the sea, his figure a well-defined verti-
cal against the sea's limitless horizontal:

As he [Aschenbach] sat there dreaming thus, deep, deep into the
void, suddenly the margin line of the shore was cut by a human
form. He gathered up his gaze and withdrew it from the illimit-
able, and lo, it was the lovely boy who crossed his vision coming
from the left along the sand. (31)*

Or again:

A wanton sun showered splendor on him [Tadzio], and the
noble distances [die erhabene Tiefsicht] *of the sea formed the
background which set off his figure. . . . There he stood at the
water's edge, alone*, removed from his family, quite close to

---

* Parenthetical page numbers of the following extracts refer to *Death in
Venice and Seven Other Stories*, trans. H. T. Lowe-Porter (New York:
Knopf, 1930).

Aschenbach, *stood there erect*, his hands clasped at the back of his neck, rocking slowly on the balls of his feet, and dreamed away into blue space while little waves ran up and bathed his toes. The ringlets of honey-colored hair clung to his temples and neck, the fine down along the upper vertebrae was yellow in the sunlight; the thin envelope of flesh covering the torso betrayed the delicate outlines of the ribs and the symmetric conformation of his chest. His armpits were still as smooth as a statue's, smooth the glistening hollows back of his knees, where the blue network of veins suggested that this body was formed of some stuff more transparent than mere flesh. (43–44. Italics mine.)

With Mann, such inspired description of the physical always carried spiritual implications and was charged with symbolic significance. Aschenbach's rapturous contemplation of the Apollonian perfection of Tadzio's body as it stands poised, significantly, against the noble distances of the sea must be recognized in its function as metaphor of the ineffable twofold source of Aschenbach's creative inspiration: The flawless perfection of the youth's body which rouses his desire to emulate its "articulation and proportion [Gliederung und Mass]" in a work of art of his creation, together with the limitless vastness of the sea that draws Aschenbach's gaze "deep, deep into the void," entices him into the alluring vagueness beyond all form and measure, there to "hover and weave in the infinite." It is in moments of such enigmatical interaction between the urgent impulse for the utmost creative concentration and the enticement to languorous, irresponsible surrender to the voluptuous bliss of inarticulate emotion that the miracle of art is consummated and Aschenbach's spirit lifted to a never-before-experienced pitch of inspiration. This climax is at once apogee of Aschenbach's creativeness and his incipient deterioration into sensuous excess and final collapse:

Mirror and image! His [Aschenbach's] eyes took in the proud bearing of that figure there at the blue water's edge; with an outburst of rapture he told himself that what he saw was beauty's very essence; form as divine thought, the single and pure perfection which resides in the mind, of which an image and likeness, rare and holy, was here raised up for adoration. This was very frenzy—and without a scruple, nay, eagerly, the aging artist bade it come. His mind was in travail, his whole mental background in a state of flux. Memory flung up in him the primordial thoughts which are youth's inheritance, but which with him had remained latent, never leaping up into a blaze. (44)

This portrayal of Aschenbach's climacteric is preceded by another highly significant description of the artist. Aschenbach had observed Tadzio from the window of the hotel as the boy was returning from the shore, and suddenly he had felt the first surge of rapture for the beautiful youth. He sat quite still, unseen in his "lofty place":

His features were alive with emotion, his eyebrows lifted, and a smile, alert, inquiring, spirited, tensed his mouth. Then he raised his head, and with both hands hanging relaxed over the armrest of his easychair, he described a slow motion, palms outward, a lifting and turning movement, as though to indicate a wide embrace. It was a gesture of welcome, of calm and deliberate acceptance. (40)

This description of Aschenbach calls to mind, with that sudden start of recognition produced by Mann's leitmotifs, an earlier account of Aschenbach by a perceptive observer. There the clenched fist was symbolic of the writer's excessive drive for accomplishment—of his stern discipline and rigid self-control, which finally ended in his sterility as a creative artist:

"You see," that observer had said, "Aschenbach has always lived like this"—here the speaker closed the fingers of his left hand to a fist—"never like this"—and he let his open hand hang relaxed from the armrest of his chair. (9)

Now for the first time in his life, under the influence of the waking passion for the beautiful youth, Aschenbach does let his relaxed hand hang comfortably from the chair's armrest. He opens his clenched fist into "a gesture of welcome, of calm and deliberate acceptance." Welcome for whom? Acceptance of what? Of life, love, and the inspiration that the poet feels wondrously kindled in his heart. The sterility that had been clamped on his mind and feelings by an all too insistent, all too rigid and systematic, consciously controlled effort to get on with the work is now magically released; his overstrained mind, his barren emotions are recharged with new vigor for the creative act. "Who shall unriddle the enigma of the artist's nature? Who understands that mingling of discipline and license in which it stands so deeply rooted?" (47) At this supreme creative moment, Aschenbach

thrilled with power to command and wield a thought that throbbed with emotion, an emotion as precise and concentrated as thought. . . . He felt the sudden desire to write. He would write in Tadzio's presence. This lad should be his model, his style should follow the lines of his figure that to him seemed divine. . . . Never had the pride of the word been so sweet to him, never had he known so well that Eros is in the word, as in those perilous and precious hours. (46)

We would not force Mann's self-identification with Aschenbach and with his artistry—though Mann has more than once acknowledged a significant degree of such identification.[10] Yet we would submit that Aschenbach's clenched fist is a most effective symbol of Mann's categorical imperative to achievement, and Aschenbach's opening gesture the symbol of Mann's willing surrender to the mystery of inspiration, which could not be commanded or forced by an act of will, but could only be welcomed and received as a gift divine. We would further claim that Aschenbach's highest joy is Mann's very own: the artist's supreme fulfillment when in his creation thought is wholly merged with feeling and feeling is endowed with the precision and clarity of thought. With Aschenbach this state of "sober passion [nüchterne Leidenschaft]," [11] this infinitely delicate balance and tension between the will to work and the passive open receptiveness to inspiration, this fertile interaction of the androgynous elements in the artist's nature, is but a fleeting moment. He is unable to sustain that creative tension, cannot maintain himself at that pitch of perfection; soon he is plunged into the excess of Dionysiac passions that engulf him in the promiscuous Bacchanalia of his dream. Tadzio's name echoes and reechoes through that fateful dream in the cry of the frenzied revellers, a cry "composed of soft consonants with a long-drawn *u*-sound at the end,"* a cry that draws Aschenbach irresistibly into total self-surrender to "the stranger god," until "in his very soul he tastes the bestial degradation of his fall." (67–68) This dream breaks the resistance of Aschenbach's spirit. "It passed him through and left him, left the whole cultural structure of a lifetime trampled on, ravaged, and destroyed." (67) Aschenbach permits himself to sink into lasciviousness, licentiousness, sickness, and death.

Thomas Mann in contrast, had the strength to maintain himself in "his lofty place," to sustain that precarious balance and awful tension; he did not sink into the abyss of lassitude and license. But neither was he insensitive to the dangers besetting the path of the artist. He was conscious of the awful threat. The words he has his dying poet utter aim beyond the person of Aschenbach; they are couched in the form of maxims and characterize the artist's problematical quest for the ideals of truth and beauty by way of the senses with Eros an inescapable companion and a questionable guide:

For you must know that we poets cannot walk the way of beauty without Eros as our companion and peremptory guide. We may be heroic after our fashion, disciplined warriors of our craft, yet we are all like women, for we exult in passion, and love is still our desire—our craving and our shame. (72)

* The interlinking of Tadzio's name with the bacchantic cry is carefully prepared by Mann. Aschenbach, when he first hears the name "can make out nothing more exact than two musical syllables, something like Adgio—or, oftener still, Adjiu, *with a long-drawn-out u at the end*. He liked the melodious sound and found it fitting and said it over to himself a few times." (32. Italics mine.) We recognize the preparation as being both stylistic (leitmotif) and psychological ("found it fitting and said it over to himself a few times.")

And he addresses a question to little Phaidros, and through him to us, leaving the decision to our judgment:

But now tell me, my dear boy, do you believe that such a man can ever attain wisdom and true manly worth, for whom the path to the spirit must lead through the senses? Or do you rather think —for I leave the decision to you—that it is a path of perilous sweetness, a way of transgression, and must surely lead him who walks it astray? (72)

Aschenbach, for his part, in explanation and defense of his own tragic downfall, argues the artist's inescapable doom:

Do you now understand that we poets cannot possibly be wise, that we can never attain to dignity? That we must inescapably lose our way and go astray, that we shall forever remain dissolute and adventurers in the realm of the emotions? (72)

Are we to take this calamitous prognosis of the artist's fate for Mann's final judgment? Undoubtedly it reflects his awareness of the artist's tragically problematical nature, an awareness that was conditioned by Nietzsche's skeptical view. This skepticism was to be, in the main, characteristic for the pre-*Zauberberg* (*The Magic Mountain*) phase in Mann's development, subsequently to be modified and moderated as we shall have occasion to show. This theme finds its most pessimistic articulation and its culmination in *Death in Venice*.

Mann was aware of this culmination and deeply troubled. He recognized it for what it was—a threat to his very existence as an artist. He was tortured by the question whether one could keep one's productivity alive and broaden one's intellectual horizons so as to meet the challenge of a new era, or whether one would be forced to repeat oneself or to fall silent. He knew that with this novella he had reached, along that particular line of his development, a *ne plus ultra*, and in moments of depression he was convinced that his career had come to its inescapable end.

We find these fears poignantly expressed in Mann's lecture "On Myself," delivered to the students of Princeton University in 1940. Here, in retrospect from the vantage point of crisis surmounted, he points to *Death in Venice* as a climax. This novella, he told the students,

represented a final and most extreme effort. In its content and form this work was the most sharply contoured, the most concentrated formulation of the problematical nature of decadence and of the [danger-beset] artist, which had been the leading theme of my production ever since the *Buddenbrooks*. . . . On the personal path which led me to *Death in Venice* there was no possibility of progress and transcending [gab es kein Weiter, kein Darüber-Hinaus], and I could fully sympathize with those friends of my work who expressed their concern and posed the question of how I could possibly carry on.[12]

Thomas Mann, we know, did find a way of carrying on. His preoccupation with the artist's enigma, though never completely resolved, was transformed and transcended into a far more comprehensive quest after the meaning of life. As *Der Zauberberg* (*The Magic Mountain*) grew far beyond the originally planned novella—a humorous companion piece to *Death in Venice*—it came to encompass ever widening circles of thought and experience. Hans Castorp's motto *Placet experiri*—to experiment with all the phases and modes of existence—was Mann's own. Whatever the loss in introspective inwardness, in the lyrical mood (of *Tonio Kröger*, for instance), it was more than made up by a newly gained limpidness of style, by gaiety and humor, by an ironic mastery over matter and by an openness toward the world [Weltoffenheit] that marked the mature artist. A thoroughly modern novel came into being, embracing contemporaneity in all its kaleidoscopic facets.

And then, with the *Joseph* tetralogy, came Mann's turn to the world of myth and legend. The poet made his descent into the "bottomless well of the past," from there to trace the imposing spiral of man's ascent from its mythical childhood in Joseph the Narcissus to his socially conscious maturity in Joseph the Provider.

Mann's will to work never flagged; if anything, it grew more intense with the years, searching out, assimilating, and shaping into the stuff of art ever vaster reaches of contemporary life, history, and myth. Mann never wavered in his determination to get on with his life's work. He remained forever faithful to the categorical imperative of perseverance. Still, he was conscious of a great malaise. He knew that a central, overriding problem remained to be constantly dealt with. He realized that, at bottom, it was not a question of *how much* material was gathered or how much world was encompassed; the basic question facing the modern artist was *how* to accomplish the transmutation of this material into a viable, meaningful, living work of art. The problem of the artist who faces the growing difficulty of original artistic production in times of cultural decay and stagnation, deeply troubled Thomas Mann. Of course, he was not alone with this awareness and profound concern, but in the perceptiveness, profundity, and dramatic intensity with which he posed the problem and offered his solution, he had few peers. He did this with every one of his mature creations, beginning with *The Magic Mountain;* but in none did he do it more perceptively, more subtly, with greater intensity and personal commitment than in his last great finished novel, *Doktor Faustus, Das Leben des deutschen Tonsetzers Adrian Leverkühn, erzählt von einem Freunde;* (*Doctor Faustus. The Life of the German Composer Adrian Leverkühn as Told by a Friend*).

Adrian Leverkühn is the archetypal artist-born-late, the artist *in extremis*. His haughty, ever critical mind, excessive sophistication, self-conscious insistence on perfection—all these characteristics arrest his spontaneity and threaten him with total stagnation of his productivity:

For with every work which the artist puts behind him, he complicates his life and, finally, destroys it altogether. It is his self-indulgence with the extraordinary that spoils his taste for all that has been or could ever be accomplished. This self-indulgence is sure to drive him, ultimately, to the completely unachievable and, in the end, seal his fate in total derangement and disintegration.[13]

Adrian looks back upon his accomplishments with hypercritical disapproval, even with disgust. The vast accumulation of man's cultural heritage is for him no longer the precious source of uplift and inspiration. It weighs down upon him as a heap of lifeless stuff, utterly used up, a veritable blight on his creative spirit. How to escape the fate of being an epigon, how to achieve the breakthrough into a new innocence, how to cast off cold ratiocination and regain emotional freedom and intensity, these are the quandaries that torture the modern artist as the ultimate problem:

In the final analysis there is but *one* problem in this world and it has this name: How does one achieve the breakthrough? How does one escape into freedom? How does one burst the chrysalis and become a butterfly? The total human situation is conditioned by this question.[14]

Mann's fictional answer is pessimistic in the extreme: Adrian enters the pact with the devil, surrenders his soul in payment for an inspirational breakthrough by way of euphoric uplift and demonic exultation, only to be plunged by the evil one into insanity and death. Yet, embedded in this tragic fictional answer is another answer by our poet, a complex aesthetic and philosophical solution to the modern artist's dilemma. Its effectiveness is vindicated by the emotional and intellectual impact upon the readers of the work that gives it artistic expression and is, at the same time, its product.

What is this solution? Mann called it a miracle, the "miracle of a dialectical process by means of which the strictest formalism is changed into the free language of emotion, the miracle of the birth of freedom from total conformity and order." [15] Precisely through the most complete formal control

over his material—by dint of the highest possible artistic sophistication—can the artist regain for his medium its original
function as a language of the emotions. Only by way of extreme complexity can language be returned to a new simplicity, can the artist liberate his art from sterile exclusivity and
communicate with the people. Only the most advanced rationality enables the artist to regain his state of innocence,
and in that state be once again capable of spontaneous creativity. Thomas Mann tells us:

The creator of *Dr. Fausti Lamentation* can surrender himself
with full abandon to his subjectivity, unconcerned with problems
of structure, now that these had been solved in advance; thus it is
that his work, which is a work of strictest formalism, a work of
the most extreme control and calculation, can yet be, at the same
time, a work of pure expressiveness.[16]

Speaking about the creator of the *Lamentation,* Mann actually is speaking about the creator of *Doctor Faustus,* about
himself. Mann characterizes his work in words that clearly
echo the solution he offers us in the pages of his tale. He calls
Doctor Faustus a work "which is a confession and a life's
sacrifice through and through, and as such knows of no concessions; it presents itself as the most form-conscious and
structurally controlled work and yet, at the same time, it steps
out of the realm of art and is reality." [17]

This, then, is Thomas Mann's solution: The arcane magic
of a dialectical process enabled the author without recourse
to black art or a devil's pact to carry forward his immense
life's work to ever more startling achievements. He reached a
high point in the novel that holds the key to the triumph of
the modern artist over seemingly insurmountable difficulties.
In writing this "book of the end," Mann has, in fact, made a
new beginning for the novel. He proved that this form of art
is indeed still possible, perhaps not in its traditional aspect,
but as a work that combines self-conscious artistry with intensity of feeling and Romantic irony with objective epic narration. Mann demonstrated that the modern novel, on its mul-

tiple interrelated levels, can offer the reader the sophisticated pleasure of an oratorio, magically recreated in words, together with as unsophisticated and popular a thrill as an eyewitness account of betrayed love avenged by murder in a streetcar.

"Should we not call the one who accomplished the *breakthrough* from intellectual coldness into a daring world of new emotionality, should we not call him," Mann asks, "the redeemer and savior of art?" [18] We ask, in turn, has not Mann achieved this breakthrough? Has he not entered that daring world of new emotionality with such emotion-charged episodes as the advent, suffering, and death of little Echo and the agony of Adrian Leverkühn at the loss of this beloved child to the devil?

Critics have accused Mann of sentimentality in the portrayal of Echo and his tragic death.[19] These critics fail to recognize this portrayal's true meaning as the achievement of a new emotional freedom, a freedom regained by the author on the level of utmost intellectual clarity, of self-consciously sophisticated artistry, and of absolute control of form.

Mann achieved this breakthrough at a frightful price of personal suffering. In little Echo he drew an idealized portrait of his favorite grandchild, Frido, Michael Mann's eldest son. When Echo had to be surrendered to the devil under the compulsion of the inexorable logic of the poet's fictive world, Mann felt the loss as deeply as if he had suffered it in palpable reality. He has told of this suffering in *Die Entstehung des Doktor Faustus: Roman eines Romans* (*The Story of a Novel*). We catch a rare glimpse of his diary—which is to remain sealed until 1975—when he quotes the following entry: "Worked on Echo's mortal illness—with suffering!" "The 'divine child' was to be taken from the man of 'coldness,' " [20] from Adrian, who was forbidden to love, and from Thomas Mann, who, with suffering, had decreed that tragic fate: "This was decreed and decided from way back" as a crucial development in the structure of the plot. "To carry this out," Mann confesses, "was a bitter task for me." [21] His pain in portraying Echo's death, he tells us, is mirrored in Adrian's soul-searing agony at the loss of the child.

H. T. Lowe-Porter, the translator of Mann's works, deeply moved by Echo's tragic fate, confronted the author with the challenging question, "How could you do it?" [22] How could Mann deliver the angelic child into the clutches of the devil? And the author replied by urging her to "read the answer in Adrian's despair, in his disavowal of all hope, in his words of 'taking back' [annulling]," [23] Beethoven's *Ninth Symphony* with its paean to friendship, brotherhood, and love.

Magical alchemy of the creative process: A charming boy is transformed into the divine, angelic child, the "elfin child," as Mann calls Echo, into a messenger from Heaven whose fate is sealed by a fiat of the poet's imagination. This dreadful fate, in turn, releases in the artist an upsurge of pain and suffering that serves as the creative impulse for the portrayal of the mind- and soul-destroying agony of Adrian and charges the scene with an emotional intensity rarely found in Mann's work, or, for that matter, in world literature. When such power of feeling, such ability to project that feeling in a superbly controlled composition is found in an artist of utmost sophistication, can one not speak, in such a case, of the miracle of redemption of art from intellectual coldness into a daring world of new emotionality? We would answer in the affirmative and would acclaim Thomas Mann as one of the saviors of art and of the artist *in extremis* from threatening emotional sterility in self-destructive cynicism.

Heritage

Among Mann's early jottings in one of his notebooks, we find the Latin dictum, *"Pereant qui ante nos nostra dixerunt."* * Such drastic laconism must have appealed to Mann; yet, surely, he could not have sympathized with its sentiment. On the contrary, overwhelming evidence reveals Mann as a grateful admirer of those who before him, had given immortal expression to thoughts and feelings that he considered his own. Mann's reliance on guidance, aid, and inspiration was always great. Especially in the early stage of his writing, he "felt dependent on great models and dared not take a step without constant contact with admired masters." [1]

Thomas Mann valued what he called his capacity for admiration as a gift to which he owed the greater part of his success. "I have always been an *admirer*," he wrote the literary critic and historian Hans Mayer. "I consider the gift of admiration to be, by all odds, the most indispensable for self-improvement. Frankly, I cannot imagine where I would now

* "May those perish who have expressed before us the thoughts that are our own!" (*Studien*, p. 290.)

be without the benefit of that precious gift." [2] And in his essay "Wagners 'Ring des Nibelungen'" ("Richard Wagner
and the *Ring*") he expands on this experience:

If anyone were to ask me which emotional attitude toward the
phenomena of this world, toward art and life, I consider the most
beautiful, the happiest, the most creative, and the most indispensable, I would answer without a moment's hesitation: *It is the
gift of admiration*. Where it is lacking, where it has withered and
died, there will be no burgeoning and no blooming; there will be
nothing but impoverishment and the desert.[3]

From practical experience, Mann knew "how productive it is
to accept with genuine love that which others have to contribute and, admiring it, to learn from it." [4]

Thomas Mann thought little of so-called original inven-
tion. For him the true mark of genius was the ability to discover, adopt, and adapt: "I do not recognize in the gift to
invent figures and intrigues the criterion of poetic talent. . . .
Very great poets have never in their lives invented anything
but, rather, have filled traditional themes with their soul and
have formed them anew." [5] Of course, he was at the same
time keenly aware of the fact that such adoption could
never be an act of mechanical borrowing, but that it had to
enliven borrowed materials with a new life. To be capable of
such animation an artist had to *be* someone, that is, a personality gifted with an instinct for spiritual kinship. He had to
know how to select his models and how to recognize their
affinities to his spiritual make-up; for nothing totally alien to
his nature would ever yield to creative assimilation. "Every
'organic incorporation [organische Einbeziehung]' of foreign
cultural values presupposes a personality . . . with the capacity for individual selection, assimilation, and transformation of the cultural heritage into something singularly one's
own." [6] Mann possessed this capacity to select and transform
to an unusual degree. As he adopted the cultural heritage he
reshaped and enhanced it into something altogether new and
singularly his own.

Thomas Mann recognized himself to be essentially a child of the nineteenth century. "Romanticism, nationalism, burgherdom, music, pessimism, humor—these are the atmospheric elements of the past century which, in the main, form the nonpersonal constituents of my make-up." [7] He felt his intellectual roots to be deeply implanted "in Goethe's autobiographical and pedagogical world, in the world of bourgeois culture, in the world of Romanticism." Yet, at the same time, he knew that "by dint of [his] profound experience of Nietzsche's personality and work, [he] had part in the self-transcendence of Romanticism." [8]

NIETZSCHE, WAGNER, AND SCHOPENHAUER

As Thomas Mann looked up to his intellectual heaven, he recognized there a constellation of three stars, *ein Dreigestirn*, which shone with special brilliance. These guiding stars were Nietzsche, Wagner, and Schopenhauer. Mann found it quite impossible to establish the preeminence of any of these three. Not only were their impacts on his eagerly receptive mind virtually simultaneous, but he experienced all three as an intellectual and artistic whole so unified, fused, and interlinked that they defied all efforts at clear-cut separation. Mann reminds us how much each of these geniuses owed the other. Nietzsche, for instance, called Schopenhauer his great teacher, while Wagner extolled Schopenhauer's metaphysics as a veritable gift from heaven, *ein wahres Himmelsgeschenk*. The three are one for the young poet. "The reverential student for whom their mighty lives had become synonymous with culture itself, would like to speak of all three at one and the same time." [9] And so he does. In his self-searching *Betrachtungen eines Unpolitischen* (*Reflections of a Nonpolitical Man*), Mann vividly describes the indelible impression which these intellectual giants and gifted artists made on him. From Schopenhauer, he tells us, he "derived the moralism—popularly termed 'pessimism'—which characterizes his philosophy, that mood of 'cross, death, and tomb' [Kreuz, Tod und Gruft] in Nietzsche's definition." [10] Yet Mann admits that he found that very same mood in Wagner's art and that he might have singled out Wagner's overpowering influence on him as the true source of this ethical atmosphere. And Mann continues this admission of an inseparable threefold indebtedness by pointing to Nietzsche's part in far-reachingly determining his view of life and art:

If this mood and attitude made of me a psychologist of *decadence* . . . then it was due to Friedrich Nietzsche, who was my guide and master. For I recognized in him from the very beginning not so much the prophet of some vaguely conceived superman . . . but rather the incomparably greatest and most astute psychologist of decadence.[11]

Friedrich Nietzsche

Instinctively young Thomas resisted the hysterical cult of power and beauty and of the zestful life that Nietzsche celebrated most fervently in his later works—beginning with *Also sprach Zarathustra* (*Thus Spake Zarathustra*)—and to which so many of Mann's contemporaries totally succumbed.[12] Mann quickly learned to recognize in Nietzsche's Will-to-Power the hectic wish-dream of a restless spirit that felt and knew itself to be inescapably the decadent offspring of a culture in its dying phase.[13] Mann unmasked Nietzsche's glorification of the superman as the yearnings of a decadent for a life in youthful vigor, free of all debilitating self-knowledge and sentimentive impulses of self-analysis and doubt. This clear view of Nietzsche's true character, this "ironic" understanding of the deeper meaning of his message, greatly increased the importance of the philosopher to his young admirer.

Mann shared with Nietzsche his longing for life, that self-denial of the spirit in favor of life. But with Mann this longing assumed a totally different emotional tone. It was tuned in a minor key; it expressed itself not in Nietzsche's strident, hectic, all but hysterical accents, but in far more subtly ironic tones. Mann did not yearn for the virility and beauty of the ruthless heroes of the Italian Renaissance. Instead, he longed for "the bliss of normalcy [die Wonnen der Gewöhnlichkeit]." The objects of his love were the thoroughly bourgeois figures of "the blond and the blue-eyed"—Hans Hansens and Ingeborg Holms of his native Lübeck. In contrast to Nietzsche's concept of life as the ruthless vitality of the blond beast, of the superman, Thomas Mann understood life to mean the charm, happiness, strength, grace, and pleasant normalcy that are characteristic of the nonspiritual, the nonintellectual, the commonplace people of the burgher world. This, surely, is a striking instance of creative borrowing. It is a form of borrowing that adopts the thoughts and feelings of a great predecessor and, in adopting them, adapts them to the borrower's temperament—his sensibilities and intellect.

Thomas Mann also derived from Friedrich Nietzsche his early critical view of the modern artist as a mixture of Lucifer and clown whose existence was based on make-believe and dissimulation and who was a constant affront to society. Here again Mann certainly did not borrow slavishly. His critique of the modern artist was, from its outset, less vitriolic than Nietzsche's. Moreover, this negative view was gradually to change, mainly under the influence of Goethe, to acceptance of the artist and to recognition of his role as a leader of mankind toward a more humane future.

Another aspect of Nietzsche's work that Mann greatly admired and sought to emulate was that writer's style in its unheard of modernity. The very *form* of Nietzsche's message, its language, influenced Mann perhaps more even than its philosophical content:

Under Nietzsche's tutelage we grew accustomed to fuse and to integrate in our minds the concepts of "artist" and "thinker," of "poet" and "man of cognition [den Erkennenden]," so that the hard and fast line separating art from criticism became altogether blurred. He was the one who reminded us of the Apollonian instruments, the bow and the lyre. He taught us to hit the mark and to hit it with deadly accuracy. He gave German prose a sensitivity, an artistic limpidness, beauty, precision, musicality, emphasis, and passion that had never been heard before. His style inescapably influenced every one of us who was bold enough to write German after him.[14]

Unquestionably, Nietzsche's influence as Mann's great teacher was immense. Mann never tired of expressing his gratitude to the guide and mentor of his youth. And yet, in the course of time, Mann's interpretation of Nietzsche's message did become more critical as it grew more penetrating and profound in the light of unfolding events. The experience of the Nazi nightmare and the horrors of World War II made Mann aware that Nietzsche's glorification of the irrational, of man's Will-to-Power, and the instinct-driven, rapacious blond beast, the *blonde Bestie* endangered man's sanity and his very existence. Thomas Mann was now ready to subject Nietzsche's dangerous errors to a far more severe and unsparing criticism. He exposed the philosopher's "error of willfully misrepresenting the true relationship of instinct and intellect by condemning intellect as a dangerous and domineering power while protecting instinct as the weak, endangered part of man's make-up";[15] he criticized Nietzsche's error of perverting the true relationship between morality and life by depicting morality as a mortal enemy of life. Mann could no longer endure any of these baleful perversions of truth. He wanted us to know that intellect, not instinct, had been and would always be in need of protection from the irrational drives in us, and that morality, far from being the mortal enemy of life, was its faithful ally. Against Nietzsche's dangerous views, Mann stressed the simple truth that "morality and life belonged inseparably together, that ethics was the proper support of life, and that the moral individual was life's rightful citizen." [16]

Mann now rejected uncompromisingly Nietzsche's romantic glorification of war:

In our times Nietzsche's rodomontades on the culture-sustaining function of war can be recognized for what they really are—the

fantasies of a child grown up in the shelter of an epoch of peace
. . . which had begun to grow bored with itself. . . . When,
in the end [in Nietzsche's late works] there resounds the song
glorifying the "blond beast," the "triumphant monster," that
type of man "who, in high spirits, returns home from terrible
excesses of murder, arson, rape, and torture as if he were returning from a student prank," then, indeed, the picture of the
infantile sadist [Nietzsche] is complete and our soul writhes in
agony.[17]

This quotation is taken from Thomas Mann's essay,
"Nietzsches Philosophie im Lichte unserer Erfahrung." [18]
This essay, written in 1945, shows clearly that Mann, at that
time, portrayed the poet-philosopher in a more stark and
ominous manner than he did in the Betrachtungen (1916–
1918). And yet this late portrait was also drawn with a profound sympathy for and deep understanding of the agonies
Nietzsche had suffered in his efforts to break with the past in
order to usher in the glorious future of a zestful, beautiful
life. As a critic, Mann focused sharp lights on the "dizzying
heights of error" to which this noble spirit had been driven
in his quest for a new truth. As an apologist, Mann strove to
explain, if not to justify, these errors. Here is Mann's defense
of the admired guide and teacher of his youth:

Nietzsche's aestheticism represents the insane negation of
"spirit" in favor of the beautiful, the strong, and the ruthless
"life." As such this aestheticism represents the self-negation of a
man deeply suffering in life. This aestheticism, I say, imbues all
of Nietzsche's philosophical outpourings with an element of the
most profound irony and stamps them for what they really are:
something altogether unreal and irresponsible, a passionately
acted make-believe [ein Leidenschaftlich-Gespieltes].[19]

In these words one can clearly hear the echo of Mann's voice
when he defined, some three decades earlier, in the Betrachtungen his view of the poet-philosopher and his teachings.
That view was even then, and has always remained, profoundly ironic; never did Mann take Nietzsche's philosophiz-

ing at its face value, but he always recognized it as the dream of a modern Don Quixote courting the strumpet Dulcinea del Toboso.

Richard Wagner

From the outset of this discussion, the inextricable unity of Nietzsche, Wagner, and Schopenhauer in their influence on Thomas Mann has been emphasized. It is altogether in keeping with this unity that Mann would see Richard Wagner and his art, from the first contact with him, with the critical eyes of Nietzsche. In his *Betrachtungen* Mann admits this fact with his usual candor. "Nietzsche," he tells us, "had experienced the phenomenon of the artist and of art itself altogether through Wagner. Just so did I, his far less significant descendant, experience Wagner's art through the critical eyes of Nietzsche." [20] Primarily because of these critical eyes Mann's opinion of Wagner's personality and work remained ambivalent throughout his life. As late as 1942 he wrote to his friend and confidante Agnes Meyer, answering to her query about his attitude toward the composer: "My way of speaking about Wagner has nothing to do with chronology or development. It is and always will be 'ambivalent,' and I can write about him this way today and that way tomorrow." [21] This attitude was at once skeptical and passionate. Filled with suspicion for the reprehensible magician,[22] Mann found himself nonetheless drawn irresistibly to Wagner's indescribably enchanting art. "Passion" is the term Mann uses most frequently to characterize this attitude because this term alone comes close to defining such a complex relationship. "Any lesser term such as 'love' or 'enthusiasm' would fail," he assures us, "to properly describe my attitude. . . . Surrender to it [Wagner's art] together with critical comprehension of it —that is what I call 'passion' and that is precisely my attitude." [23]

Under the influence of Nietzsche's essays "Nietzsche contra Wagner" (Nietzsche Against Wagner) and "Der Fall Wagner" (The Case of Wagner) Mann formed his critical view of the composer. But the author's empathic immersion in Schopenhauer's romantic philosophy served to intensify his infatuation with the metaphysical eroticism of Wagner's music. Thus, this twofold influence furthered the ambivalence that was to remain characteristic of Mann's attitude toward Wagner's genius.

Wagner exercised his influence on the receptive youth "not as a musician or as a dramatist, not even as an operatic dramatist [Musikdramatiker], but rather as a modern artist *par excellence* . . . and most significantly, as a prosaist of musico-epic compositions and as a symbolist [musikalisch-epischer Prosaiker und Symboliker]." With considerable exaggeration of his debt to Wagner, Mann continues:

Whatever I know of the epic spirit, of how to begin and how to end, of style as that mysterious accommodation of the personal to the objective, of symbol formation, of that organic unity of the single work and the total *oeuvre*—all that . . . I owe to my dedication to this [Wagner's] art.[24]

Mann has given an emotionally charged expression to this passion in unforgettably vivid pages of the *Betrachtungen*.[25] Young Thomas is standing on the Piazza Colonna in Rome during an outdoor concert. A lonely stranger in a foreign land, his face pale, his throat tight with emotion, tears of rapture welling up in his eyes, he is listening to the overture to Wagner's *Lohengrin*. Round about him the piazza is ringing with the *bis* and the *bastas* of Wagner's lovers and haters in their battle of tastes until the *Notung* motif, rising to its triumphant crescendo amidst the frenetic *Evvivas* and *Abbassos* of friend and foe, drives all opposition before it, and sweeps up in its surge our ecstatic Wagnerite.

Yes, Mann's passion for Wagner's art ran deep; it was a passion such as mere gratitude for guidance received could never have roused. Wagner had far more to give the young beginner than mere instruction. Wagner's art was able to still Mann's deepest longings and satisfy his highest expectations. It could forever remain a source of supreme challenge and inspiration because for him it was an art that in a magical way welded countless seemingly disparate elements into an unprecedented unity. Mann never tired of experiencing, exploring, defining, criticizing, and praising this all-embracing polarity of Wagner's personality and his works. Among the many characterizations of Wagner which Mann has written[26] there is hardly one that does not stress this many faceted ambivalence typical of the man and his art. Mann has called Wagner's work "the most fascinating phenomenon in the world of art, . . . a thoroughly unique eruption of talent and genius, the most profound and the most enchanting creation of a soulful magician inebriated with wisdom." One should observe the characteristic oxymorons in this definition, which stand out even more strikingly in the German original: *"eines ebenso seelenvollen wie von Klugheit trunkenen Magiers."* [27] Here is the key to Mann's passion for Wagner. It is the magical fusion of intellect *and* feeling, of soul *and* mind, of elemental inspiration *and* artistic intelligence, of instinct *and* shrewd calculation that roused in Mann ambivalent emotions, passionate acceptance, and critical reserve. To Hermann Hesse, Mann made a statement that throws a startling light upon his relationship to Wagner:

The popular elements in *Königliche Hoheit* (*Royal Highness*), for example, are quite as honest and instinctive with me as the artistic—as far as I know. I believe that what you call "playing up to the public" is the result of my long-standing, passionately critical enthusiasm for the art of Richard Wagner—for that art which is quite as exclusive as it is demagogic and which has determined—not to say corrupted—my ideal of art, probably forever. Nietzsche speaks once of Wagner's "changing optic" as being at one time focused on the crudest needs and at another on the most refined. This is the influence that I have in mind, and I really don't know whether I shall ever find the strength of will to rid myself of it. I tend to value those artists rather low who strive merely for esoteric effects. *I reach out for the stupid public as well.*[28]

What becomes clear in this self-analytical statement is the fact that Mann's relation to Wagner was far more than a case of influence by the musician upon the poet; in these lines it is not difficult to recognize a startling admission by Mann of a singular affinity with the "soulful magician." On an emotional level, far less intense, less flamboyant, and less extravagant, Mann's genius does exhibit to a surprising degree that very ambivalence and those very polarities that characterize Wagner's personality and art. Can one fail to recognize the kinship of Thomas Mann, the poet, who felt himself to be a musician, to Richard Wagner, that musician and poet in one, whose "music," in Mann's words, "was literature and whose libretti were music?" When Mann describes Wagner's technique of the leitmotif in the *Ring,* he might as well be describing the giant tapestry of motifs of his own *Joseph* tetralogy. When he extols Wagner as the incomparable psychologist *and* the most profound mythologist, as the "redeemer of opera through myth," [29] he is praising a twofold endowment that is Mann's very own.[30] Mann speaks of the willful ambition that animates Wagner's works and makes the artist subservient to their bidding so that in the end the creator exclaims before his creature in utter amazement: "No, *that* I did not intend to create, but now I *must,* God help me!" [31] When Mann describes this autonomous will inherent in Wagner's creations, he is at the same time describing his own experience with *his* works, which also had that stubborn will of their own and that ambition to grow beyond the originally planned slim novellas into multivolume novels. Mann shares with Wagner the "penchant for the monumental curiously paired with the love for the very small, the minuscule psychological detail";[32] Mann's Naturalism, like Wagner's, transcends itself into symbol and myth.[33] Mann's genius, again like Wagner's, was oriented toward the past, the mythical past, while it was, at the same time, eagerly receptive of the new and the experimental.[34] One could even maintain that Mann's Germanism was "analytical, intellectual, and capable of a worldwide effect," [35] precisely as Wagner's was.

Other instances of Mann's affinity to Wagner could be cited. These, however, should suffice to establish the fact that Mann's attitude toward the composer and his art was in a significant measure conditioned by emotional and intellectual rapport. A creative temperament had unerringly discovered in another artist "his own" and had adopted and adapted this cultural heritage with singular success.

Arthur Schopenhauer

The third star in Mann's spiritual constellation was Arthur Schopenhauer. Mann's experience of Schopenhauer's philosophy was a deeply emotional one—"an experience of the soul of the first magnitude [ein seelisches Erlebnis ersten Ranges]"—whereas he defined his experience of Nietzsche's world as a "rather more intellectual and artistic one." [36] Young Thomas read, so he tells us in the revelatory chapter "Einkehr" (Introspection) of his *Betrachtungen*, for days on end Schopenhauer's masterpiece of a world- and will-denying philosophy, *Die Welt als Wille und Vorstellung* (*The World as Will and Idea*). "Lonely, refractory youth, youth yearning for life and death, how passionately he imbibed that metaphysics, the innermost essence of which was the erotic, and which, moreover, he had come to recognize as the spiritual source of the music of [Wagner's] *Tristan*." [37] It was not the complex logic or the subtleties of the philosophical argument that held young Thomas spellbound. He was fascinated by the philosopher's central message, which unmasked this best of all possible worlds for what it was, the worst of all possible worlds, worthy of being denied and transcended in aloof contemplation. This was a message that had a profound meaning for Thomas Mann, whose affinity to the quietism of the East and whose longing for Nirvana we discovered to be deeply rooted elements of his nature.[38]

It is this message that the poet gives as a precious gift to Thomas, the suffering hero of the novel *Buddenbrooks:* "I made my precious experience and high adventure a gift to him, placing it into his life shortly before its end; I wove it into the narrative and let him find life in death, the freedom from the fetters of his worn individuality." [39] By chance, Thomas Buddenbrook comes upon Schopenhauer's masterpiece and reads with incredulous amazement one of its greatest chapters, "Über den Tod und sein Verhältnis zur Unzerstörbarkeit unseres Wesens an sich." ("Of Death and its Relation to the Indestructibility of our 'Intelligible' Being").[40] He reads it and puts the book aside in puzzlement. But some time later, in the stillness of the night, he awakens thrilled with a happiness he had never before experienced. Schopenhauer's message resounded in his soul as a deeply felt and undeniable truth vouchsaved to him by an intelligence far more powerful than his own. This message of the philosopher utterly justified his yearning for escape from this life of toil and tribulations, from that gnawing sense of insufficiency and limitation, and from the ever growing agony of an unbearable weariness. In that ecstatic moment the suffering hero knows with utmost certainty and truly celestial joy that his fate is not to be the continuation of his existence in the feeble ego of his decadent son, poor little Hanno, but that he will find his reincarnation in "all those who have ever said 'I' and *especially in those, who have said 'I' with fuller voice, with greater strength, and with greater joy. . . .* Have I hated life, this pure, this cruel and strong life?" Thomas asks and gives his triumphant answer:

Foolishness and misunderstanding! Only myself did I hate because I could not endure life. But I love you all, all of you, you happy ones, and soon I shall cease to be separated from you by the narrow confinement within my individuality; soon my love for you will be released to be with and in you . . . with and in you all! [41]

Schopenhauer's philosophy has undergone a strange transformation in the creative mind of the poet. Thomas Buddenbrook's wish to escape the narrow limits of individuation and the toils of life is indeed in keeping with the teachings of Schopenhauer. But the hero's jubilant resolve to join all those who have ever affirmed a zestful and beautiful life with the strongest and the most joyous voices, this resolve is a clear echo of Friedrich Nietzsche's affirmation of life. Such is

Mann's fusion and synthesis of two worlds of thought, his adoption and the adaption of cultural heritage. This is the artist's freedom to borrow from his great predecessors and to transmute the gratefully received heritage into his own. Thomas Mann commented on this freedom of the artist:

One can think in the spirit of a philosopher without in the least thinking *in accordance* with his system. That is to say: One can make use of his thoughts and at the same time think in a manner in which he would not have led us to think. In this passage [of the *Buddenbrooks*] we have the thoughts of one who has read Nietzsche in addition to Schopenhauer and, by introducing one experience into the other, has created a most curious admixture of the two.[42]

Schopenhauer's masterpiece held a twofold fascination for Thomas Mann. Not only did its central message appeal to him, but he was also fascinated by its structure and style, by the musical quality of its composition and language. He admired in it a model of the type of artistic creation he himself was striving for:

A book, totally self-contained that reaffirms itself constantly by being and doing what it says and teaches: Whichever page you may turn to, it is there in its entirety, although it requires its whole manifold complexity of appearance to realize itself in time and space.[43]

Mann greets this "book of wisdom," as he calls it, as a "novel of the spirit [Geistesroman] and as a symphony of ideas [Ideensymphonie] wondrously wrought from a single ideational core [Gedankenkern] present at every point of its composition.[44] This work became for Thomas Mann what it had been for Wagner, truly a gift from Heaven, a source of self-cognition and self-justification and—for the beginner laboring over his first great novel—aid and inspiration and a fruitful challenge. As in Nietzsche, Mann discovered in Schopenhauer a *bel esprit*, a master of the language, who was able to create the most wide-ranging literary effects, a prose writer of European stature, like whom there had been perhaps two or three among the German poets and none at all among the philosophers." [45]

Later in life Thomas Mann was to turn again to the admired poet-philosopher to welcome him as a fellow champion of that new humanism Mann so fervently strove to bring to a troubled world. He could extend this welcome to Schopenhauer because he discovered in the moralism of this philosopher a profoundly humanistic element. Mann hailed Schopenhauer as a profound thinker of the conservative past with a message for the future. He was not blind to Schopenhauer's reactionary attitude toward politics, his open disdain of all those who sought their own and mankind's salvation in political action, either in the glorification of the state (as Hegel did in his late period) or in espousal of revolution (as with Marx and Engels). Mann does not belittle the antisocial bias in Schopenhauer's metaphysics. Yet he did find it possible to greet this philosopher as a modern thinker and as a great humanist because he recognized that Schopenhauer, this apparent pessimist, had a profoundly revolutionary message. Aware of man's shortcoming and failing, Schopenhauer nevertheless respected him as the only creature on this earth that had been able to conceive the possibility of overthrowing the cruel tyranny of the will and thus to gain the only victory worth striving for. Despite his essentially pessimistic view of life, Schopenhauer found the strength to believe in a future when man's essential nature would change, in which the wall between the "I" and the "thou" would be torn down, and man would finally recognize in fellow-man a fellow-sufferer in need of sympathy and love.

Mann hailed this pessimistic humanism as a humanism of the future precisely for its pessimism. The humanism of the classical period in German thought, Mann found to be overly optimistic. It failed to discern or else sought to gloss over the dreadful brutality, selfishness, envy, hatred, and all the other vices innate in man. Schopenhauer, the modern depth psychologist, as Thomas Mann called him, had gained insight into man's instinctual and irrational nature and yet, far from despairing, had found the strength to praise him as the crowning glory of creation, as the last and best hope of life's liberation from a blind and irrational will.[46]

Not only Schopenhauer's philosophy but his very character impressed Mann as being of the future:

The elements of his [Schopenhauer's] personality in their harmony of light and dark, that mixture of Voltaire and Jakob Böhme, that paradox of his classically clear prose, which yet reveals the lowest and the darkest depths of human nature, his proud misanthropy, which yet never lets him deny his reverence for the ideal of man, in brief, his "pessimistic humanism," all that appears to me replete with an aura of the future [Zukunftsstimmung]. . . . His intellectual sensuality, his teaching that was his life, they both proclaim that cognition, cogitation, and philosophizing are not a matter of the mind alone, but of the whole human being, of the heart as well as the senses, of the body as well as the soul. This artistry belongs to a humanity that has moved beyond the onesided extremes of rationalistic desiccation [Vernunftdürre] on the one hand, and of the deification of man's instinctual drives [Instinktvergottung] on the other. It is an artistry that will prove helpful in creating a humanity of the future." [47]

This is Mann's final tribute to Schopenhauer for his unique contribution to man's painful progress toward a more harmonious life, freed from the overwhelming tyranny of blind will, guided by a steadier light of intellect.

THE HOLY RUSSIAN LITERATURE

Young Thomas Mann gratefully accepted another great gift and heritage, which impressed him deeply and influenced his work from its very beginning. It was, in his words, "the beloved, the holy Russian literature." [1] His admiration for the great Russian masters was always to remain undimmed.

Of course, there were other bright stars of world literature that offered guidance and inspiration, but none of them had quite the luster in Mann's spiritual heaven. From among the great number of French writers Mann singled out for special mention the brothers de Goncourt, whose novel *Renée Mauperin* had impressed him with its subtle character portrayals, and specifically with the deft arrangement of its considerable bulk into appetizingly brief chapters, a structural feature that our young poet adopted in his *Buddenbrooks*. Klaus Schröter has made a plausible case for considerable influence by Paul Bourget on the beginner.[2] In those early years, young Thomas found Guy de Maupassant's brilliant narrative skill much to his liking, while Balzac, Flaubert and Zola came relatively late to his attention. He wrote to Philipp Witkop in retrospect: "I am hardly aware of any real influence [by them]. To be sure, Flaubert's severely artistic stance left its mark on me. It counts among the educational experience of my *later* youth."[3] Closely linked to the influence of the Goncourt brothers and of the North German novelist Fritz Reuter on the *Buddenbrooks* was that of the Scandinavian genealogical novels of Alexander Kielland (especially his sea merchant novel *Garman and Worse*, 1880), Jonas Lie (*The Family at Gilje*, 1883), and Herman Bang.[4] Needless to say, there were many other writers who came to the attention and aroused the interest of this omnivorous reader in search of models. Yet all of them fade into relative insignificance when compared with young Mann's interest in the grand men of Russian letters.

It was in the summer of 1898 during his stay with his brother Heinrich in Rome and Palestrina that Mann immersed himself in the works of the great Russians. Tolstoy, Turgenev, Dostoevsky, Gogol, Goncharov—their young admirer and eager student of their message and their style "devoured" them all.[5] Their spirit, specifically the somber tones of Dostoevsky, can be detected in the writer's earliest novellas, in such pre-*Buddenbrooks* stories as *Tobias Mindernickel, Luischen* (*Little Lizzie*), and *Der Bajazzo* (*The Dilettante*). While working on *Buddenbrooks*, Mann "was sustained," as he tells us, "by Tolstoy, the Homer of Jasnaya Poliana, that bearer of epic burdens of gigantic weight," while Ivan Turgenev lent him "the lyrical exactness of his bewitching style" in aid of the composition of Mann's most lyrical novella, *Tonio Kröger*.[6]

His learned guide in the vast world of Russian letters was Dmitri Merezhkovsky, an eminent literary critic and foremost world psychologist, as Mann called him. He profoundly influenced not only Mann's opinion of Tolstoy, Dostoevsky, and Gogol with his penetrating studies of these authors, but also Mann's view of Russia's national character and culture in general.[7] To the very end that view remained essentially unchanged.

Thomas Mann's professions of love and admiration for Russian literature were truly rhapsodic. He equated in importance his discovery of that beloved sphere with his momentous introduction to the philosophy of Nietzsche. Both "ushered the son of the nineteenth century into a new era, protected him from torpidity and spiritual death, and built for him bridges to the future." [8] Nietzsche had sought to realize the age-old dream of the Third Kingdom where spirit would attain corporeality and matter would be spiritualized. Gogol and Tolstoy had carried on this same search only to sink back into an ascetic radicalism which preached that to live in God, man would have to lead a life of strict asceticism. Yet "that struggle was being continued," according to Mann, "in the Russia of Gogol as it was in the Germany of Nietzsche, and to recognize this struggle—to take part in it with insight and with passion"—that was for Mann "a matter of existential significance." [9] For him Russian literature remained throughout his life essentially the grand arena of that confrontation between spirit and nature and of the eternal quest for the synthesis of these polar opposites, for the spiritualization of nature and the naturalization of spirit.

Leo Nikolaevich Tolstoy was extolled by Thomas Mann as the incomparable "seer of the body [Seher des Leibes]." [10] Mann placed him in the tradition of epic poetry, tracing his lineage back to Homer. He represented for Mann "the plastic principle in art." [11] At the same time, Mann saw in him an "arch-Russian of enormous ethnic genuineness and of colossal eastwardness [Östlichkeit]." [12] Maxim Gorky, the great disciple of Tolstoy, had compared him in his *Recollections* with "a sort of Russian God . . . who, though perhaps not very majestic, was shrewder than other gods." [13] Mann thought this characterization of Tolstoy particularly apt.[14] He saw in Tolstoy traits of amazing shrewdness, unpredictable whimsicality, elemental "moral indifference, and frightening nihilism." [15] He went beyond Gorky in his characterization of Tolstoy as a pagan, a "spritelike [elbische], elemental nature." [16]

Tolstoy's greatness was, according to Mann, of a proto-heathen kind—wild, antedating civilization, and lacking the humane element [das Menschliche].[17] It derived from Tolstoy's intimate contact with the Russian soil. His efforts at sublimation, spiritualization, and moralization of his Antean energies were doomed to failure; they had something child-like, even ridiculous about them. Whenever Tolstoy lost touch with mother earth, his creative forces ebbed, his voice rang unconvincing. On the other hand, Mann assures us, "there are passages in the Russian's works where Tolstoy touches mother earth, and suddenly his words—which rang wooden and were incoherent while he was theorizing—become filled with a vitality and freshness that no soul could resist." [18] Mann's awe-struck admiration for Tolstoy's narrative genius never diminished. In a letter dated as late as June 16, 1952, the same enthusiasm still rings out: "By God," he exclaims upon having reread Tolstoy's thrilling tale of Hadshi Murat, "By God, I am but a shrew-mouse [Spitzmaus] compared with *such* a lion. Let them bestow on me, for my achievements, whatever further world prizes they choose—I will always know what is truly great and what is, at best, middling. All we can do is sit there, all of us together, quite small and look up in admiration!" [19]

Fedor Mikhailovich Dostoevsky represented for Thomas Mann a type of artist who was antithetical to Tolstoy in every respect. Tolstoy, a kindred spirit to Homer, was the epic writer *par excellence*. Dostoevsky, in contrast, overwhelmed Mann as a phenomenon altogether *sui generis*: "In Dostoevsky I could not but see . . . a completely extraordinary, wild, monstrous, and terrifying event [!] totally outside all epic tradition." [20] Tolstoy was for Mann the "pagan god on a maple throne under the golden linden tree," [21] whereas Dostoevsky appeared to him as the "saint of holy Russia," as the "Holy Sinner," a tortured soul with dark demonic depths and yearnings for celestial purity. In a letter to his poet-friend Stefan Zweig, Mann even went so far as to admit that he had "always preferred to call Dostoevsky a great sinner rather than a great artist." [22] And yet Mann saw Dostoevsky standing far above Tolstoy as "the infinitely more profound and experienced moralist." [23]

Dostoevsky, suffering from poverty and poor health, was yet uplifted by an indomitable, incandescent spirit that frowned on mediocrity and reached out for all that was extreme, intense—for hellish depths and heavenly heights— even at the risk of losing touch with mother earth, of being swept into the far-out world of grotesque and apocalyptic visions. He possessed the religious greatness of the accursed. He taught Mann to recognize in the sickness of genius the very source of his creativity. Mann was convinced that "however much Dostoevsky's sickness sapped his physical energies, his genius was, nonetheless, intimately bound up with it and conditioned by it." [24] His personality and life, in much the same way as Nietzsche's, presented the phenomenon of illness as greatness and a stupendous intellectual achievement as the product of disease. "His psychological astuteness, his intimate knowledge of the criminal psyche, of those depths that the apocalypse calls the 'satanic,' and above all, his uncanny ability to suggest the sense of a mysterious *guilt* as forming the background of the life of his protagonists many of whom are truly terrifying,"—all this was for Thomas Mann indissolubly bound up with Dostoevsky's "holy sickness, with his epilepsy." [25]

Mann recognized as Dostoevsky's central message a humanism that was "altogether new, far more profound and unrhetorical for having passed through the hell of suffering and cognition." [26] With this definition of Dostoevsky's humanism, Mann placed the Russian poet and thinker at the side of Schopenhauer as another great prophet of a humanism of the future.

In Nikolai Vasilievich Gogol, Mann greeted the harbinger of a new epoch of Russian literature—one in which Alexander Pushkin's "sensuously radiant, naïve, and serenely poetic world" is replaced by criticism, a resurgent religiosity, and a humor that does not spring, as did Pushkin's, from blissful serenity but, rather, from a "desire to make a laughing-stock of the devil." [27] This is the grotesque comicality, that pervades Gogol's *Dead Souls* and *The Inspector General.* Gogol exposed evil and corruption in all their devilish guises to make laughingstocks of them. It is this Russian humor with its truthfulness and warmth, its fantastic quality and winning drollery, that Mann considered to be the most lovable and most delightful in the world. He valued this humor higher than the English and the Jean-Paulesque and most emphatically higher than the French, which he called, with a pejorative accent, dry, sec.

Another great Russian, Anton Pavlovich Chekhov, came late into Mann's favor. To be sure, as a young man Mann had read some of Chekhov's novellas and at least one of them, *The Duel,* "with enormous interest." [28] Yet in those early days, as he is frank to admit, he had set himself higher goals. He sought to equal, if not to surpass, the monumental epic achievements of Tolstoy.[29] Only later did he come to appreciate fully the supreme skill required to fashion the flawless form of Chekhov's short stories and plays, which in their brevity grew out of a more comprehensive and penetrating view of life than many a voluminous novel by a less perceptive and gifted writer.

What impressed the mature Mann in the personality and work of Chekhov were his modesty, unbending veracity, total lack of all false pathos and pomposity, and especially his skeptical view of art as a reliable guide in times of social crisis such as the one that cast its shadows on the Russian's life. As Mann was browsing through Chekhov's correspondence, one of the Russian writer's phrases struck him with the shock of sudden recognition and sent him on an exploration of Chekhov's life and works. The particular phrase had been Chekhov's characteristically self-searching query, "Am I not fooling my readers since, after all, I am completely unable to answer their most important questions?" [30] This doubt tormented Mann quite as intensely as it did the Russian. Moreover, Mann discovered in Chekhov the same stubborn perseverance that he knew to be his very own—a tenacity that enabled him to carry on despite gnawing doubts about the apparent futility of his labors. And finally Mann found in Chekhov a quality that he would not have appreciated in his younger days, but which he had learned to admire as a mature observer of and active participant in the sociopolitical life of his times. That quality was Chekhov's concern with Russia's social conditions—its abysmal economic injustice, obscurant legal system, and vile political corruption. In short, Mann learned to admire the writer's intense social consciousness—that "democracy of the heart" in which he had come to recognize a thoroughly Russian trait. Already in his *Betrachtungen* he had declared that "Russia had always been, in the depth of its soul, democratic yes, even Christian-communistic [christlichkommunistisch], that it had always been imbued with the spirit of brotherliness." [31] In Chekhov's pages there spoke that voice of brotherliness, which so gladdened Mann's heart.

The following brief summary recapitulates the essential features of Russia, its literature and national character, that impressed Mann most deeply. Russia was for him first and foremost a land of profound soulfulness, *"das weite seelenvolle Land"*—that land where the most human of humans live, full of an unsapped vitality, close to nature and their fellow-men, scarcely touched, to be sure, by the humanistic culture of the western world, but gifted with an intuitive knowledge of the soul, a profound social consciousness, and inborn tact [Herzenstakt]. Even in the bitter social critique, in the satire, and irony of Russian literature Mann found this deep humanity of the Russians reflected; for in his view the Russians' satire and irony did not spring from Mephistophelian nihilism and cold cynicism or from hate and intolerance; rather they were engendered by a profound sympathy and love for fellow-men and by the fervent desire to succor, set free, educate, and elevate. Mann recognized and admired in the Russian writers the bold explorers of metaphysical and social problems who had the courage to strike out beyond the stifling, stagnant confines of bourgeois morality and conventions and to press forward toward radical solutions of basic human problems, fearless of censure and condemnation, exile or even death. These men strove to achieve in their personalities and works the fusion of spirit and nature. They dreamt of the "Third Kingdom."

Mann marveled at the easy accord in the writings of the great Russians of an intense sensuous enjoyment of nature, of a happy, healthy sense of life with the most profound insights into the world of sickness, with the personally experienced "torments of a Dantesque Hell." [32] "Is not the Russian litera-ture," Mann exclaims ecstatically, "is it not the most human of all—holy in its humanity?" [33] It is this all-embracing, this fierce and withal tender humanity, this holiness alive in the Russian soul that held the deepest fascination for Mann. The passionate force of Russia's deeply human, soul-searching and ever questing spirit built for young Thomas bridges to the future; it inspired the maturing poet and helped protect him from torpidity and spiritual death.

FRIEDRICH SCHILLER AND
JOHANN WOLFGANG
VON GOETHE

Thomas Mann's knowledge of Schiller's and Goethe's works and of German literature in general was all the more impressive for being thoroughly personal and never bookish. He was truly at home with German poetry. Among his favor-ite lyricists were August von Platen, whose poem "Tristan" he praised as the most profound and personal expression of the Romantic spirit; Theodor Storm, whose inimitable lyrical tone found its nostalgic echo in the novella *Tonio Kröger;* and Novalis, in whose poetry Mann not only admired the glorification of death and the transcendent peace of night, but also discovered a forward-looking spirit celebrating a future humanity united in a rekindled common faith and culture. Erika Mann tells us that her father knew well over 300 poems by heart. Mann, agreeing, adds that he knew enough German poetry to recite from memory on the longest of his beloved walks without ever running out of material.[1]

The masters of German prose, with the exception of Theodor Storm and Theodor Fontane, came to Thomas Mann's attention surprisingly late. Not until 1916 did Mann finally become aware of Adalbert Stifter, when he was introduced to him by his wartime friend and confidant, Ernst Bertram, who at the time was planning a study of the writer. Mann became deeply engrossed in this great stylist's work and was particularly impressed by his descriptions of nature, which he found "phenomenal, especially those of unusual and extreme events, such as snow- and ice-catastrophes, thunderstorms, etc." [2] In a letter to the literary historian Fritz Strich he defined the "magic" of this poet as a "quiet, pale, pedantic kind . . . , which captivates more deeply than most so-called interesting writing. . . . And yet, beyond and despite this, what an exciting, extraordinary narrator this fellow really is, one who ventures, at any moment, into the extreme, the truly pathological." [3] He praised Stifter's prose as "altogether unique," and felt that "no other type of reading could teach . . . a German writer in a more beautiful way to preserve the purity of his language and to serve it in faithful dedication." [4]

Gottfried Keller's novel, *Der Grüne Heinrich* (*Green Henry*), Mann seems to have read in its entirety for the first time during his convalescence from the lung operation he underwent in 1946. It turned out to be "a work after [his] own heart, despite certain weaknesses and irritating *longeurs*." [5] Nor did Conrad Ferdinand Meyer, that other Swiss master of German prose, come early to his attention. It was during World War I that Mann finally turned to him as to an ally in his struggle against the hated *Zivilisationsliterat,* that quasi-artist serving ideological ends rather than poetry and culture. At that time Mann came to know Meyer as a "man and an artist with a most profound conscience, a non-political man who had renounced in his 'Pescara' and his 'Angela Borgia' *passion, brutality,* and *ruthlessness.*" [6] Mann wrote empathetic studies of Gotthold Ephraim Lessing,[7] Heinrich von Kleist,[8] Eichendorff's *Taugenichts,*[9] and Adalbert von Chamisso.[10] Yet none of these novelists and dramatists seems to have impressed young Thomas as early and as deeply as did Theodor Fontane.

In Fontane, Thomas Mann welcomed a kindred spirit.[11] He discovered in Fontane's late works a benevolently skeptical view of life, a keen awareness of its puzzling complexities, a cautious avoidance of easy generalizations and apodictic judgments, as well as a realistic style that eschewed all grandiloquence and bathos, the only style between Romanticism and Nietzsche that satisfied Mann's inborn artistic needs. He praised Fontane's masterpiece, *Effi Briest,* as the best German novel since Goethe's *Elective Affinities*—very high praise indeed from a person who had placed Goethe's work among the immortal creations of world literature. The dramatic thrust, the lucidity and precision, the wit and *pointe* of Mann's dialogue in *Buddenbrooks* as well as his portrayal of the novel's pert little heroine, the indomitable Tony, owe a great deal to this admired model.[12]

It is impossible in this context to record, evaluate, and analyze Mann's countless contacts with the works of German writers. However, two figures stand out as prominently in Thomas Mann's spiritual world as in Germany's cultural past, and call for special attention: Friedrich Schiller and Johann Wolfgang von Goethe.

Among the earliest impressions Mann received in his contacts with German literature were Schiller's dramas, which were read to the young boy by his mother, an ardent admirer of the poet. In his last essay, the ambitious "Versuch über Schiller" ("Essay on Schiller"), Mann recalls these early "loves." They included, typically for Mann, Schiller's little-known earliest effort, *Semele, Operette in zwo Scenen* (Semele, Operetta in Two Scenes), which has as its central theme "the passion of the artist for his creation," a theme that was capable, as Mann tells us, "of arousing the childlike enthusiasm of the boy." [13] But above all it was *Don Carlos*, Schiller's dramatic masterpiece, that "kindled in the fifteen-year-old his first infatuation with language [die erste Sprach-begeisterung]." [14] The tears Tonio Kröger sheds over the tragic fate of King Phillip—the lonely monarch betrayed by Marquis Posa, the only man he could trust and admire— those tears were Mann's very own.

On the occasion of the centennial of Schiller's death in 1905, Mann presented the idol of his youth with a most moving monument. In the study with the revealing title "Schwere Stunde" ("A Weary Hour")[15] Mann drew his first portrait of the poet. He extolled him as the man of an unbending ethos of achievement, whose accomplishments were victories gained by a soaring spirit and an indomitable will over a frail body wracked by illness. In this early study Goethe remained in the background as the object of Schiller's "yearning hostility." One cannot but feel that Goethe, the prince of life and favorite of the gods, who gathered his laurels with an easy hand as fair gifts from heaven, had not as yet won Thomas Mann's admiration. Schiller was clearly the idol of Mann at this stage of his development. This evident predilection for Schiller, the saintly hero of the spirit, was not to last, however. Not that he ever completely fell from Mann's favors, although there were those brief years at the turn of the century during which Mann regarded him through the eyes of Nietzsche and his brother Heinrich as a rather ridiculous "moralizer with the sky-blue nose." [16] But even in the long perspective, the preeminence of Schiller over Goethe was to yield to a far fairer valuation of the true greatness of these poets.

By 1922, in the essay "Goethe und Tolstoi: Fragmente zum Problem der Humanität" ("Goethe and Tolstoy: Fragments to the Problem of Humanism"), Schiller and Goethe found themselves juxtaposed as figures of equal stature. In fact, the impossibility of establishing the preeminence of either was the central theme of this essay. Mann was no longer willing or able to bestow his accolade on Schiller, the hero of the spirit, to the exclusion of Goethe, the prince of life. Mann became convinced that there were in fact, two ways and not just one to enhance human nature:

One way is man's elevation to a godlike state by the grace of nature, the other is his ennoblement to sainthood by the grace of another power opposed to nature and representing the emancipation from and the eternal revolt against it—by the grace of the spirit.[17]

Mann would not dare pass judgment as to which was the loftier way. "What is nobler," he asks, "freedom or constraint [Gebundenheit], free will or obedience, the ethical stance or the naïve? If we refuse to answer, it is because of our conviction that this question will never be answered with any degree of finality." [18] Of one thing, however, Mann was certain. Neither form of enhancement and ennoblement can ever be accomplished without a supreme effort on the part of man:

What matters [in man's spiritual growth] is that nothing be given to man without effort. Effortless nature amounts to crudeness; effortless spirit to rootlessness and to lack of substance. A lofty meeting of spirit and nature on their way to each other in yearning and longing: that is man in all his nobility.[19]

In this process of maturation man is in need of aid and challenge by an admired guide.

Goethe's central role in Mann's life as such a guide providing aid and challenge has been emphasized by Bernhard Blume in his excellent study Thomas Mann und Goethe:[20]

In the supreme task of enhancing and forming his personality Goethe became Mann's admired model; the progress of Mann's development and his constant striving for growth and fulfilment can be viewed as the process of a growing proximity to Goethe.[21]

One cannot, of course, belittle Mann's admiration for Goethe's enormous artistic achievements. Goethe's *Faust*[22] and *Die Wahlverwandtschaften* (*Elective Affinities*), with their unique combination of plasticity of imagery and ideational richness, Mann repeatedly singled out for praise as sources of poetic inspiration. Nevertheless, we would maintain, that Goethe exerted his chief influence on Thomas Mann with his singularly balanced and harmonious personality. In Goethe Mann recognized and admired "the poet in league equally with both powers, with 'nature' and with 'spirit.' Such a poet could well be called the *master* of mankind." [23] As such a master of mankind, as the incomparable exemplar of a fruitful balance between all extremes—between refinement and strength, intellect and vitality, reason and imagination, rapture and common sense—Goethe entered Mann's life to become quite literally his "father image." [24] With every passing year, Mann strove harder to emulate the great man, this "friend of life" and "darling of mankind [Liebling der Menschheit]" until at the summit of his career, in his work on the *Joseph* tetralogy and the Goethe novel *Lotte in Weimar* (*The Beloved Returns*) he did achieve a veritable *unio mystica* with the revered master.[25]

Mann was able to achieve such a spiritual union because in fundamental ways he was a true citizen of Goethe's world. He was very conscious of this. To Käte Hamburger he wrote:

The feeling of kinship, the consciousness of a similar stamp and stance, of a certain mystical imitation and of walking in the other's [Goethe's] footsteps are vividly alive in me. . . . There can be no mistaking it; as Stifter had written, "To be sure, I am no Goethe. But I am one of his family." [26]

Mann shared Goethe's aristocratic patrician family background, his German bourgeois provenience [deutschbürgerliche Herkunft] and his inborn humanism.[27] Even Goethe's lively sense of obligation to cope with the challenges of the times and his open-mindedness toward the world Mann felt to be his own, dormant at first, but ever present in his personality and awaiting stimulation to assert themselves. This needed stimulus was furnished him in large measure by Goethe's challenging example.

In 1949, Mann prepared and broadcast for BBC a speech on "Goethe, the German Miracle." In those years Goethe had truly become a miracle for Mann. He admired in Goethe the man and poet who had achieved the all but impossible. Goethe had been able to represent in his person and in his work the monumental German, and had accomplished this "not in pathetic tones and with great gestures, but in the most winning, the most lovable, and the most blessedly inspired form [musisch-gesegnetsten Form]; thus he established the happiest union between Germany and the world." [28] Mann admired Goethe as a born aristocrat endowed with a lively affinity for and an understanding of the democratic spirit of the epoch[29] and as a leader of the Germans from their congenital inwardness toward a new sense of engagement in the social problems of the day. Goethe's Wilhelm Meister in his progress through the years of his apprenticeship (*Lehrjahre*) and through his years as a journeyman (*Wanderjahre*) demonstrated for Mann this liberation from asocial egocentricity to a new sociality. This novel of education Mann wanted us to recognize as a work

of a far more fully developed humanism than the German bourgeois reader could possibly conceive, who would take this work merely for a monument of personal development and Pietistic autobiography. To be sure, it begins with the individualistic education of the self, but it ends in a political utopia. . . . This work teaches us how to view the innermost meaning of education as the process of an organic transition from the world of inwardness to the objective world. It demonstrates . . . how the concept of education, having its origin in the idea of self-education, leads man into the social sphere and affords him a view of what unquestionably is the highest stage in human existence, namely, the state.[30]

What was it that made such a reorientation in Goethe's view of the world possible—this change in his intellectual stance from self-centeredness to a sense of communality, from the aristocratic principle of unlimited self-fulfillment to the democratic insistence on specialization in a specific occupation or profession as a productive member of society? Mann singles out as the deepest source and the most forceful impulse for this change Goethe's "ethos of renunciation [Ethos der Entsagung]," which gradually developed into a central theme in the works of the mature poet, in his dramas *Iphigenie auf Tauris* and *Torquato Tasso* and in the novel *Wilhelm Meisters Wanderjahre*. In developing this ethos Goethe found himself fulfilling an "inborn imperative." "Is not the pedagogical duty of renunciation," Mann asks, "is not the duty that Goethe fulfilled something more than personal? Is it not the decree of fate, the inborn imperative that must be obeyed lest grave spiritual punishment be incurred?" [31] Mann too followed the decree of fate and an inborn imperative when he overcame his romantic inwardness and, emulating Goethe, turned his energies as man and artist outward toward the world in social and political activity.

It is one of the numerous instances of an amazing "fittingness of circumstances [Stimmigkeiten]" in Mann's long and eventful life that the voice of Schiller, which had spoken to him in his youth with so much appeal, would speak again to the venerable poet in the last year of his life. Symbolically the grand circle of his life was closing.

The initial impulse for Mann to turn once again to the works of Schiller had been the approach of the 150th anniversary of the poet's death. From Germany had come insistent requests that Thomas Mann, the greatest representative of German culture, be the official speaker on this festive occasion. At first Mann was reluctant to accept the invitations. Finally he committed himself, and as he pondered the speech and became immersed in the world of Schiller, he felt himself swept up again to the soaring heights of this spirit.

Mann experienced with astounding youthful vigor Schiller's creative genius in all its manifestations. Once again he entered the world of the dramatist to characterize for us deftly and succinctly each of the many plays, pausing to offer us his insights into the *Wallenstein* trilogy that held for Mann "such a grand sweep of tragedy, both in the intimately personal sphere and on the grand stage of history." [32] Schiller's portrayal of Wallenstein Mann extolled as the product of an intuitive psychological insight far in advance of the historical investigations of Schiller's day. Genius had penetrated to the core of personality to reveal Wallenstein in his "grandiose ambivalence" [33] as a nature ruled by the twofold astrological constellation of Saturn, that brooding, treacherous God lusting for power, and of Jupiter the radiantly majestic benevolent father-image. As his Jovian self, Wallenstein embraces Max Piccolomini with a genuine, fatherly, more than fatherly love; at the same time, as a Saturnian nature, he is driven to use Max, that flower of his life, as a pawn in his ruthlessly scheming game of power politics. Mann would have us know that he "believe[s] in the ingenious aptness of Schiller's portrayal of Wallenstein and that [he] disbelieve[s] all those who profess to know that the 'real' Wallenstein was 'different.' " [34] Under the spell of Schiller's drama, one cannot but agree with Mann.

Reading once again, or rather experiencing with lively empathy, Schiller's poetry, Mann wondered why so sublime a poem as "Das Glück" ("Good Fortune") had been inexplicably neglected, seldom appearing in the countless Schiller anthologies. How could the critics fail to recognize in these verses the imperishable monument Schiller had set to his envy-tortured love for Goethe, that darling of the gods,

> Whose eyes had been opened by Phoebus, whose lips by Hermes
> And on whose brow Zeus had planted the symbol of power.[35]

For Thomas Mann there was nothing more beautiful, more noble, more holy in the whole realm of feeling and of speech than this poem. He would have "gladly sacrificed entire anthologies of erotic verse for this one love poem of the spirit, of determination and toil, addressed to the godlike, who creates without effort." [36]

Schiller's aesthetics preoccupied Mann once again.[37] He recalled how Schiller's excitedly antithetical thinking had fascinated him in his youth, how it had left its mark on his own antithetical style, especially Schiller's essay "Über naive und sentimentalische Dichtung, ("On Naïve and Sentimentive Poetry"), which in Mann's rather too generous view "made all subsequent efforts superfluous," having once and for all defined the twofold nature of genius.[38]

Goethe had been Mann's guide to the fullness and splendor of life. He had taught the maturing poet to be loyal to life and to dedicate himself to its service. Now Schiller stepped again to his side, this time to lead the octogenarian to a sphere beyond mundane concerns. It is no exaggeration and no far-fetched metaphor to say that while Goethe had been Mann's pedagogue in the art of living life to the fullest, Schiller became, at the end of Mann's life, his psychagogue into the realm of transcendence. Not that Schiller failed to inspire Mann in his longings and strivings for a nobler future for mankind in the here and now, for a political utopia, as had Goethe. Certainly the "Singer of Freedom" had fortified Mann in his belief that the hour had struck for mankind to transcend the narrow confines of regional interests and to unite in the cosmopolitanism of a world-wide brotherhood. Mann acclaimed Schiller as "the very element that our body politic so desperately needs, the vitamin that is so sadly lacking in our life's economy, in the organism of our society." [39] Mann paraphrased and quoted at length from Schiller's preface to the periodical *Die Horen* where the poet warns *his* time, *our* time, not to surrender to selfish interests but instead to recognize the dire need for instilling in men the longing for a "universal, higher interest—a purely human one beyond the influence of time and to unite a divided world under the banner of truth and beauty." [40]

Unquestionably this cosmopolitan and altruistic aspect of Schiller's genius influenced Mann. Yet as we read his late letters and study his last great essay, "Versuch über Schiller," we cannot escape the impression that the ethereal part of Schiller's nature came to hold even greater fascination for our poet. Mann was profoundly impressed with Schiller's idealism, which not only left behind the sociopolitical realm, the workaday world, but also yearned to emancipate itself—an absolutely untrammeled spirit—from the telluric elements altogether. For Mann,

Schiller's greatness was so generous, soaring, incandescent and uplifting that even Goethe's wiser nature-majesty [Natur-Majestät] could not reach up to it. . . . His was a greatness most manly in every respect, not at all starry-eyed [verschwärmt], but endowed with a strong sense of reality, destined for great success, quite equal to the demands of this world [erdentüchtig] and yet, in its deepest depths, yearning for Heaven, thirsting for transfiguration, eager to divest itself of all earthly dross.[41]

As the most noteworthy, revealing, and moving letter that had gripped him most extraordinarily, Mann singled out from Schiller's correspondence the poet's epistle to Wilhelm von Humboldt. There Schiller confided to his great friend his plan of writing a scene on Olympus, the marriage of the demigod Hercules with the goddess Hebe. This was Schiller's "deepest wish," his "loftiest ambition," and his "ultimate dream: everything mortal dissolved, *nothing but light, absolute freedom, limitless power—no shadows, no limits*, nothing of all that to be seen any longer." In the realization of this dream Schiller was ready "to marshal once more all [his] creative powers and the *entire ethereal part of* [*his*] *nature*, even if on that occasion it should be altogether consumed." [42] Thomas Mann had come upon this letter after he had completed his essay. Yet such was the importance he attached to this expression of Schiller's deepest wish and loftiest ambition that he returned to his work and inserted the letter and his interpretation of it as a prominent theme of his study.[43] Deeply moved by Schiller's dream, Mann exclaimed: "Mighty, upsurging soul! When would it be, when could it be 'totally free'? When would and could the ethereal part of his nature have freed itself, a pure flame, from the mortal man, to pour forth in the celestial poem?" Never, of course, save in self-immolation! Schiller's dream was for Mann "completely transcendent, no longer belonging to life, transworldly; it seemed reserved for a blessed spirit." [44] Why did this dream of the poet move Mann so deeply, if not for the reason that he felt it to be, perhaps subconsciously, his own dream at the threshold of death. It was indeed an all but miraculous fittingness in Mann's life, that at its end his thoughts should have been focused on Schiller's luminous world, that his emotions should have become so fully attuned to the poet's soaring spirit.

Looking back over Mann's spiritual heritage, one is impressed with the autobiographical note, which is rarely missing from the essays, letters, and speeches that record for us Mann's appreciation of his favorite poets and thinkers. These records are obviously not meant to be scholarly treatises, though they are based on a thorough knowledge of their subjects; rather, they are evocations of creative personalities with whom Mann could identify. To achieve these evocations, to paint these portraits, Mann had to become personally involved with the lives and thoughts of his models; a most intimate contact had to be established. In his novel *The Beloved Returns*, the author had Goethe characterize such a typically Mannian experience: "This making contact [Contactnahme], this delving self-immersion into the sphere and the object . . . this digging and burrowing of an obsessive sympathy makes you an initiate of that world which you have lovingly grasped." [45]

Undoubtedly this intense self-immersion and identification with the object of obsessive sympathy holds its peculiar dangers for the chronicler and critic. It may well become so intense—and it often did with our essayist—that the figures which he portrayed became oddly distorted and assumed a startling resemblance to their biographer. The record of their lives became in significant part the story of the chronicler's spiritual development. Thomas Mann would not have it otherwise. His evocations of the great are intended to be *auto*biographically conditioned, products of an intense personal involvement. Mann considered "criticism worthless unless it is at the same time a personal confession. Genuine, deep, emotion-charged criticism is nothing less than an act of creative writing in the sense of Ibsen's, 'Judgment Day *over one's own self!'* " [46]

In the preface to the collection of his essays, *Altes und Neues* (Old and New), Mann elaborated upon this thought:

Everything in this collection is autobiography and whatever fascination this book holds for me derives from the fact that it lays hold of life and preserves situations that had to be faced, in large part with full personal involvement—situations to which I look back with that curious satisfaction with which one is apt to recall a life steadfastly endured.[47]

With Mann's essayistic and epistolary writings as a record of such a steadfastly endured life in mind, this study was made in order to trace in perspective Mann's personal involvement with the thoughts and emotions of his great predecessors as he made them his own, enriching his life with this great cultural heritage.

3

Thomas Mann and His
Contemporaries

THE NATURALISTS

Thomas Mann's intellectual awakening took place in the decade of the 1880s, in the years of the rise and ephemeral triumph of Naturalism. He made early contact with the representative members and journals of the movement. At eighteen he had his first novella, *Gefallen* (*The Fallen One*),* accepted by Michael Georg Conrad's vanguard periodical, *Die Gesellschaft*, which championed Emile Zola, Tolstoy, and Dostoevsky. At twenty, he contributed to the *Neue Rundschau*, which had inherited the program of the *Freie Bühne*, Berlin's radically Naturalistic journal. It certainly cannot be said that Mann kept aloof from the movement. And yet his attitude toward it remained critical; he could not accept its literary goals and predilections. The Naturalists' heavy-handed stress on photographic rendering of everyday reality, their obsession with the sordid life, their penchant for the analysis of the social ills of the day—all this held little attraction for him. In his first masterpiece, *Buddenbrooks*, Mann's "main concern," as he recalled it in his *Betrachtungen*, "was with the intimately human. The sociopolitical aspects of life

* In the meaning of dishonored, morally bankrupt.

[he] took along on the side, half consciously; they were of little concern to [him]." [1] He found the works of the dogmatic Naturalists sadly lacking in psychological subtlety, in limpid gaiety, in aesthetic refinement, and in a sure sense of form—that is, those very elements he considered essential in a work of art. He sharply criticized Georg Hirschfeld's typically Naturalistic style: "This style is no style! There is no play, no esprit, no irony, no joy in language, no gaiety, none of the magic of art!" He did credit the Naturalists with "a tendency toward the monumental and with a highly developed social consciousness." [2] Naturalism from the pen of genius, of a Dostoevsky, a Tolstoy, an Ibsen, even of a Zola, whom Mann did not count among the really great, he accepted for the reason that such Naturalism was always transcending itself into the symbolic and the mythical to become, in that magical process, inspired art. Of Tolstoy Mann wrote:

As an artist and as the son of his epoch, of the nineteenth century, Tolstoy was a Naturalist. . . . But as an intellectual he was beyond (or rather he struggled and tormented himself to reach beyond) the new [Naturalism] toward something still loftier, toward something the other side of his century, beyond Naturalism. He was striving for a concept of art that was much nearer to "spirit," "insight," and "critique" than to nature. [3]

This quotation is at least as applicable to Mann's own efforts. Even in his earliest novellas as well as in *Buddenbrooks* he sought to transform the heavy and somber Naturalism that he had inherited from the nineteenth century into a work of art at once intellectual, symbolic, and transparent to ideas. He strove to achieve this by transforming the inherited style into something far more limpid, light, and meaningful; by lending it a bright gaiety; by elevating it. Readers of *The Magic Mountain* hardly need Mann's warning not to take the work for a realistic novel:

The Magic Mountain does employ the methods of the realistic novel but, for all that, it really is not one. It constantly transcends realism, elevating reality to the symbolic and making its surface appearance transparent to the spiritual, to the intellectual importance. This even applies to the portrayal of characters in whom the reader senses a deeper meaning. They are, in fact citizens, representatives, emissaries of intellectual domains, principalities, and worlds.[4]

Even in Mann's early works we recognize this striving for the typical, this often unconscious tendency to enhance the merely individual and empirical into the universally significant. Thus the "Naturalistic" *Buddenbrooks* not only gives us the decline of a specific burgher family of Lübeck, but also portrays it in such manner as to make it recognizeably typical for European bourgeois society.[5] The central theme of the novel reflects, moreover, the generally valid insight Mann derived from his study of Schopenhauer that a decline in physical vitality induces, through sublimation, an increase in refinement, artistic bent, and aesthetic sensibility. A writer with these tendencies and predilections could find little to learn from the social novels of a Max Kretzer or the plays of Hermann Sudermann, and felt a Naturalistic drama, such as Gerhart Hauptmann's *The Weavers,* despite its excellence on its own terms, to lie outside the sphere of his main artistic concern. In fact, the only "Naturalist" Mann greatly admired and from whom he was eager to learn was Theodor Fontane who, while being the benevolent father figure of the movement, certainly was not one of its militants.

Mann was a keenly perceptive observer of the literary scene at the turn of the century, of that productive period in which so many trends ran counter to, crossed, and merged with each other. He deftly characterized his contemporaries:

Naturalism was the literary current of the day and Gerhart Hauptmann its champion. . . . But at the same time there was something astir . . . that was very far from the simplistic reproduction of nature, something running altogether counter to this practice and method: There was the somber suggestiveness of Ibsen's late plays, Stefan George's esoteric stylistic innovations, which derived from the French *Parnassiens,* a group quite as radical and challenging as the Naturalists had been in their terroristic attack on the bourgeoisie; there were the early Symbolist dramas of Maeterlinck with their deeply troubled, dream-like language, and the culture-saturated, sublimated, age-mellowed Viennese art of Hugo von Hofmannsthal; there was the moralizing sex-circus of Frank Wedekind; Rilke was there with his new, seductive lyricism—and all that existed, side by side, was the expression of these stirring times, in which so many currents . . . crossed and merged.[6]

It would be surprising indeed if so keen an observer would have been left completely uninfluenced by his fellow writers' works, at least insofar as these works were compatible with Mann's artistic temperament, his ambitions and goals, and his aesthetic tenets. To be sure, Mann could not subject his individuality to any school or movement, or to any "ism." He could not even bring himself to join literary clubs or organizations that courted his membership. To his friend Kurt Martens, Mann once confided that after repeated attempts which, he admitted, were made partly out of vanity and partly from a sense of duty, he had become firmly convinced that he "simply was not made for the whole business," [7] and in the *Betrachtungen* he characterizes his "independence [as] truly that of a Bohemian." [8] "I am a solitary, a loner; I stand aside and observe." [9]

Though never a joiner, Mann had a vast range of interests and contacts. He passionately took part in the controversies of the day and was always eagerly and sensitively receptive to new ideas.[10] He freely admitted, to mention but one specific instance, that he had learned a great deal from the Impressionistic novel of Hermann Bahr with the apt title *Die Gute Schule* (The Good School). Some early poems that Mann did not include in his collected works perhaps because of their all too obviously derivative nature ("Zweimaliger Abschied" and "Vision," for example) clearly show the influence of Symbolism as well as of Neoromanticism. Even his later works, the novella *Der Kleiderschrank* (*The Wardrobe*), for example, or so inimitable a masterpiece as *Tonio Kröger* share in content and style certain characteristics with typical Neoromantic works. Yet in all fairness it must be stressed that we are dealing here with instances of affinity rather than with cases of virtuosic imitation or direct influence. Mann's works simply cannot be pigeonholed under any of the convenient "isms."

SIGMUND FREUD

One would expect a writer so predominantly interested in the intimately human side of life, as Thomas Mann was, to turn eagerly to Freud's teachings. In fact, Mann's approach was hesitant and cautious; from initial criticism, the poet moved gradually to guarded acceptance of the psychoanalyst's methods and ideas.

Thomas Mann's first encounter with psychoanalysis took place surprisingly late in his life, about the time he was working on *Death in Venice* (1911–1912). Mann confessed that on first contact he, "as an artist, was far from satisfied with Freud's ideas." He felt "disturbed, even diminished [verkleinert] by them, because these ideas, much like a bundle of x-rays, irradiated [durchleuchteten] the artist, violating the secret of his creative act." [1] This initial defensive reaction was due, to some extent at least, to Mann's superficial acquaintance at that time with Freud's work. He frankly admitted that he had not gone in search of Freud but that the psychoanalyst's ideas had come to him by way of hearsay mostly through Freud's disciples, who had developed an interest in certain of his works, especially in the novella *Death in Venice*. In a letter written in 1944, Mann recalls that in those days "one could be influenced by Freud's ideas without any direct contact with his works because for a long time the air had been filled with the thoughts and results of the psychoanalytical school." [2] Long after the completion of *Death in Venice* and after having written his second great novel, *The Magic Mountain*, in which Mann's ambiguous attitude toward psychoanalysis is mirrored in the questionable figure of

Krokowski,[3] did Mann finally turn to a serious study of Freud.

He soon realized how much he was being helped in this study by his early immersion in Nietzsche's and Schopenhauer's thoughts. "In the works of Nietzsche," he tells us, "especially in [Nietzsche's] critique of Wagner, [he] had experienced the very essence of psychoanalysis. In the form of irony it had become an integral part of [his] spiritual orientation and of [his] works." [4] As Mann penetrated more deeply into Sigmund Freud's thoughts he discovered a close kinship of the psychologist to Arthur Schopenhauer. Much like Schopenhauer, Freud strove to dispel the shallow optimism about the human condition; he also showed man as he really was, a slave to the instincts and drives buried deep in his subconscious. And quoting Freud's optimistic battle cry, "Where there was Id, there shall be Ego!" Mann proceeds to demonstrate that Freud's Id is in essence Schopenhauer's concept of the will and that the psychoanalyst's Ego is the philosopher's intellect.[5]

Mann had early extolled the *philosopher* as a champion of a profound enlightenment. Now he was prepared to extol the *psychologist* as the liberator of mankind from the tyranny of blind instinct, as the leader of man toward a truer self-cognition. Mann had become convinced that Freud in his descent into the dark depths of human nature had never aimed at glorifying man's instinctual drives, that he had never played them out against the intellect, as had some scholars in their misguided support of the so-called conservative revolution proclaimed by the Nazi movement. On the contrary, Freud had taken an unyielding stand against the champions of obscurantism and neo-barbarism. This courageous stand deeply impressed Thomas Mann. In his speeches given for the great scientist's eightieth birthday in Vienna in 1936, Mann expressed his admiration for Freud's "colonizing spirit" and compared it with the ever striving spirit of Goethe's "colonizing" Faust.[6] He praised Freud's work as "one of the most important cornerstones ever laid in the foundation of the future, in the construction of the dwelling place of a liberated, far wiser, and far more knowledgeable humanity." [7]

Clearly, Mann's attitude to Freud was a highly complex one. It began in sharp criticism and ended in acceptance, even in admiration, which, however, was never quite free of a cautious reserve. And yet, in a deeper sense, Mann had always been a Freudian. By his very nature, he had always practiced the most subtle, if unprofessional, kind of psychoanalysis. The searching glance with which he looked at life in order to penetrate to its problematical depths was in a more than metaphorical sense the glance of psychoanalysis. The more mature Mann's artistry grew, the more consciously did the poet adopt and adapt Freudian insights to his creative purpose, on the grandest scale in the *Joseph* tetralogy. Henry Hatfield, a perceptive student of Mann's life and works, may well be right in arguing that in his narration of the Joseph story, "Mann is much closer to Freud than to the Bible." [8] Unquestionably, Freud's discoveries in the realm of the subconscious are pervasively present in Mann's mature works; they aided the poet in his subtle transformations of the shadowy figures of a distant past—of Mut-Em-Enet, Joseph's suffering temptress, for instance, or of Saint Gregorius, that holy sinner—into the deeply problematical and thoroughly modern protagonists of his novels and novellas.

THE NEOCLASSICISTS

Thomas Mann's early suspicion of psychoanalysis went quite naturally hand in hand with the attraction that the young author felt for the Neoclassical movement introduced in the first decade of our century into German letters by such writers as Paul Ernst, Wilhelm von Scholz, Rudolf Pannwitz, and Samuel Lublinski, among others. Thomas Mann greeted this movement as a welcome renaissance of form-consciousness in life and letters, which could act as a countervailing force to the rising influence of the psychoanalytical school in which Mann thought he detected a dangerous challenge to traditional standards and values sacrificing them for an all-pervasive tolerance and total relativism in the spirit of *"Tout comprendre c'est tout pardonner."**

Mann's recently published letters to Samuel Lublinski help us gain a clearer view of his sympathetic reaction to the artistic canon of the Neoclassicists. In one of these letters written in 1908, the year marking the high tide of the movement, Mann speaks of his projected novel on Frederick the Great and emphasizes his intention to compose this work with greater attention to selection and form than in his *Buddenbrooks:* "As to my Frederick dreams, you are absolutely right to insist on selection and form. I am clear on one point—namely that under no circumstances may that book be of the external formlessness of the *Buddenbrooks*." [1] Though the planned novel was never written, Mann did carry out the self-imposed imperative of scrupulous regard for form—of rigorous attention to faultless structure and elevated style in the major works of these years: with an all too programmatic insistence in the verse drama *Fiorenza*, with happier results in the novel *Königliche Hoheit* (*Royal Highness*), and with supreme mastery in the novella *Death in Venice*. It is interesting to note that the works of his Neoclassical contemporaries seem not to have served Thomas Mann as direct sources of inspiration. Instead, he found this inspiration in Goethe's *Elective Affinities*. He had early recognized this novel as a classical work, as the creation of a highly developed sense of formal perfection. In its organic fusion of "form and thought, plasticity and idea, sublimation and corporeality [Plastik und Idee, Vergeistigung und Verleiblichung]," [2] this masterpiece became a supreme model for our poet in his labors on his own masterful novella. In it Mann not only gave expression to his ideal of selection and form but also mirrored something of his own development toward a new Classicism in the hero's, Gustav von Aschenbach's, determination "to reject all lassitude in morality and aesthetics, and to cultivate the ideal of beauty and noble purity, simplicity and balance in artistic formulation." [3]

* "To understand everything is to pardon (to tolerate) everything."

Contending this degree of identity between the author and the fictional *persona* Aschenbach, we are by no means unaware of Mann's warning, which he sounded in the *Betrachtungen*, not to mistake Aschenbach's masterstyle [Meisterstil] and the hieratic atmosphere surrounding him for Mann's own attitude and style. Yet despite this explicit denial of outright identity of his own person with Aschenbach, Mann nevertheless admitted a significant degree of resemblance. In the very source (*Betrachtungen*) in which he sounded his warning, he also offered conclusive evidence of his significant part in Aschenbach's personality and life. The reference to *Death in Venice* is unmistakable in the following passage:

In a narrative I have experimented with the rejection of the psychologism and relativism of the ebbing epoch. I had an artist [Aschenbach!] dismiss "cognition for its own sake." I had him withdraw his sympathy from "the abyss" and turn toward will, value judgment, intolerance, and "resoluteness."

And Mann continues:

I know full well that this "new will" could never have become a problem for me, an object of my artistic impulse, had *I not had my part in it, for there is no objective knowledge and cognition in the realm of art, but only an intuitive and a lyrical one.*[4]

And as if this were not sufficient proof of personal participation in the new will to value judgment in life and art, Mann offered us additional evidence in his Preface to the *Betrachtungen*. Here he wrote:

In various passages of the work I have sought to make it clear in how far *I too had in my make-up something of that "resoluteness," of that rejection of an "obscene psychologism" rampant in the bygone epoch, of its lax and amorphous tout comprendre.*[5]

Mann was intent on establishing the degree of his participation in that will, which he characterized as being "anti-

Naturalistic, anti-Impressionistic, and anti-relativistic." [6]
That participation, he concluded, "has manifested itself
clearly enough in my case—not because of any want or need
to join and to participate, but because all I had to do was
listen to my own inner voice to hear the voice of my times." [7]

In the chapter "Einkehr" of the *Betrachtungen*, Thomas
Mann repeatedly draws our attention to that voice in his
works of the prewar period. We have quoted his reference to
Death in Venice. In the drama *Fiorenza*, it is, according to
Mann, the Prior Girolamo Savonarola who champions this
new morality and preaches the gospel of resoluteness and intolerance in the name of the spirit. Savonarola's will is passionately anti-Naturalistic, anti-Impressionistic, and anti-
relativistic. He is a far more radical brother in spirit of Gustav
von Aschenbach, fanatically demanding the total rejection of
the obscene psychologism, the laxness in morality and aesthetics rampant in his Florence, nurtured by the coterie of
effete aesthetes at the decadent court of Lorenzo de' Medici.

In the limpid fairy-tale novel, as Mann has called *Royal
Highness*, he also wanted us to recognize a product of this
insistence on selection and form:

Here, all of a sudden, is a book which did not at all "become"
and "grow," a book very far removed from the exuberant and
rank proliferation [Wucherndem und Strotzendem] of the earlier one [*Buddenbrooks*], a thoroughly formed book, consciously
structured on the principles of measure and proportion . . . a
play of art, not life.[8]

Does one catch in this quotation an echo of that passage in
Mann's letter to Samuel Lublinski announcing the author's
resolve to adhere strictly to the principles of selection and
form and condemning the external formlessness of his Naturalistic first novel? So great was our author's desire to see German belles-lettres ennobled that he even proposed the rein-
troduction of Classical masks on the modern stage. "They
would," he argued, "greatly further the spiritualization, styli-
zation, and purification of the stage. In short, they would
help elevate the theater." [9]

Envisaging the masterpiece of the twentieth century, Mann saw it as a work of art that would be "primarily logical, of faultless structure, and clear." That chef-d'oeuvre would be both disciplined and cheerful, of no less tension of the will than Wagner's art, but of a more detached, a more aristocratic, of a healthier mentality. Mann fully expected the dawn of a new Classicism to break: "A new Classicism, it seems to me, must come!" [10]

THE EXPRESSIONISTS

No doubt our poet did hear the voice of those of his contemporaries who sought to usher in a renaissance in ethics and aesthetics. Did he also hear the voice of that other group which succeeded Neoclassicism, the voice of Expressionism? Or was that voice so out of tune with Mann's, so alien to his nature, that it remained inaudible for him, inaudible, that is, in a productive sense? This has often been claimed. But one must be most careful in making such an assertion. It is true that the Expressionist's voice was alien, perturbing, even repellent to Mann, not the least because it was the voice of his brother Heinrich to whom he was so violently opposed in the years of the movement's rise and early flowering. He detested what he derisively called the "Vienna-Prague-Berlin explosions," referring to the Expressionistic works appearing in those cities. Their political activism, the violence and crassness of their language, he found "dreadful [grässlich]." [1] Their voices and attitudes left him full of suspicion and resentment:

An art movement [Expressionism] with violently activistic tendencies, a movement derisively critical of contemplativeness, of calm, objectivity, gaiety, and humor, incapable of appreciating epic tranquillity, a movement bent on a frantic dynamism of style, on crass expressivity, on vehement mobility, this movement suddenly demands that "spirit turn to action." That could make a right fine mess.[2]

The Expressionists' professions of pacifism failed to convince Mann. Their explosive, humorless, hard-bitten, wildly flamboyant style was to Mann its own best proof against their activistic peace proposals and programs. Mann's conviction that their voices actually preached war would not be shaken. "*Hier ist der Krieg!*" he stated with an impassioned emphasis quite unusual for him. He was particularly critical of the Expressionistic satirical social novel. The writers producing this "pseudo art" he accused of utter lack of conscience:

An Expressionism critical of social conditions [in Germany], lacking altogether in conscience and a sense of responsibility, depicting enterpreneurs who never existed, workers who do not exist, social "conditions" which, perchance, may have existed in England in 1850, an Expressionism that brews out of such ingredients its inflamatory-amatory murder stories, such a social satire is, indeed, utter humbug.[3]

In a letter to Ernst Bertram, Mann's judgment on the movement was again of a rare curtness and finality: "Expressionism aids and abets sloppiness of style; it is the ruin of prose!" [4]

On evidence such as this, it can hardly be argued that Mann was favorably disposed toward the movement, at least not during the war years when he expressed these opinions. Yet even during those years, Mann's sense of scrupulous fairness, his penchant for judging each person and each work of art for its own inherent value and not by its associations with a school, movement, or group, his perceptiveness in matters of artistic excellence asserted themselves and enabled him to recognize real merit.

He admired the tortured genius of Frank Wedekind, defended his drama *Die Büchse der Pandora* (*Pandora's Box*) against a philistine censorship, and acclaimed his dramatic masterpiece *Marquis von Keith* in a penetrating interpretation as one of the great works of modern German literature.[5] He held Franz Werfel, Franz Kafka,[6] and Max Brod in high esteem, and he admired Alfred Döblin's *Berlin Alexander-*

platz, even though this work belonged to the hated genre of
the expressionistic-satirical, social novel. He greatly loved
Hermann Hesse's *Demian*[7] and acclaimed his *Der Steppen-
wolf* as "the most interesting German novel of recent
times." [8] Above all, it must be remembered that Mann had
penetrated deeply and passionately into the realm of Expressionism during his intense preoccupation with the works of
Nietzsche and Dostoevsky, the two greatest Expressionists.

It certainly cannot be said that the voice of Expressionism
had not been heard by Mann, that this realm was altogether
closed to him. Had this been the case, he could never have
written *Doctor Faustus;* he could never have created the
character of Adrian Leverkühn, whose life and art are those
of an arch-Expressionist. His "wildest" novel, as he called it,
offers ample proof of how deeply, with what a sharply observing eye, and with what intense empathy Mann had experienced the mind and soul of the Expressionistic generation,
the temper of the times from which the movement sprang
and in which it developed. Compared with Mann's portrayal
of the modern artist, his frustrations, and his ultimate breakthrough into the demoniacally intense, ice-cold, hellishly
burning, ecstatic world—the world of the Expressionists—
even the most knowledgeable literary study of the movement
strikes us as academic and remote. Here, in Thomas Mann's
terrifying novel, in this book of pain, born in the tortured and
torturing days of the Nazi nightmare, we experience with
Adrian Leverkühn his agonizing struggles for new modes of
expression in an epigonous era of a devitalized, desiccated
traditionalism, in which art had run into a cul-de-sac and
seemed doomed to total stagnation. We experience with him
his dearly bought breakthrough into a new world of the
primitive, the elemental, and the intensely emotional, to the
protoform of expression: the cry of heartrending despair and
the shout of supreme exaltation. We share Adrian's deliver-
ance from the pale cast of thought; we experience with him
the resurrection of the soul with all its grief and joy, its love
and hate and its religious ecstasy—sensations that throb in the
works of such Expressionists as Dostoevsky, Barlach, Werfel,

Kornfeld. While composing his "devil's book," Mann felt much closer to Dostoevsky's apocalyptically grotesque world of suffering than to Tolstoy's Homeric protopower, for which at other times he had a definite predilection. Mann felt that in the composition of this work, this "life's sacrifice [Lebensopfer]," art had ceased to be a gay and lofty game and had suddenly become creation in dead earnest—a soul-rending labor of personal dedication, self-cognition, and confession. Painfully involved in the Expressionists' existential condition, Mann looked back with longing to the period in his life when he composed the *Joseph* tetralogy in the free and playful spirit of the artist safely sheltered in art's higher gaiety.

And yet, such is the paradoxical nature of this artist that, in spite of the deeply experienced self-identification with *Doctor Faustus*, Mann was nevertheless able to maintain something of that feeling of remoteness from his hero and his world that is so typical of all his writings. He could maintain the objective stance of the biographer and chronicler. He stood above his work, not primarily because his genius encompassed both the Expressionistic temperament of Leverkühn *and* the tempered Humanism of Serenus Zeitblom, but because his very nature demanded that skeptical distance even from the object of his deepest sympathy, his warmest admiration and love. While the chronicler's hand trembles with emotional involvement as he is setting down the awful fate of Adrian, his intellect remains clear and sharply focused enabling him to observe, analyze, and record with unerring precision. This attitude characterizes to some extent the biographer *within* the work, Serenus Zeitblom, but far more precisely, the chronicler *outside* and *above* it, the poet Thomas Mann.

When the young author said of himself that he was no joiner, that he stood aside and observed, he had expressed in homely words a profound truth about his nature as a man and artist. And yet, he had revealed only half the truth. For this inveterate observer was capable of intense sympathy and empathy, of sincere love and admiration. The reader is here face to face with the artist's enigma—with that paradoxical combination in a creative personality of the need for critical distance from life together with a longing for identification and participation in life.

Speaking of Theodor Fontane's ambivalent attitude toward Bismarck, Mann defined for us with fine precision his own "heartfelt ambivalence [herzbewegende Ambivalenz]," his own "skeptical love" for greatness:

I find that greatness is not only worthy of respect and honor, but that it is above all *interesting*, and I find that one can love, honor, and, at the same time, *doubt*; yes, I find that this kind of love and respect is the deepest of all.[9]

This seeing, knowing, skeptical love, this doubting love, with the stress falling with equal emphasis on the adjectives and on the noun, basically determined Mann's view of the world; it characterized his attitude toward the great figures of the past as well as toward his contemporaries. This paradoxical combination of skepticism and empathy, of distance and identification destined Thomas Mann to be the great chronicler of life, of the deep reaches of man's history, and of his own epoch—a chronicler and biographer, supremely observant, critical, detached, and yet, at the same time, capable of profound empathy and unstinting admiration.

4

The Hallmark of the Artist

From the moment Thomas Mann appeared on the literary scene, he showed himself possessed of a mature soberness, of circumspection, and of artistic tact startling in so young a writer. Mann's earliest literary activity—passing over his less-than-typical beginnings as coeditor of the student periodical, *Frühlingssturm* (Springstorm), and as coauthor with his brother Heinrich of the *Bilderbuch für artige Kinder* (Picture-book for Well-Behaved Children)—is surprisingly free of that ebullience typical of the rebellious spirit of youth. The dogmatic accent, grandiloquence, and pompous gesturing of *Sturm und Drang* are altogether absent from Mann's early work. Samuel Lublinski, a talented poet in his own right and a perspicacious critic, was the first to recognize and stress this quality of Mann's style. He characterized it as a "gentle persuasiveness [sanfte Überredung]." Reviewing Mann's *Buddenbrooks*, he praised the novel as an imperishable book, as one of those works that truly transcend the day and the epoch, that "do not carry us away with a tempestuous rush, but rather overwhelm us gradually and irresistibly with their gentle persuasiveness." [1]

The highly developed sense of order and responsibility of Thomas Mann's forebears has already been mentioned.[2] These qualities reappeared in the artist-son as hypertrophic punctiliousness and conscientiousness in the execution of his work. To an intimate friend of his youth, Paul Ehrenberg, Mann complained of the pains this idiosyncrasy was causing him: "Yes, I too have been working. That is, I have been hemming and hawing and have been torturing myself in an all but unbearable manner with doubts and hesitations, with my insatiability for perfection and the hypersensitivity of my artistic conscience."[3] And in his novella *Tristan* Mann coined, with a smiling glance at himself, that confessional witticism: "The writer is a man who has more difficulty with writing than all other people."[4]

Of course, Mann knew the surge and uplift of inspiration, of creative élan. Yet he would not rely on them. He possessed an astonishing perseverance, an unflagging determination to carry on his work whatever his mood and circumstance. When questioned on his manner of writing, Mann gave his reasons for keeping himself free from the influence of moods, of weather and the seasons. Otherwise, he explains, "because of my slow and stepwise manner of working, I would never be able to complete the large-scale compositions into which my initially modest projects have a way of growing."[5] We know the many modest projects that had this way of growing, which developed a will and direction of their own beyond the conscious control of their author. Mann has furnished an impressive list of the more striking examples in his lecture on *The Magic Mountain* to the students of Princeton University:

My first novel, *Buddenbrooks*, was meant to be a book of some 250 pages, after the pattern of Scandinavian novels of family and merchant life. It grew into two fat volumes. *Death in Venice* was to be a short short-story for the Munich periodical *Simplicissimus*. The same proved to be the case with the *Joseph* novels, which had been originally envisaged as a novella the size of *Death in Venice*.[6]

The Magic Mountain had been planned as a humorous companion piece to *Death in Venice* and was to be about the same length: a sort of satire on the tragedy just finished. Even his *Doctor Faustus*, which was to grow into one of his weightiest works both in its physical size and in its intellectual and emotional impact, was at first referred to as a mere "artist novella." [7]

Repeatedly Mann has described his manner of writing. Every morning he would spend three to four hours—from nine to about half past twelve—in complete seclusion with his creative work. Having an ingrained aversion to dictation, he always wrote in longhand. One and a half pages of manuscript was his usual daily output. So thoroughly were his texts prepared in his mind—usually on his favorite walks—that he could put them on paper with a minimum of corrections and deliver the first drafts, including those of his longest novels, directly to the typist and, in earlier days, even to the printer. [8]

Most of his works were very slow in developing, their plans and early drafts dating far back in his life. In fact, unless a work was deeply rooted in his personal experiences, Mann felt it could not be authentically his own. "A work must have long roots in my life," he explained in his speech on the *Joseph* novels. "Secret connections must lead from it to the earliest childhood dreams, if I am to claim a right to it, if I am to believe in the legitimacy of my undertaking. The arbitrary choice of a subject to which one has no longstanding claims of affection and knowledge, appears to me senseless and dilettantish." [9] Thus, the inception of his *Joseph* tetralogy actually reached back to his childhood [10] and, as he tells us in the *Story of a Novel*, the *Faust* theme also was one of those conceptions with secret links to boyhood dreams requiring a lifetime of experience and the agonizing nightmare of the Nazi years to reach its final realization. [11] What constancy in the creation of a work of art!

Perseverance—steadfastness in the performance of one's mission even on the verge of exhaustion—in this attitude Mann recognized his ideal of the heroic. His heroes are not men of bulging muscles and inexhaustible energies, not a

Hercules, not a Siegfried. For him heroism exists as an "in spite": *in spite* of weakness, *in spite* of frustrations, *in spite* of physical and mental suffering. For Thomas Mann the truly heroic is inextricably linked to pain; his heroes are of a delicate and highly sensitive constitution, which, despite its great delicateness is nonetheless capable of withstanding extreme tension.[12] Mann's legendary hero was Saint Sebastian, that personification of an "intellectual and virginal manliness, which clenches its teeth and stands in modest defiance of the swords and spears that pierce its side." [13] This "heroism from weakness" Mann has ennobled far beyond all popular heroics of brute strength and crude sensibilities. In his drama *Fiorenza* he has the heroine of the play share his disdain for brute strength. Fiore dismisses Piero, Lorenzo's power-drunk, muscly fop of a son with the cutting remark, "You are no hero! You are merely strong. And you bore me." And when Piero, accustomed to instant triumphs with ladies, protests in dumb disbelief, "Only strong? Only strong? Isn't he who is strong, isn't he a hero?!" Fiore retorts with a curt "No!" Then, relenting, she explains to the crushed princeling, "He who is weak and yet of such a glowing spirit as to win the prize—he is a hero." [14]

In Thomas Buddenbrook, Mann created his first *Leistungsethiker*, as he called this type of hero. Painfully aware of the uncontrollable decline of his energies and of his fortunes, Thomas tenaciously preserves the appearance of the successful man of social, political, and business affairs who steadfastly upholds the honor of his family against disruptive forces from within and without. The great majority of Mann's chief protagonists are kith and kin of such a man who, unflinchingly, carries on his mission even beyond his native capabilities: Girolamo Savonarola, the fanatical monk of the drama *Fiorenza* is such a man—weak of body but sustained by an indomitable will; Gustav von Aschenbach obeys the categorical imperative of achievement, ruthlessly taxing his spiritual energies beyond endurance; Klaus Heinrich, the unheroic hero of *Royal Highness*, who with his one sound hand—the other being shrivelled—accomplishes for his land more than most other people with their two. Even Perçeval, the high-bred aristocratic collie of *Royal Highness*, has his share of this heroism, suffering pain in stoic silence while ordinary canines yip and yowl.

The theme of the *Leistungsethiker* is indeed one of those that appear throughout the belletristic and essayistic writings of Thomas Mann. Friedrich Schiller of the short short-story "A Weary Hour," (1905) is a typical *Leistungsethiker*, and in so late a work as *Der Erwählte* (*The Holy Sinner*), completed in 1951, the characteristics of the hero from weakness are still in evidence, extolled in the figure of Grigorius, whose steadfastness in adversity and whose tenacious will turn native weakness into a strength capable of the seemingly impossible. As a boy, Grigorius defeats his older and much stronger foster-brother Flann in a boxing match by all but superhuman concentration of his psychophysical energies. He gains this victory, as the narrator of his extraordinary life explains, "because he knew how to concentrate 'his all' at every instant of the contest and to fight not only with his physical strength but with still other energies." [15] At another high point of the narrative, Grigorius again proves the superiority of a determined will over physical power. Defending his mother and bride-to-be, Sibylla, against the overbearing advances of the Red Knight Roger, he takes his hulking adversary captive by holding fast to the knight's sword and to his charger with "an unconditional grip [mit unbedingtem Griff]" [16] and dragging knight and horse into the fortress.

Mann shared with his heroes this pertinacity, this ability to concentrate "his all" unconditionally on the task at hand. Such concentration helped the poet to compensate for a less than robust constitution, to withstand turbulent times, the shock of revolution, exile, and war and, in the face of these dire adversities, to carry on his work. On arriving in Princeton, his first home in America, Thomas Mann sent this typical message to his friend Erich Kahler: "I am determined to carry on my accustomed life and work here with the greatest possible perseverance, unruffled by the events that can harm but never confuse or humiliate me." [17] Together with a highly developed sense of responsibility in his creative efforts such persistance basically determined his manner of work: "Every forenoon a step, every forenoon a phrase—that happens to be my way, and it has its inner necessity. . . . Not that this is a matter of timidity or of inertia; rather it is the result of an extremely lively sense of responsibility." [18] Moreover, there was still another important reason for punctilious attention to every detail of composition—the leitmotif. This stylistic device, Mann told us,

demands an extremely alert surveillance of the form and content of every sentence, for one can never tell beforehand whether a sentence or even a part of it might not be destined to recur, to serve as a motif, a significant link, a symbol, a quotation, an association. And a sentence that is to be heard twice must be raised to a high degree of significance, must . . . possess a symbolical mood. [19]

Small wonder that Mann developed a deep-seated suspicion of all facile productivity, and especially of the spurious inspiration that is triggered by alcohol, opiates, and other artificial stimuli and produces in the would-be artist a deceptive sense of omnipotence while removing all self-control and dulling the faculty of self-criticism. Thomas Mann strongly condemned such a state of mind. In a revealing and, as it turned out, prophetic critical reaction to Aldous Huxley's provocative book *The Doors of Perception*, Mann took issue with the author's recommendation of mescaline as a pleasant means of escape from a life that at best offers stultifying stupor and at worst pain and suffering. Mann would have none of such escapism. He frowned on any kind of trip, successful or botched, happy or terrifying: "It would disgust me to drug myself into a condition in which everything human would grow indifferent to me and I would find myself surrendering to moral turpitude in aesthetic self-indulgence." He was convinced that rapt contemplation of the existential miracle, the *Daseinswunder* of a chair or of sundry delectable color mirages, has far more to do with mental dullness than Huxley would care to admit. Already in 1954 Mann foresaw with grave misgivings the day "when a great number of English and especially American youths would try the experiment so eloquently espoused by the famous writer." [20] Mann condemned Huxley's best seller as "a book without conscience, a book which is sure to contribute its share to the intellectual stultification of the world, fatefully reducing its ability to face the deadly serious problems of our times with reasoned understanding." [21] Vladimir Nabokov, a writer with a very different background and of a very different artistic temperament, nonetheless held equally negative views on this matter of drug abuse. For him "there is nothing more philistine, more ovine, more bourgeois than this business of drug duncery." Nabokov recalled that "half a century ago, a similar fashion among the smart set of St. Petersburg was cocaine sniffing combined with phony orientalities." He was confident that "the better and brighter minds of [his] young American readers are far removed from those juvenile fads and faddists." [22]

Mastery of the artist's métier, brilliance of structure and style—these, Mann well knew, could be achieved only in total dedication, in "addiction" to one's work, not to alcohol or drugs:

Love of the subject, passion for it, a state of being filled and charged with the subject [that to Mann is the] only true source of all formal brilliance and beauty of style which are not—as one might believe—a mere addition, frill, and flourish, but the natural and inherent form of every thought worthy of being uttered.[23]

Love of the subject and passion for it, are indeed the driving forces that produced the monumental life work of Thomas Mann. Love and passion are the wellsprings of the untiring zeal with which Mann expanded, embellished, lent charm, humor, and transcending significance to a minimal plot. Did not Mann demonstrate this passionate zeal and loving devotion most impressively in his amplification and elaboration of the "all too brief narrative,"—in Goethe's words—"of the

biblical *Joseph* tale?" As Peter Heller, a perspicacious interpreter of Mann's work, observed with reference to this feat of
narrative skill: "To achieve such closeness of vision, to draw a
world of shapes so completely and fully into one's circle, requires a primary desire and delight, which is the opposite of
hostile indifference and thus a great erotic attachment be-
neath and beyond all modifications." [24]

Thomas Mann thought little of the artist's knack of in-
venting elaborate, thrilling plots. With Schopenhauer he
held that the epic writer's chief aim should be the conjuring
up of the richest inner life by means of a minimum of external action. In his essay on the "Art of the Novel," Mann
spelled out this conviction: "Art consists in the writer's
affecting our inner life most strongly with the least display of
outer life; for the inner is essentially the object of our interest." [25] Thus, in drawing his characters, it behooves the artist
to choose the details of outward life with the greatest of care,
to select only those elements of plot that carry the widest symbolical meaning and are capable of illuminating the deepest
recesses of the characters' psyches. For Mann, the hallmark
of a great writer was his power of observation and interpretation, which was gained at a terrible price of suffering, for such
clairvoyance unmasks the sweet lie of life and penetrates to
those agonizing depths of being that are mercifully concealed
from ordinary mortals. Thomas Mann wrote of this Pandora
gift to the poet:

The gaze which you fix as an artist upon the objects of the inner
and outer world is of a different sort than the one with which you
as a human being behold these very same objects; that gaze is at
once colder and more passionate. . . . Your demon forces you
to "observe," to perceive and record in a flash, with painful malice, every detail of life that is characteristic in a literary sense, has
typical signification, opens perspectives, marks distinctively the
racial, sociological, the psychological elements. It is your demon
that forces you to the task of observation just as if you had no
human ties whatever to the objects observed. It is thus that in a
work of art everything stands unmasked and revealed.[26]

But together with this gift of unmerciful exposure, the true artist, according to Mann, is endowed with the beneficent gift of animation, of *Beseelung*. "It is this power of animation that makes the great poet. . . . It is this unique ability to imbue matter with soul, to infuse it with what is inherently the poet's that makes matter become uniquely his own." [27] Mann possessed this gift to an unusual degree. Through his power of animation he assimilated into his own the vast body of material that entered his life's work. By means of it he placed the unmistakable imprint of his personality, of his soul, on his monumental *oeuvre*.

It has become fashionable to speak of Thomas Mann as the ironic German *par excellence*. One likes to dwell on his ambivalence, his reservation, his *Vorbehalt*. Often one comes close to making of our poet an outright nihilist. Herbert Lehnert certainly does not entertain any such extreme views, yet, in his valuable study, *Thomas Mann—Fiktion, Mythos, Religion*, he does speak of the "non-involvement of the narrator Thomas Mann," ascribing this non-involvement to the author's "poetic justice." [28] Poetic justice is indeed typical of Mann, yet it cannot be argued that it subverted his will to involvement, certainly not in the sociopolitical sphere, nor even in the playful freedom of his fictive world. To be sure, Mann has proclaimed as the truly fruitful principle of art that irony which plays subtly and undecidedly with opposites and is in no great hurry to arrive at conclusions. And yet, in the very process of the seemingly noncommittal free artistic play, the narrator Mann does, in fact, arrive at decisions, does give his answer and take his stand—not in dogmatic accents or in prophetic tones, but by way of the portrayal of such positive figures as, for example, Joseph the Provider. One need but compare Mann's *Joseph* tetralogy with Kafka's *The Castle* or *The Trial* to become instantly aware of Mann's great distance from a position of unrelieved ambivalence.

Thomas Mann has warned explicitly not to reduce the spirit that animates his creative work all too narrowly to a spirit of irony. In a radio speech on "Humor and Irony," he told his audience that he "had always felt rather bored when confronted with criticism which sought to reduce [his] work to the concept of irony and to make of [him] the ironic author par excellence." He was happy when his readers "recognized in [him] less the ironist and more the humorist"; he was anxious that they would not "disregard the element of humor in [his] works." [29] His *Joseph* tetralogy, perhaps his greatest achievement, he consistently called a humorous epic with a basic tonality of higher gaiety. Nor would he have us miss this basic tonality, this *Sangeston*, in his other works, in *Royal Highness*, for instance, or in *The Magic Mountain, Felix Krull,* or *The Holy Sinner.* Even so somber a novel as *Doctor Faustus* Mann strove to "lighten and brighten with humor," [30] convinced that without it any creative effort would be doomed to failure.

This is the reason Mann demanded so urgently that he be recognized for the humorist he was. He insisted on this proper appreciation of his art, for it concerned the very core of his being, his life's philosophy, the salvation of his soul: "The comical—laughter, humor—these reveal themselves to me more and more as the very salvation of the soul; I thirst after them." [31] He wanted us to know that humor does not spring from alienation, disillusion, bitterness, or the cynicism of nihilism as irony often does, being close kin to satire and caricature.

Thomas Mann would have wholeheartedly agreed with Mark van Doren's high praise of a sense of humor as the hallmark of the man with openness of mind and greatness of soul:

Nothing in man is more serious than his sense of humor; it is the sign that he wants all the truth, and sees more sides of it than can be soberly and systematically stated; it is the sign, furthermore, that he can remember one idea even while he entertains another, and that he can live with contradictions. It is the reason at any rate that we cannot take seriously one whose mind and heart have never been known to smile. The gods do not weep; they smile. Eternity is something like the sun.[32]

Van Doren recognized in this sense of humor, the key to a proper understanding of Mann's skeptical genius—of his ability to comprehend and entertain together a host of diverse ideas, his capacity for a kaleidoscopic change of mood. "These transformations of his mood will bewilder anyone," van Doren is convinced, "who does not comprehend how serious at last the comic spirit is." [33] Such a reader surely will misinterpret Mann's skepticism as nihilistic disdain for ideas and feelings. Yet, once he discovers the pervasive humor in Mann's works, he will be able to appreciate van Doren's apt characterization of Thomas Mann as a truly tolerant spirit:

It was not that he [Mann] believed nothing; he believed everything; he liked ideas, and could live with all of them at once. No sooner did one start up in his brain than another came to reinforce, illuminate, or check it. This was why he could turn so soon from tenderness to pathos, and why he could mock the very man he loved most.[34]

Of course, Mann knew well how to mock and how to wield the devastating weapon of scathing sarcasm. He was quite capable of sardonic invective and outbursts of deadly hatred, as he proved in his attacks on the Nazis, whom he called on more than one occasion the devil's excrement (*Teufelsdreck*). Satire is by no means absent from his work; it usually appears in association with caricature and the grotesque. We find it in Mann's sketches and snatches of verse preserved for us by Victor Mann from the lost *Bilderbuch für artige Kinder*; in his portrayal of Detlev Spinell, the "decayed infant," and of Klöterjahn, the arch philistine in the novella *Tristan*; in Lobgott Piepsam—note the satiric, well-nigh Gogolian play with names—of *Der Weg zum Friedhof* (*Way to the Cemetery*); or again in the Dwarf Dûdû of the *Joseph* tetralogy, that caricature of the strutting, sex-proud, chauvinistic Nazi nincompoop. And finally, to mention one more example, one detects that same satiric portrayal in the loquacious impressario Saul Fitelberg, Adrian Leverkühn's satanic tempter, with his unmistakable resemblance to Lessing's satirical takeoff on volubility, cupidity, pretense, and vainglory in the Chevalier Riccaut de la Marlinière, Seigneur de Prat-au-val of his comedy *Minna von Barnhelm*.[35] And yet, when we examine Mann's characters closely, we recognize that even those drawn in his most satirical vein are experienced and portrayed with a sympathy and an empathy that are never completely absent in this author's works.

The same holds true for Mann's parodistic style, which he developed in the works of his middle and late period, beginning with *The Magic Mountain*. His parody was not to be the destructive kind exemplified by the scathingly parodistic takeoff on Schiller's Storm and Stress drama, *Die Räuber* (*The Robbers*), from the pen of Heinrich Mann and young Thomas which Victor Mann has rescued from oblivion in his family reminiscences.[36] Whatever part Thomas may have had in the authorship of these and similar immature efforts—and it was probably minor, he having been at that time under the influence of his older brother—this type of parody disappeared from the writings of the mature artist. His parody developed into a subtle kind, discernible only to the initiated reader with an ear attuned to the cadences of classical German. It is, for instance, not at all easy to recognize the parodistic nature of *The Magic Mountain* or the *Confessions of Felix Krull, Confidence Man*. And yet these works are just that, subtle parodies of a classical model, of the time-honored but also time-worn novel of education, the *Bildungsroman*, which had been carried to its triumphant climax by Goethe in his *Wilhelm Meister*. Of *Felix Krull* Mann helpfully told us that it was built "on the parodistic idea of transposing an element of beloved tradition, the Goethean autopedagogical, autobiographical, aristocratic tradition . . . into the sphere of criminality." [37] Note the adjective "beloved" in this quotation. While *parodying* content and form of the venerable exemplar, Mann *loved* it all the while. This parodist's basic impulse is not to destroy but to preserve cultural values, while yet transforming their structure and their style into a more viably modern form.

How did Mann achieve this transformation and regeneration of traditional forms? Perhaps his clearest answer is the one the poet gave us in *Doctor Faustus,* in Adrian's conversation with the devil. Here Adrian ponders on ways of escaping from the dreadful cul-de-sac in which he finds himself. "One could," he muses, "potentiate the game [of artistic creation] by playing with the very forms from which, as we well know, all life has vanished." The devil, to be sure, dismisses this solution with derision. "I know, I know," he counters, "Parody! That could be fun, if only parody were not so dismally boring in its aristocratic nihilism." He proposes instead a truly diabolical breakthrough into an art that "springs from inspiration that is not sicklied over with the blight of debilitating circumspection, of criticism and deadening intellectual control." [38] Adrian accepts the devil's proposition and enters the pact to become the tortured victim of black magic.

To Thomas Mann the devil's proposition was unacceptable. He would not be the creator of an art that spurns the sobering control of intellect. We have a letter by the poet to his musician-son Michael, in which he described with candor and precision his relation to Adrian's hell-inspired music. He characterized his attitude as "composed of feelings of compassion and respect rather than of affection" and stressed that he would never have written such music. He had felt much happier, he told his son, "when describing very different compositions, for example the *Leonore* Overture or the Prelude to *Die Meistersinger* . . . than when describing [Adrian's] Oratorio Series," which he recognized to be an art of despair. To be sure, he had "experience with this type of art, but never had [he] fallen prey to it." [39]

No, Mann never became a victim of this art of despair. Instead, he took the very pathway of escape Adrian had caught sight of. Mann would not be deterred by the devil's argument against experimenting with the device of parody. He did potentiate the game of artistic creation by playing with the very forms from which life had vanished. Far from surrendering to orgies of irrationalism, he cultivated an art of higher gaiety, which is an apt definition of Mann's type of parody. This parody did not destroy traditional structures and styles, but gave them new life by refusing to take them in dead earnest, by infusing them with the gaiety of wit and humor, by playing with them. This parody produced its subtle effect by such devices as mock exegesis of traditional themes, elaborate commentaries by the author on the sources of his tale, and adroit allusions to, and apt quotations from, the masterpieces of the past[40] that evoke a smile of recognition in the informed and attentive reader. The most extreme, even if (for that very reason) not the most satisfying example of this style, is Mann's playful parody of Hartmann von Aue's *Gregorius* in *The Holy Sinner*. This novel Mann characterized as "a late work in every sense, not only in view of the advanced hour of history [Spätzeit] in which it was written. It is a work that carries on its playful game with the ancient, venerable values of a long tradition." He admits that "there is much of travesty here" but is quick to add that "this travesty is not loveless." [41] Here all the devices of Mann's parodistic manner are in full play, transforming content and form of the venerable model into the highly sophisticated, thoroughly self-conscious orchestration of Mann's prose, which suddenly, as at the touch of a magician, proves capable of expressing with limpid precision and scintillating verve the depth and breadth of modern sensibility in all its baffling psychological complexity.

Obviously, the sardonic, scathing, sarcastic tone was not characteristic of Thomas Mann. In the *Betrachtungen* he explained:

I was perhaps too positively oriented to have been predisposed for negative characterization, for the pamphlet, and for satire lacking in sympathy. I am aware of the fact that without sympathy nothing can be created in three-dimensional form, that mere negation is bound to end in shallowly flat caricature [flächiger Karikatur].[42]

The type of irony characteristic for him, Mann has called "loving irony." At other times he defined it as "epic irony," in order to characterize with that term the artist's attitude from which such irony springs, namely, his ability to observe life with epic equanimity, mit *epischem Gleichmut*. Mann hastened to explain that such epic irony by no means excludes or even inhibits the artist's sympathy for, and empathy in, life. We should not, he warned, associate with it aloofness or derisiveness. "One should not, hearing this word, think of coldness of heart, of lovelessness, of mockery and derision; rather, this epic irony is an irony coming from the heart, it is loving irony, it is that magnanimity that is full of tenderness toward all that is small." [43] Or as Mann phrased it in a later essay, "The Artist and Society":

Art does not thrust the devil's cold fist . . . into the face of life. Rather, it is created to infuse life with spirit. Art is allied with goodness and in its depths there is a kindliness closely akin to wisdom and even more closely to love.[44]

Despite these warnings, perhaps even challenged by them, some critics continue to claim that Mann's irony prevented the author's empathy with life, that as an artist Mann lacked warmth, humor, and kindliness and was incapable of a loving appreciation and a realistic, positive portrayal of man and nature. An extreme statement of this view we find in Klaus-Jürgen Rothenberg's recent study of the problem of Realism in Thomas Mann's work.[45] The author argues that Mann's manner of observing and recording life is not that of a realist but rather that of an inveterate cynic: "The observing eye of the artist Thomas Mann is as malicious as it is brutal. . . . In the last analysis everything comes down to pursuing, spying on, and catching in the act [Verfolgen, Belauern und Ertappen]." [46] And for good measure Rothenberg adds: "To the maliciousness is joined the viciousness of Mann's stance. . . . It is not the exact eye, it is the hyper-exact, the 'evil' eye [der 'böse Blick'] that is characteristic of Thomas Mann." [47] This gravely prejudiced view of Mann's artistry leads this critic to see in the poet's work nothing but "comedy and wretchedness," a veritable panopticum of grotesquely distorted caricatures and evil parodies of reality; it leaves him totally unable to appreciate the many portraits that Mann drew with genuine empathy, yes even with love. Just one such scene as Rachel's death in the *Geschichten Jaakobs* (IV, 384–389), over which this supposed cold and malicious author shed tears of deeply felt loss,[48] should suffice to convince any sensitive reader of the wrongheadedness of the type of criticism presented in Rothenberg's study.

Reinhard Baumgart in his thoughtful analysis of irony in Mann's works[49] approaches the illusive problem with far greater fairness, caution, and circumspection. Yet even he sees Thomas Mann's irony as blocking the artist's access to life. He states categorically: "His [Mann's] Eros can and must never reach 'life' precisely because this Eros wants to remain irony." [50] There is, of course, no denying the fact that Mann's Eros contains the element of irony. But is this irony really the cause for Mann's inability to reach life? Does his Eros really *want* to remain irony? We would rather agree with Mann that, on the contrary, his Eros fused and intermingled with his irony to establish his loving contact with life while yet guarding against his blindly emotional surrender to it. We have it on Goethe's authority that "one does not escape the world more surely than through art, and one does not link oneself more surely to it than through art." [51] It would appear to us that Goethe's words characterize with fine precision the stance of the poet Thomas Mann: able to maintain a distance to the slice of life he wishes to form and shape, yet linked to it all the more firmly through this paradoxical power of art.

Progressive Universal Poesy

In his lively, challenging book, *The Ironic German: A Study of Thomas Mann*, Erich Heller acclaimed our poet as "the perfect Romantic of Friedrich Schlegel's expectations" [1] and demonstrated how well Schlegel's definition of Progressive Universal Poesy[2] fits Mann's *The Magic Mountain*. It is truly astonishing how close most of Mann's works, including such relatively minor efforts as *The Beloved Returns* and *The Holy Sinner* come to fulfilling the extravagant demands of the Romanticists. Thus, quite in accordance with romantic expectations, Mann's works are sensitively attuned to every modern trend even though they are rooted in tradition. They "reunite the separate genres of literature and blend epic, lyric, and dramatic modes"; they "mix and mingle creative spontaneity with critique" and "satiate the medium of art with solid learning of every kind," to quote from Schlegel's recipe for his "masterpiece of Romanticism." [3]

Thomas Mann certainly fulfilled the ideal of using "solid learning of every kind" in his masterpieces. One is hard put to enumerate, much less trace in detail, all the excursions Mann has made into the most diverse disciplines. Thus in the preparation of *The Magic Mountain* he undertook the study of medicine, biology, and the occult; in his "descent into the bottomless well of time" in the *Joseph* tetralogy he explored Judaic and Egyptian myth and history; and in setting out on the composition of *Doctor Faustus* he immersed himself once again into history and myth, this time of the medieval and the most modern periods, into sociology and philosophy, politics and music, and the terrifying pathology of an individual and of a nation. Mann was convinced that only narration that was detailed and exact could be truly entertaining. In this conviction he perused whole libraries and unhesitatingly enlisted the aid of experts in order to obtain the desired factual information.

Such an emphasis on details was Mann's standing practice from his earliest beginnings to his last great works. For the *Buddenbrooks* he collected a mass of memorabilia by untiring research into family records, into the history of Lübeck and by way of a far-flung correspondence with relatives, friends, and acquaintances. While fashioning the vast *Joseph* tetralogy, he sought and obtained advice and information from his friend and collaborator Karl Kerényi,[4] the great Hungarian mythologist and historian of religious thought; in his labors on *Doctor Faustus* he drew to his side the musicologist Theodor W. Adorno as counselor and participating instructor. Mann never hesitated to admit his dependence on professional assistance and did not spare commendation of faithful advisers. Adorno he praised as "the helper, counselor, and participating instructor who—by dint of his extraordinary professional competence and intellectual rank, proved to be precisely the right one." [5] "The right one" to furnish the most advanced and sophisticated information that could serve as the solid factual base and framework for the modern novel. In a letter to me, Thomas Mann wrote:

From the very beginning [of the composition of *Doctor Faustus*] it was clear to me that one can no longer write an "artist novel" in which the genius of the hero is merely asserted. I had to prove it, had to make it real; I had to demand exactness of myself—at any cost, even at the price of obtaining help from specialists, so that every detail would be unassailable.[6]

This stress on the reliability of the factual material that Mann worked into his compositions should not deceive us, however, about the true nature of the author's erudition and the function of solid facts in his fiction. Mann repeatedly sought to disillusion those who would think of him as a savant, a specialist, an encyclopedic mind eager to gather and retain scientific facts for their own sake. In a revealing letter to Irita Van Doren, he humorously dispelled this impression. He admitted that in the grip of inspiration, under the compulsion of a large-scale artistic project, he would collect and absorb an enormous mass of information. However, as soon as the work had been completed, he promptly jettisoned all that laboriously gathered wisdom:

When it was a matter of laying the scientific foundation for a work of art, when it was necessary to collect positive information in order then to play with it in the spirit of art . . . I could develop a bee-like industry. Thus I had been, in turn, a learned physician, a biologist, an orientalist well-versed in my specialty, an Egyptologist, a mythologist, a historian of religious thought, a specialist for medieval culture and poetry, and more of the like. The sad fact, however, is that just as soon as the work for the sake of which I had plunged into all that research was done and finished with, I would forget all that ad hoc acquired wisdom with unbelievable alacrity and would walk about empty-headed, in the wretched knowledge of my total ignorance.[7]

Mann is, of course, exaggerating. And yet there is in his statement more than a grain of truth. He did "forget" and that forgetting was a therapeutic, probably subconscious, stratagem by means of which the poet unburdened his mind of useless freight and thus kept it alert and ever receptive of new challenges and spiritual adventures.

Mann treated facts not as a scientist who gathers data for their own intrinsic value, but as an artist whose genius compels him to lend to the world of his imagination the flesh-and-bone substance of factual reality, and to fashion novels that would *be*—as he put it—what they *speak* about: *be* music, *be* philosophy, *be* myth and legend and history, yet, above all, *be* the gay and lofty game of art. Of course, the facts are there in Mann's fictional world, solid and in rich array. Yet, reading Mann's creations or, for that matter, belles-lettres in general, it is important to keep in mind that the facts of fiction are the stuff of art and so cannot be judged or even enjoyed for their intrinsic value or reliability. As Mann has warned us:

The intellectual message in a work of art is not properly understood if it is taken as a message for its own sake—it derives its purpose solely from its relation to the artistic composition; it stands and affirms itself only with reference to it. . . . Taken in an absolute sense, as a literal statement, it may be banal, and yet, within the structure of the work of art, that same statement can be witty and full of meaning.[8]

A poet takes liberties with facts; he arranges, shapes, and stylizes them. Mann defined this sovereign freedom of the artist in his essay "Bilse und ich" ("Bilse and I"). Defending himself against accusations of falsification in the *Buddenbrooks* of Lübeck's social history and familial facts, he stated flatly, "When I have made a sentence out of a thing—what does this thing still have to do with the sentence!?" And he went on to explain:

The reality which an author draws upon for his purposes may be his daily life, it may be the people who are nearest and dearest to him. He may observe with utmost precision all the circumstances furnished by reality; he may make use of each one of them in detail, avidly. And yet, there will remain for him (and should remain for all the world) an abysmal difference between that reality and his representation of it: the kind of difference that separates forever the world of reality from the world of art.[9]

It cannot surprise us to find the good burghers of Lübeck feeling abused and insulted upon discovering that their personal lives had been exposed in the guise of art to the inquisitive gaze of an ever-growing international audience. It is rather more startling to realize that even eminent professional men took strenuous exception to the manner in which Mann had treated facts in their special areas of competence: physicians, for instance, disapproved of the depiction in *The Magic Mountain* of the life in a Davos sanatorium and were particularly incensed at Mann's portrayal of Doctor Behrens, considering that portrayal an insult to their profession. A German prince felt moved to take exception to Mann's depiction of his "class" in the novel *Royal Highness*. Germanists took umbrage with Mann's treatment of Goethe in *The Beloved Returns*, accusing Mann of historical inaccuracies and of a lack of reverence for the sacrosanct figure of the greatest of German poets. Theologians resented the secularization of the gospels in the *Joseph* tetralogy. Nor could all musicians agree with the way Mann had presented their art and profession in *Doctor Faustus*; Schoenberg even went so far as to accuse the author publicly of having plagiarized his twelve-tone system. On some occasions, when basic misunderstandings of the message of his work were involved, Mann felt moved to reply. He did so in a conciliatory spirit, in the sincere desire to remove misunderstandings, to assuage angry passions and to clarify issues.[10] Mostly, however, he reacted with silence in pained resignation, unable to comprehend how intelligent men could fail to recognize and value his books for what they were—works of art and not of scholarship.

Käte Hamburger, a conscientious and sensitive interpreter of Mann's works, in a searching study of the *Joseph* tetralogy[11] points out a basic anachronism the poet committed by placing his Joseph figure into the reigns of the Pharaohs Amenhotep III and IV which postdate Joseph's years in Egypt by at least two centuries according to the all but unanimous opinion of the experts. But Miss Hamburger takes no offense. She has the sensibility and good sense to appreciate the triumph of Mann's art in creating, despite or, rather, by dint of, this very anachronism, a heightened image of the figures and their times. As a perceptive critic, she was able to accept and enjoy the artist as he shaped and fashioned his narrative with its own logic and accuracy, with the playful logic of art.

Hermann Weigand called *The Magic Mountain* "the most highly integrated of all novels conceived on a grand scale," [12] and Erich Heller has admirably illustrated how one chapter of that novel "mirrors" the work in its totality. He used for illustration the chapter "Snow," [13] but other chapters, "Soup of Eternity" and "Sudden Clarity," for instance, or "Humaniora" could have served his purpose quite as well. However, not only chapters but also far smaller units of the narrative are capable of such mirroring, down to sentences or even to expressions made up of merely two or three words. These units, called leitmotifs, acquire this power by being charged with the emotional and ideational content of the entire work by the subtle process of association as they appear and reappear at various crucial points in the narrative. As these leitmotifs recur they cause in the attentive reader's mind an instant recall of much that has passed before. Readers enjoying the work a second time will be able, with their help, to anticipate what is still to come; they will be able to foresee the epic future of the narrative. Thus the sequential flow of narration is transformed into a *nunc stans*, a constant presence of the entire novel in the reader's mind. It is of such an effect, of such integration, that Friedrich Schlegel must have thought when he asked the accomplished poet "to infuse every part of his creation with the identity of the whole . . . to multiply reflection as if in an infinite series of mirrors." [14]

It has been frequently observed that Mann's leitmotif technique underwent a long and complex development.[15] Initially, in the *Buddenbrooks*, Mann employed the leitmotif as a purely descriptive device, the kind that has been used by such diverse poets as Homer in the *Iliad* or Otto Ludwig in the novel *Zwischen Himmel und Erde* (*Between Heaven and Earth*). Here the leitmotif is a fixed epithet firmly attached to a person (*grey-eyed* Athene, *brilliant* Achilleus) or to an object (*black* ships of the Argives), or it is an unvarying descriptive pattern of action (*He fell, thunderously, and his armour clattered upon him.*) These epithets fix in our memory, by way of insistent repetition, certain aspects of a person or of a happening that may or may not carry a deeper meaning. With Mann, even in his earliest works, they usually did have a more profound, a symbolical significance, as, for instance, the blue veins on the hands of Gerda and Hanno Buddenbrook, which are suggestive of decadence, or Tony's pertly upturned nose, which signifies, none too subtly, the unsapped vitality and undaunted pride of this steadfast Buddenbrook.

Already in *Tonio Kröger* (1902), however, the leitmotif assumes a distinctly musical function. Here Thomas Mann successfully took up the challenge of Wagner's leitmotif and strove to achieve in the verbal medium its magical effect. As Mann has explained, "the leitmotif is here no longer a purely physiognomical-naturalistic device which it still was in the *Buddenbrooks*; it has now acquired an ideal emotional transparency [eine ideelle Gefühlstransparenz] which frees it from a merely mechanical function and raises it to the musical plane." [16] How well Mann succeeded with this transformation is demonstrated by one of the central motifs of the novella which grows in its accoustic effect with each repetition and achieves its "musical" climax as the closing sentence of the work: "Schelten Sie diese Liebe nicht, Lisaweta; sie ist gut und fruchtbar. *Sehnsucht ist darin und schwermütiger Neid und ein klein wenig Verachtung und eine ganze keusche Seligkeit.*" *

It is characteristic for these "musical" leitmotifs to become rhythmic, syntactical molds, as it were, into which Mann poured the most diverse ideational content. Thus, to give but one example, when we read in the essay, "Von deutscher Republik" ("The German Republic"), written in 1922, the sentence, "*Goethe ist darin und das Beste, Zukünftigste, Erzieherischste, was Nietzsche war, und die*

---

* "Do not chide this love, Lisaweta; it is good and fertile. Longing is in it and melancholy envy and no little chaste blissfulness." (*Tonio Kröger*. VIII, 338.)

Tempelandacht des Novalis," † we are at once made conscious of the fact that despite an altogether different thought
which the passage conveys its rhythmic pattern is, basically,
that of the italicized portion of the *Tonio* motif. Naturally, it
is not and is not intended to be, an exact mechanical reproduction of the original pattern; rather it is a variation on it.
Nonetheless, the ear attuned to verbal cadences can not possibly miss the close kinship. As Mann was fashioning this sentence there was echoing in his mind—across some fifteen intervening years—the "music" of the exquisite leitmotif of the
novella.

This type of acoustic and/or ideational self-quotation over
wide stretches of time satisfied, in a subtle way, a basic desire
of our poet: to link the totality of his life's work into one
enormous composition which would, ideally, be present as a
whole at any given moment in the attentive reader's mind—a
"magical *nunc stans.*" [17]

In *The Magic Mountain,* the leitmotif becomes primarily,
if not exclusively, a vehicle of ideas. I have attempted to illus-
trate and analyze this stage in its development in my essay
"Ein 'symbolisches Formelwort' in Thomas Mann's *Zauberberg,*" [18] where I demonstrate how such leitmotif phrases as
"up here," "down there," "up here with you," "up here with
them," and "up here with us" by subtle reappearance at critical points in the composition are gradually endowed with the
power of "mirroring" the development and growth of Hans
Castorp. They help trace his progress into the Hermetic
sphere of the mountain and his efforts to free himself from
its enigmatical spell.

In the *Joseph* tetralogy, the leitmotif experiences a transcendence from its function as a stylistic device to that of a
life philosophy, the highly romantic world view of life as a
cycle or, rather, life as a spiral, characterized by the emer-
gence and reappearance of certain mythical "orbiting images"

† "Goethe is in it and the best, the most progressive, and the most
  educative that was in Nietzsche, and the temple devotion of Novalis."
  ("Von deutscher Republik." XI, 846–847.)

[Kreislaufbilder]. The ever-repeated appellation of this world view as the "revolving sphere" [rollende Sphäre] is a very apt definition of the nature and function of the leitmotif as occurrence and reoccurrence of orbiting images on earth, in the Heavens, and back on earth again, in subtly varied shapes and forms. Thus the ever-recurring pattern of redemptive sacrifice, as Mann developed it in the images of Osiris, Tamuz, and Adonis, and in young Joseph's descent into the well, the pit, the grave, the prison, and his ultimate elevation to the side of Pharaoh, is an orbiting image that points, by a multitude of leitmotif cues, to its ultimate realization in Christ's sacrificial death, His descent into Hell, and His ascension into Heaven.

Beyond this stage, it becomes very difficult to trace the development of Mann's leitmotif technique. To be sure, the leitmotif's continued presence can be detected in *Doctor Faustus*. Yet the very complexity of its interrelating associations, cross-affiliations, and subtle permutations in the intricate texture of this novel contributes greatly to the blurring of the leitmotif's characteristic quality as the readily recognizable reoccurrence and progressive development of a specific image or an idea verbalized in unmistakably repetitive terms. In brief, it has no longer the clearly demonstrable function in the composition of a formula firmly associated throughout the work with a particular person, situation, or sentiment, to use the *Oxford Dictionary* definition of the leitmotif. Thus the leitmotif tends to lose its function as a stylistic device, its musical or ideational thrust and effect, precisely because of the high degree of sophistication it reaches at this late stage of its development.

Moreover, the leitmotif in *Doctor Faustus* became associated with, if not replaced by another stylistic device that Mann adopted in the composition of this novel. He called it "montage." This device, embarrassingly close to plagiarism,[19] was nevertheless freely used by Mann, for it was his overriding aim to lend his novel the highest possible degree of verisimilitude and actuality precisely by means of more or less verbatim excerpts from works of literary history and criticism as well as from historical and contemporary documents of all types. The author has enumerated some of the many instances of the

intertwining of the tragedy of Leverkühn with that of Nietzsche. . . . There is the verbatim introduction of Nietzsche's brothel experience in Cologne as well as the record of all the symptoms of his sickness; there are, in addition, the *Ecce Homo* quotations delivered by the devil, there is the exact reproduction of the dietary menus as given by Nietzsche in his letters from Nizza, or again, there is the unobtrusive account of Deussen's last visit to the mentally deranged [Nietzsche] with the bouquet of flowers.[20]

Mann wove these and a multitude of other extracts so skillfully into the texture of his composition that the fictive world could no longer be distinguished from the world of palpable reality. Mann admitted the questionable nature of this montage technique; it continued to trouble him, and yet he was firmly convinced that this device "belonged to the very conception, to the central 'idea of the novel.' " [21] He wrote to his son Michael, "I was determined to use all forms of 'montage,' because what we both call by that name is intimately involved in this book's transcendence of the merely literary, in its 'shedding of the illusion of art,' its realism." [22]

Mann drew the psycho-philosophical justification for this type of borrowing from his conviction that facts and ideas, once they are incorporated into a work of art, lose their original signification, assume a new identity, and derive their effect solely from their function within the structure of the work. In Mann's opinion an artist could and should not respect the stamp of copyright on the material he draws from the realm of life, or, for that matter, from the realm of letters. "An idea," Mann argued, "will never possess much intrinsic value for the artist. What matters to him is the capacity of the idea to perform its function in the spiritual context of his work." [23]

Further clarification and precise definition of the nature both of the leitmotif and of the montage technique in

Mann's infinitely complex late works will have to await detailed studies more comprehensive than the excellent contributions by Gunilla Bergsten and Hans Wysling, which point the way both in a scholarly and an imaginative manner.[24]

In the masterpieces of his mature period and old age, Thomas Mann seems to smile down upon his creations in the manner of Goethe who—in a memorable characterization by Friedrich Schlegel—had "smiled down" on the vast world of his *Wilhelm Meister*. In Goethe's novel, Schlegel had recognized the foremost example of "universal poesy in the making." [25] One wonders what Schlegel would have thought of Mann's *The Magic Mountain*, the *Joseph* tetralogy, *Doctor Faustus*, and *Felix Krull*. He might well have acclaimed these works as universal poesy not merely in the making but actually accomplished.

In the spirit of Romantic irony Mann played with these compositions. He took his stance outside and above them, contemplating them with loving irony. Playfully he would assume the role of audience, commentator, and critic of his own productions, and in this role would carry on a witty dialogue with the readers, designed to dissolve the epic integrity of the naive narrative and to transform it into a self-conscious, that is, a modern, reflective work of art, in terms of Friedrich Schlegel's famous definition.

Erich Heller furnishes several well-chosen examples of Mann's Romantic irony in *The Magic Mountain*. He shows, for instance, how Mann effectively breaks the objectivity of his narrative by speaking *in propria persona*, addressing the reader and warning him of what there is to come: "At this point the author [Mann] feels it would be advisable for him to express his surprise at what is coming next, or else the reader might try to do it for himself and overdo it." [26] One could cull many other equally apt passages from this and other works, but one additional example can stand for many. Thus we read the opening sentence of the *Joseph* stories and are at once made aware of a sophisticated narrator: "Deep is the well of the past. Should one not call it bottomless?" With this question a direct involvement of the reader with the author is immediately established. The author steps out of the frame of the epic narrative to address his audience directly with a request for agreement. The objectivity of the epic mode is intentionally broken. Thomas Mann then proceeds to explain the utter futility of his attempt to plumb the depths of the past. Such an "explanation" is, of course, another device employed by the author to further transmute the traditional form of the novel. The wonder is that the epic quality of Mann's narrations is not lost but rather enhanced into a thoroughly modern form. The reason for this unique phenomenon may be found in the fact that Mann's playful approach to his work in the spirit of Romantic irony is constantly checked and counterpoised by his sincere involvement with his creations. This paradoxical combination of freedom and involvement, which we had already occasion to characterize as typical of the poet, may well be the ultimate source for the unique stylistic quality of Mann's work, which manages to combine the life-like realism of epic narration with audacious flights of imagination, with the lyrical timbre and with the intellectual lustre and sophistication of romantic art at its best.

Friedrich Schlegel had demanded of the modern author, who would attempt to create the masterpiece of Romanticism and furnish with it the grand model of progressive universal poesy, that he be above all "a wholly free and educated person capable of attuning himself at will to philosophy or philology, to criticism or poetry, to history or rhetoric, to the ancient or the modern—just as one tunes an instrument." [27] Granting that even Mann's instrumentation was not of such a scope, one must nevertheless admit that he all but satisfied this ideal of Schlegel's imagination. In his works he is historian and critic, philosopher and poet, rhetorician and philologist, and he does adjust himself to the ancient and the modern; he is both the mythologist and the psychologist in a unique union of talents. Moreover, Mann has exactly the stance that Schlegel ascribes to the romantic poet. According to him, such a poet "writes his autobiography and, in writing it, sets forth the image of his epoch." [28] This is exactly what our poet did in every one of his major works, and even in some minor ones, beginning with the early novellas. In the *Buddenbrooks*, to single out but one striking example, Mann had dealt with events and developments that profoundly concerned and agitated him, problems that were part of his intensely personal experience, which subsequently proved to be of general concern. The decline of a Lübeck family was soon recognized as a development of European scope, the decline of Western bourgeois society. "In Switzerland, Holland, and Denmark [Thomas Mann] had heard young people exclaim: 'This process of escape from bourgeois existence [Entbürgerlichung] by way of differentiation, by way of excessive sensibility—exactly as with us!' " [29] Illuminating and objectifying his personal experiences in artistic form, seeking and gaining deeper insight into the meaning of events impinging on his personal life, Mann helped entire generations to a clearer understanding of the cultural and social, even the political, developments of their times. In a very real sense it can be said of Mann that he was always writing his autobiography, fragments of a great confession, to use Goethe's famous phrase, and in so doing was setting forth the image of his epoch and, in his greatest creations, the timeless image of man.

It should be evident that Mann in the content and style of his works, came surprisingly close to Schlegel's ideal of progressive universal poesy. One would suspect that Schlegel's thoughts on the nature of romantic poetry had a direct influence on Mann. Yet Mann's extant writings yield no evidence of a more than cursory acquaintance with the Romanticists' theoretical discourses. And, most surprisingly, he seems not to have used anywhere in his extensive writings on romantic art the term "progressive Universalpoesie." Mann does, however, speak of the *Gesamtkunstwerk* and is obviously using this term to describe a type of art much closer to Schlegel's idea of progressive universal poesy than to Wagner's definition of the total work of art. In fact, Mann explicitly rejects Wagner's concept. Praising his friend and fellow poet René Schickele for having recognized in the art form of

the novel the total work of art, Thomas Mann expresses a
special fondness for that idea but would have none of Wagner's theory. "It [Gesamtkunstwerk] is an old favorite idea of
mine, Wagner's conception of it is laughably mechanical." [30]
In his essay "Sufferings and Greatness of Richard Wagner"
his rejection is even more explicit and emphatic. He finds
himself completely unable "to make anything of [Wagner's]
addition of music, word, painting, and gesture, which claims
to be the sole truth and the realization of all aesthetic longings." How could one possibly accept, he asks, "a theory of
art according to which [Goethe's] *Tasso* would have to take
a back seat to [Wagner's] *Siegfried*?" It is Mann's conviction
that

art is whole and perfect in each of its various aspects; one need
not add up its genres to make them perfect. Such thinking is *bad*
nineteenth century, a wickedly mechanical manner of thinking.
. . . It would be childish barbarism were one to believe that
the intensity and loftiness of the effect of art could ever result
from the impact upon our senses of its accumulated mass.[31]

Thomas Mann in creating his total works of art could not
possibly have been influenced by Wagner's *theory*, though
Wagner's *works*, as we well know, were always an inspiration
and a challenge to him. The fact is that Mann followed his
own unfailing sense for the spirit of the times, which he knew
demanded a *Gesamtkunstwerk*, a type of progressive universal poesy, as the medium capable of giving the modern *Zeit-
geist* its adequate expression. And following his bent, Mann
raised the novel to a total work of art that is far from a mechanical addition. It combines in the most subtle manner the
various literary modes: the creative impulse with the discursive and the analytical temper, poetry with philosophy, and
poetry with analysis. With the subtlety and complexity of its
mirroring levels of meaning, with its self-consciously ironic
reflections on its own form, with its lofty gaiety and its playful parody of traditional structures and styles, it equals and
often exceeds the Romanticists' most adventurous flights of

fancy. Truly, even the Romanticists' boldest experiments, Friedrich Schlegel's in his *Lucinde,* for instance, or Clemens Brentano's in his *Godwi*—that novel run wild [ein verwilderter Roman], as the subtitle announces—appear downright conventional when compared with such examples of stylistic tour de force, of sophisticated, parodistic narrative as Thomas Mann's *The Holy Sinner* or the *Confessions of Felix Krull.*

Poet and Writer—Myth Plus Psychology

One of the time-honored tenets of German literary criticism is the differentiation of authors into *Dichter* and *Schriftsteller*. Neither English nor French aestheticians have centered their thinking on this particular dichotomy; neither language has exact equivalents for the German terms. Thus in discussing Thomas Mann's attitude on this issue, highly revealing of his view of art and the artist, one finds oneself under an embarrassing terminological handicap. One is forced into unsatisfactory approximations of meaning, using the term "poet" for *Dichter* and "writer" for *Schriftsteller*, "poetic talent" for *Dichtertum* and "literary talent" for *Schriftstellertum*. Alas there is no escaping the semantic dilemma, for neither the English "poet versus writer" dichotomy nor the French *"poète* versus *écrivain"* convey the sharp antithesis expressed by the German terms, since neither the English "writer" nor the French *écrivain* carry the pejorative overtones of the German *Schriftsteller* with its implication of mere mechanical ability and, at best, of cerebral acuity—in contrast to the divine inspiration, prophetic vision, and intuitive imagination of the *Dichter*.

Thomas Mann took early and lively exception to this characteristically German classification and evaluation of literary artists; he considered it not only unfair but completely unrealistic, altogether lifeless, and downright poisonous. He had early recognized this insistence of German aestheticians on the dichotomy of *Dichter* versus *Schriftsteller* as an obscurantic aberration, frequently motivated by racial and ideological attitudes and thus totally irrelevant to the realm of art. To Mann the world of letters always had appeared as a unity. There was for him as much critique of life and of society in imaginative writing as there was artistic vision and sense of form in truly great criticism. Mann had experienced this unity in the genius of Friedrich Nietzsche who represented for him the most successful fusion of the poetic with the literary talents, of emotion, inspiration, and visionary intuition with a brightly analytical, highly critical, even skeptical, intellect. "It was in Nietzsche's school," he tells us, that he "became accustomed to interrelate the concepts of the artist and of the man of cognition [des Erkennenden], so that the borderlines between art and criticism became altogether indistinguishable." [1]

Now it cannot be denied that in his *Betrachtungen* Mann had employed this differentiation in creating the figure of the *Zivilizationsliterat*, in denigrating him for his facile *esprit* so alien to the German *Geist*, for his soullessness, for his unprincipled rootlessness. But Thomas Mann had done this in a clearly polemical spirit. Bitter, fratricidal attacks on his Germanism, his supposed parochialism, his cultural and political backwardness had provoked him into equally extreme rejoinders that were not his soberly considered opinions but rather weapons for the day and the hour of battle. We have striking evidence of Mann's basic position on the issue in a letter to the literary critic Julius Bab, which he wrote as early as 1910, years before the *Betrachtungen*:

I will not hide from you the fact that I, for my part, never sympathized with the sharp antithesis of poetic talent and literary talent. In the land of Wagner, in a land with a hostile stance toward *Literatur,* where anyone who does not stammer but tries to write coherently is insulted by being called a *Literat,* and where the mere suggestion of intellectualism is frowned upon and derided, in such a land the emphasis on this not always tenable differentiation tends to confuse rather than to clarify the issue.[2]

One cannot miss in these words a certain note of caution imposed on the writer by his realization that he is carrying his attack against his countrymen's deeply held convictions, against an all but sacrosanct tenet of German aesthetics.

He was to speak out far more emphatically against this lifeless antithesis in his "Speech on Lessing" in 1929. Here he throws caution to the wind, raising his voice against those obscurantic, parochial, bigoted critics who would deny a writer of Lessing's genius the status of a poet. He condemns these fanatics for being

. . . totally incapable of realizing how the conscious and the un-conscious impulses overlap in the creative process, how much of the unconscious, how much of naïveté, and how much of the demonic, to use their favorite terms, enter into the conscious act of creation. These benighted critics fail to understand the reason why their favorite antithesis is lifeless and unreal. It is unreal and lifeless for the simple reason that the boundary line between po-etic and literary talent does not run externally between the phe-nomena but runs instead internally, *within* the personality of an artist; it is unreal and lifeless for the simple reason that an intui-tively impelled literary talent and a brightly intellectual, thor-oughly controlled, poetic inspiration . . . that these two can and do gloriously exist joined in personal union, a fact clearly demonstrated by Lessing's classical individuality.[3]

Lessing is to Thomas Mann, "the classical representative of the *poetic intellect,* the progenitor of all intelligent and brightly awake poetic talent." [4] He is, by virtue of his pene-trating mind, predestined to the task of differentiation and analysis; his genius, however, is a unifying, synthesizing force. Lessing's best works, particularly *Nathan der Weise* (*Nathan the Wise*), are the products of intuition and conscious

thought, of soul and intellect, of faith and irony, of a cosmopolitan spirit steeped in his native cultural heritage.

This defense of Lessing was written very much as a justification, if not a glorification, of Mann's own twofold endowment as a poetic and a literary talent. The combination of
profound emotion and intellectual detachment formed a productive union in the poet-thinker Thomas Mann. It is Lessing's ideal creativity of which Mann partakes, in which the
"cold," philosophical head enters into alliance with the
"warm" heart, not to create confusion and chaos but to
achieve that highest synthesis wherein the total man is engaged in the act of creation. "Thought that can merge wholly
into feeling, feeling that can merge wholly into thought—
these are the artist's highest joy." [5] Significantly, it was this
quotation from *Death in Venice* that came most readily to
Mann's mind when he was asked for striking aphorisms that
might be culled from his works. Having cautioned his in-
quirer that his style was dialectic and strictly focused on the
characteristic, that in his works much is said that must be
credited to the person speaking and not be taken for the author's personal view, Mann then cited this particular passage
as a rare exception, as a "pure maxim," which, for once,
actually expresses his personally held opinion.[6] This pure
maxim does more; it defines with great precision Mann's twofold endowment as a poet-thinker, as a *Dichter und Denker*,
and furnishes the key to a proper appreciation of the singularly close affinity between Mann's artistic and his essayistic
creations.

An attentive reading of the discursive reflections of the
Betrachtungen and *The Magic Mountain* reveals both works
to be unmistakably the creations of the poet-thinker Thomas
Mann. This singular stylistic affinity is not to be primarily
explained by the fact that the *Betrachtungen* provide some
themes of the novel or because, as Mann put it, they disclose
the spiritual foundations of his artistry, but rather because in
the autobiographical, confessional, essayistic *Betrachtungen*
there is operative the same "poetic" talent that created the
belletristic narrative. And conversely, the same "literary" en-

dowment, the analytical, critical spirit that dominates the *Betrachtungen* is strikingly evident in the novel, which transcends precisely with the brilliance of its dialectic intellectuality, with its profoundly analytical, reflective spirit the time-honored bounds of the traditional, the "poetic" novel. It introduces a new form of narrative that combines contemplations, essayistic excursions, with vivid milieu descriptions and character portrayals of profoundly symbolic significance. To offer but one example: In a discussion such as that of Pfitzner's opera *Palestrina* in the *Betrachtungen*, we find at work the very same brightly intellectual talent as in Hans Castorp's contemplations on the meaning of life and death in his snowbound solitude atop the Magic Mountain; and conversely, in the essay on "Goethe and Tolstoy" the plasticity of the portrayal of the protagonists is quite as poetic, as vivid and vibrant with life as that of the personae of the novel. In the essay, the figures of Goethe and Tolstoy stand before the reader in their three-dimensionality almost as real and lifelike as do the protagonists of the novel— Naphta, Settembrini, or Mynheer Peeperkorn, each of them in his unmistakably individual manner a citizen, representative, and emissary of intellectual domains, principalities, and worlds. Hans Wysling, the curator of the Thomas Mann archive in Zurich, quotes the author from a hitherto unpublished manuscript: "If I may speak of myself: I have written several essays that I could include, without the least scruples, in a volume of my short stories, and the reverse is not at all unthinkable." [7] This reversibility of the classification of Mann's works is forcefully brought home to us when we consider, for example, such a composition as *Friedrich und die Grosse Koalition* (*Frederick and the Great Coalition*), a work that had been planned as a novel but was left unfinished as an "Abriss für den Tag und die Stunde" ("Sketch for the Day and the Hour") of World War I. Should this "sketch" be considered a historical treatise or a work of belles-lettres? Or, again, should the character study of Friedrich Schiller, "A Weary Hour," stand, as it does now, among the short stories or among the essays? It certainly would not be altogether out of place alongside so vivid and empathetic a character portrayal as "Der Alte Fontane" ("The Old Fontane"), which appeared in the essay volume *Rede und Antwort* (*Statement and Answer*).

While thus focusing attention on the striking stylistic affinity between Mann's essayistic and his fictional writings, we would not want to deny or gloss over the differences in structure and style which do, of course, exist. It would be a most instructive undertaking to define these differences with precision and to analyze in depth Mann's manner of forming his experiences and ideas into essays and fiction—for instance, his experiences with the occult that he recorded in the essay "Okkulte Erlebnisse" ("Occult Experiences") and shaped into the narrative of the chapter "Fragwürdigstes" ("The Most Questionable") of *The Magic Mountain*.

Even Mann's letters reveal the same poet-writer at work. Here again both Mann's poetic and his literary talents manifest themselves as he reports with astounding insight and vividness the experiences of his eventful life: his tender, gently insistent courtship of Katja Pringsheim, with its frequent echoes of the lyrical *Tonio Kröger* tone; or his visceral hatred of the Nazis; or his deeply empathetic and yet coolly controlled, at times even critical, impressions of his children, of his intimate friends, of his fellow artists, and of his numerous acquaintances; and finally, in his last letters, that autumnal mood of reminiscing, of grateful wonderment at so long, so rich a life granted him "by a benevolent guidance from above." [8] Let us listen to that inimitable *Sangeston* of musing retrospection as the poet recalls his boyhood love for Armin Martens, the Hans Hansen of his *Tonio Kröger*:

Him I have loved—he was truly my first love, and a more tender, a more blissfully painful one it was not given me to experience. One cannot forget something like this even after seventy eventful years have passed by. It may sound laughable, but I cherish the memory of that passion of innocence like a treasure. It was only too understandable that he knew not what to make of my infatuation, which I confessed to him one "great" day. That was be-

cause of me and because of him. And so it died away—long before he himself . . . as one of the very first, died, perished
somewhere. But I have set him a monument in *Tonio Kröger*.
. . . Strange to think, that the entire destiny of this human
being had been to awaken a feeling that was to turn one day into
a lasting poem.[9]

To read the best of these letters—and most of them are
very fine indeed—is an experience as absorbing, informative,
and often as moving and exciting as the perusal of Mann's
essays, novellas, and novels. It is no exaggeration to say that
all of Mann's works—belletristic, essayistic and epistolary—
are the product of Mann's twofold endowment, which lends
them their perceptive clarity *and* vibrant vitality, their mar-
velously felicitous articulation *and* musical lyricism so aptly
symbolized in the signum of Mann's opus: Apollo's bow and
lyre.

Thomas Mann's twofold endowment as a poet-writer also
helps explain his predilection for the combination of "myth
plus psychology." To Karl Kerényi Mann once confided his
growing fascination with these two realms in their fusion,
which he felt to be his native element.[10] This combination
could satisfy more fully than any other both Mann's poetic
genius and his literary, analytical, rational bent. It must be
stressed, however, that Mann understood the terms "myth"
and "psychology" in their broadest possible meanings; for
him they were shorthand symbols for two modes of experiencing life, and of giving it artistic form. Myth encompassed
for Mann the transcendent, the surrealistic and suprarational,
the realm of the occult, the visionary, dream, legend, and
fairy tale, the romantic realm; it called for a language
cleansed of the colloquial and the commonplace, a language
charged with lyric pathos or evoking the monumental and
the statuesque. Psychology, on the other hand, to Mann
meant penetrating analysis and carefully controlled report—
in an all but Naturalistic idiom—on the reality of the psychophysical world. Finally, the "plus" in the combination repre-

sented for him not a simple addition but a subtle combination and permutation of the two elements. Not only was he convinced of the feasibility of such an enhancing and intensifying permutation of myth and psychology; he recognized in it the very sign and symbol of great art.

With this conviction Mann found himself once again in opposition to an established German view that the two realms of myth and psychology were mutually exclusive. In his controversial speech, "Sufferings and Greatness of Richard Wagner," which was to be the immediate cause of his exile, Mann had attacked that prejudice in a most emphatic manner: "What is it," he asks, "that elevates the works of Wagner so high above the old-fashioned musical dramas?" And he gives the categorical answer: "It is the unique fusion [in Wagner's works] of two forces . . . and their names are *psychology* and *myth*." It seemed to him unbelievable that there should be

those who would seriously deny the compatibility of these two powers. Yet there are those critics who claim that psychology is too rational *not* to be an insurmountable obstacle on the way to myth. Psychology is seen by them to stand in flat contradiction to myth, just as it is seen to stand in contradiction to music. These obtuse critics insist on their points of view even though this very combination of myth and psychology and music stands before their eyes as an organic reality in the two great exemplars of this combination—Nietzsche and Wagner.[11]

We now can add Thomas Mann as a third illustrous exemplar of this combination. He too has splendidly achieved this fusion in his works, perhaps most convincingly in his novella, *Death in Venice*.[12] Here Mann's twofold endowment, his romantic and his realistic self, and his poetic and his intellectual talents were engaged in the most intimate collaboration; a *doppelte Optik*[13] was operative here, a bifocal view of the novella's locale, of its plot, and especially of its characters.

Venice, "the fallen queen, flattering and dubious beauty

. . . half fairy tale, half tourist trap," is caught by this bifocal vision in its sordid reality *and* in its mythical splendor. We are not spared the oppressive sultriness and fetid stench of its alleyways nor the garbage floating on its canals with their evil exhalations; yet above these very waters there rises the "airy splendor" of its palaces, bridges, churches, of its "fairy temples," [14] rendered in a rhythmical prose of exquisite limpidity and grace. This panorama is unfolded before the reader's eyes with the most painstaking precision, yet not in order to produce a naturalistic picture of the city but in order to create, by way of an alert selectivity, a highly stylized composition characterized by a tense equilibrium of realism and idealization. Into the modern Venice is skillfully blended the timeless, exotic Venice risen from the dreams of Byron, Platen, Wagner, and Nietzsche—that magical city of ruthless passions, passions unto death, of the *Liebestod*. And on this subtle composite of reality and romantic lore Mann superimposed the world of classical antiquity, its historical figures: Socrates, Phaedrus, Critobolus, and the gods from Mount Olympus.

This bifocal vision is clearly at work when Mann creates the long procession of figures, each palpably real, yet each acting out its mythical role, each endowed with symbolic significance: the stranger on the steps of the funeral hall; the gondolier—Charon, the lewd and lascivious old fop with his false teeth, painted lips, and garish hatband; the goateed captain of the ship from Pola; the mendicant singer with the stench of death; they all are realistically rendered in their individuality, yet each weaves his enigmatical spell in his mythical role of Aschenbach's tempter and seducer.

Again this principle of composition is applied, this time on a much grander scale, in Mann's portrayal of the main protagonists of the novella, of Tadzio and of Gustav von Aschenbach. In Tadzio, Mann created a human figure of flesh and blood. He carefully rendered his unique charm, his flaws and failings that rouse our sympathy and bring him close to us as a fellow human. We see him as the little Polish boy of pale complexion, with carious teeth; we hear his high-pitched voice, observe a fit of his high-strung temper. But we also behold him as the paragon of beauty whose flawless profile "conjures up mythologies; it was like a primeval legend, handed down from the beginning of time, of the birth of form, of the origin of the gods." [15] In fact, Tadzio's shortcomings serve to support—they do not weaken—the ideal qualities of the figure. The pallor of Tadzio's cheeks enhances the boy's resemblance to the famous statue of the *Boy with the Thorn in his Foot*; the collar of his sailor suit, precisely because of its poor fit, serves the more effectively to set off "the head . . . poised like a flower, in incomparable loveliness . . . the head of Eros, with the yellowish bloom of Parian marble." [16] Even the outburst of the boy's ill-controlled temper acquires, in Thomas Mann's carefully stylized description, the quality of myth, by calling to mind the image of a young god in rage:

A storm of angry scorn came over his face. His brow darkened, his lips curled; on one side of his mouth a grimace of bitterness distorted his cheek, and he knit his brows so fiercely that his eyes seemed to have been drawn in under their pressure; dark and angry, below them, they spoke the language of hate.[17]

This intensification of the realistic figure into a figure of myth is carried out with the greatest circumspection. Nowhere is the reader required to relinquish reality in favor of myth. To be sure, Tadzio is set apart from his sisters, he is desired, courted, admired. That in itself, however, would not lift him above the plane of reality. Only in Aschenbach's inflamed imagination is the figure likened to, or identified with, the immortal beings of Greek mythology. Even Tadzio's final appearance as Hermes in that impressive setting on the sea-encircled sandbar as a "figure most isolated and apart . . ." is at once rationalized as a vision of the dying poet: "But *to him it seemed* the pale and lovely summoner out there smiled at him and beckoned, *as though*, with the hand he lifted from his hip, he pointed outward as he hovered on before him into an immensity of richest expectation." [18]

Analysis of Mann's work, then, proves that psychological realism remains unbetrayed. Tadzio's identification with figures of myth can in every instance be explained on solidly rational grounds as a figment of Aschenbach's overwrought imagination. And yet, such is the vividness of Mann's evocation of the mythical figures in their identification with Tadzio that we experience their fusion as palpably real and must exert a conscious effort to disengage in our imagination the real boy from the mythical overlay of the divine figures. Thus it is that Mann achieves the characteristic enhancement of the real persona into a complex symbol whose existence is beyond time and space in the realm of eternal myth.

The author is able to accomplish the same subtle balance and tension between reality and symbol, this enhancement of reality into myth in the central figure of Gustav von Aschenbach. Mann's portrayal of his tragic hero oscillates tensely between the poles of apotheosis and deflation, of idealization and searching analysis touched with gentle irony, between rhetorical flourish and sober naturalistic prose, ever maintaining a perfect balance in the stylistic modes by subtly using each as a check on the other.

Again, this dialectic of style is predicated on Mann's two-fold endowment. Within the structure of the novella it determines Mann's ambivalent attitude toward his hero. The realistic *writer* in him tends to approach the *persona* of his work with detachment—in an analytical spirit, insisting on distance. He recognizes and depicts the problematical nature of his "hero" and deflates him to an unheroic figure. The empathetic, imaginative poet, for his part, tends to elevate him to heroic stature, to raise him to the prototypical, to transport him to the realm of myth. Thus Gustav von Aschenbach finds himself raised upon the pedestal as the poet laureate of exemplary achievement; but he also finds himself examined as a case on the psychoanalyst's couch. Aschenbach's way to his doom is traced both on the level of realism and on the level of myth. Every detail of Aschenbach's outward life is chosen to illuminate the deepest recesses of his mind *and* to furnish the richest symbolical meaning. Aschenbach is drawn, on the psychological level, as the aging man whose rational, disciplined self is overwhelmed by a late and sudden eruption of emotional drives that had been all too long and too ruthlessly suppressed. This delineation is most searching in its statement of the unique case, yet at the same time it is most effective in raising the unique to the typical. Aschenbach transcends the individual. As has been shown in the first chapter of this study, his tragic life is enhanced into a symbol of the inexorable fate of the artist who follows the danger-beset path, that "erring and sinful way" which leads by the *senses* toward the goal of cognition and beauty.

On the level of realism, Aschenbach suffers a sordid collapse, ravaged by an unnatural passion and the onslaught of cholera; on the level of myth, Tadzio-Hermes-Psychopompos, the guide of man's soul to the nether world, beckons him onward to "the immensity of richest expectation." Aschenbach's psychophysical disintegration, while observed and rendered with the objective eye of the mercilessly exact and truthful analyst, is yet informed by the poet with the dignity and beauty of apotheosis. Describing in all but naturalistic detail the old man's collapse, Mann links it by means of the leitmotif to the apotheosis of the demigod Menelaus who is "transported by the immortals to Elysium, to the ends of the earth . . . where life is easiest for man," [19] thus elevating the dying poet to a figure semi-divine.

May this interpretation suffice in demonstration of Mann's twofold talent as poet and as perceptive analyst as he fashions his psycho-mythical masterpiece, the novella *Death in Venice*. An examination of Mann's other works reveals the presence of his favorite combination of myth plus psychology already in the earliest creations. Even in these the author bursts through realistic representation, transcends psychology, and confronts the reader with the surreality of the demonic and the diabolic by way of caricature and the grotesque in such an early novella as *Luischen* (*Little Lizzie*) or with magical fairy tale motifs in the spirit of E. T. A. Hoff-

mann in *Der Kleiderschrank* (*The Wardrobe*) or of Hans
Christian Andersen in the fairy-tale novel, *Royal Highness*.
Heinrich Mann, a perceptive reader of his brother's works,
finds "more dignified matters told in the *Buddenbrooks* than
a superficial reading would reveal." He asks us to focus our
attention on Mann's manner of describing the death scenes
in the novel. Some of Mann's protagonists die, according to
Heinrich, "deaths that are surrounded by a ceremonial aura
exactly like the deaths of the heroes of imperishable sagas." [20]
More importantly, Heinrich links the central theme, the decline and fall of the house of Buddenbrooks, to the myth of
death and resurrection of the *Joseph* tetralogy: "It [the Buddenbrook family] was to rise and die, and was to be resur-
rected in the words [of the poet]—exactly like Joseph was to
rise, decline, and rise again, in accordance with a timelessly
repeated ritual." [21] Can Heinrich's discovery of the aura of
myth in this early work be dismissed out of hand?

It is, of course, in the *Joseph* novels where Mann's favorite combination is finally realized on the grandest scale and
with the greatest virtuosity. Yet to us it appears that Mann
has nowhere achieved this fusion of legend and reality, of
myth and psychology with greater spontaneity and immediacy of effect than in *Death in Venice*. In the all-but-Alexan-
drine sophistication of the *Joseph* tetralogy, the combination
was carried off with a subtlety, finesse, and playful irony not
attained—or even intended—in the novella; but by that very
finesse and playfulness, the combination necessarily lost some
of its vitality and directness. In the novella everything springs
with utter inevitability, uncontrived and effortlessly from the
realm of myth and legend; everything stands rooted, solidly,
in the world of reality. We have Mann's word that a trip to
the Lido in the spring of 1911 had furnished him

. . . all the material for his novella. . . . The wanderer by the
North Cemetery in Munich, the gloomy ship from Pola, the old
fob, the ambiguous gondolier, Tadzio and his family, the departure frustrated by the misdirected baggage, the cholera, the hon-

est clerk in the travel bureau, the malevolent street singer, and whatever other elements might be mentioned—everything was given.[22]

Yet it was the poet's imagination that seized upon this raw material furnished him by life and transformed it into this unique masterpiece. Mann tells us in "A Sketch of My Life" (1930) that he had turned to the work with such a splendid sensation of uplift as he had never experienced before or after. In a transport of inspiration rare with this deliberate, circumspect author, he reached for the treasures of myth and legend that lay dormant in his mind since his boyhood days, and vitalized them to incandescent intensity.[23] Thus the vividly experienced reality of his trip to Venice became enhanced and ennobled by myth's timeless grandeur, while myth was rescued from abstract remoteness and endowed with a vibrant immediacy and high pathos far removed from parody. Here, truly, both Mann's poetic and his literary genius fulfilled themselves in a creative collaboration that achieved the ultimate in the artistic fusion of myth and psychology.

The Mediator

In the characterization of Thomas Mann, the man and the artist, brief reference has been made to the tension the poet suffered so violently in his youth, the tension between his bourgeois heritage and his artistic temperament and mission.[1] Mann has given this experience its most poignant statement in his deeply autobiographical novella *Tonio Kröger*. He portrayed the main protagonist as a person with two souls, as a person with a close affinity to the world of art and the world of the burgher. His name neatly symbolizes this hybrid nature, this *Mischlingsnatur*, "Tonio" standing for the Romance heritage from his mother's side, "Kröger" for the German from his father's. Beyond this twofold heritage the name symbolizes its bearer's endowment with an all but endless array of antithetical traits: the burgher's probity and the artist's eccentricity, health and delicacy, sobriety and thirst for adventure, propriety and dissolution, extreme self-discipline and dissipation. Tonio suffers the pains and clearly recognizes the dangers in this midway existence between the two seemingly irreconcilable extremes of life and art. Born to be an artist, he feels himself excluded from the bliss of normalcy, from the world of Hans Hansen and Ingeborg Holm. At the same time he recognizes Adelbert's, the writer's, flight from the beguiling fragrance of spring into the neutral sphere of the coffee house as a fateful error bound ultimately to result in emotional impoverishment and artistic sterility. Thus Tonio's existential dilemma would seem impossible to resolve.

Yet, the novella does not leave us in the gloom of a tragic denouement. On the contrary, among Mann's early works it is the one with the most positive message. It stands in clear counterpoint to the other autobiographical novella, *Der Bajazzo* (*The Dilettante*). There Thomas Mann had portrayed the tragicomedy of the life of a rootless, unproductive pseudoartist ending in disillusionment and self-hatred, a fate young Thomas dreaded as a frightful possibility for himself. In *Tonio Kröger* the author of the *Buddenbrooks* celebrates the birth of a poet in triumph over self-doubt and alienation.

What power was it that worked this miracle, that liberated Tonio from the tragic fate of the "hybrid nature" doomed to exist in isolation, neither belonging to the bourgeois world nor to the world of art? This power is Tonio's love for the blond and the blue-eyed, for Hans Hansen and Ingeborg Holm and for their world of normalcy. A source of melancholy sadness and bitter pain to young Tonio, this love is experienced by the maturing artist as the power that endows him with the gift of poetic inspiration. In his letter to Lisabeta Ivanovna, his friend and confidante, Tonio apostrophizes this love in words that rise to a well-nigh apostolic pathos, to a rare intensity of diction that Mann himself has found to be dangerously close to the unartistic in its obviousness and directness. Tonio writes:

If anything is capable of changing a litterateur into a poet, it is this bourgeois love of mine for the human, the vital, and the normal. It is the source of all warmth, kindliness, and humor, and I would almost hold it to be the very love of which it is written that one could be talking with the tongues of men and of angels and, lacking it, would yet be but a sounding brass and a tinkling bell.[2]

Yes, Thomas Mann makes much of the redemptive power of Tonio's love, more than those interpreters who put excessive stress on Tonio's difficult lot as a hapless victim of his *Mischlingsnatur*, as an exile from *both* worlds, and who fail to give sufficient weight to the creative role of the mediator which his love for "life and normalcy" enables him to play through the medium of his art. Yet proper stress is essential here lest the delicate balance of loss and gain in the existence of the ironic mediator be upset. Even so perceptive a critic as Reinhard Baumgart, placing his accents with the greatest of circumspection, tends to weight the balance on the side of loss. Summarizing the results of his analysis of the novella, he defines "Tonio Kröger's new position as being beyond decadent ideology and yet not connected with 'life,' " and concludes, "It [Tonio's new position] remains forever an experimental existence, ironically free, but also ironically homeless between the 'two worlds.' " [3] Mann's text rather seems to suggest that Tonio Kröger, the artist, is about to achieve a productive contact with *both* spheres now that his poet-self has been liberated by his love for life and normalcy from the skepticism and alienation of the litterateur, now that his voice is no longer merely a sounding brass and a tinkling bell.

Confidently Tonio promises his friend Lisabeta to excel in his future work, to order and shape a world yet unborn, to redeem through the magic spell of his art a host of shadowy figures who beckon to him. "The work," he tells her, "that I have done so far is nothing or not much—as good as nothing. But I will do better, Lisabeta—this is a promise," [4] a promise the Dilettante of the earlier story could never have made, far less kept, destroyed as he was by disgust with himself and with life, overwhelmed by *Lebensekel*, lacking even the strength of will to escape his miserable existence by suicide. Contemplating these two contrasting figures, one grows aware of the basic change in Mann's attitude and mood during the intervening years, a change that enabled him to portray Tonio's hard-won liberation from a lethal disgust with himself and his rootless existence through loving acceptance of and participation in life.

Thomas Mann has explicitly supported this positive reading of the novella. In the *Betrachtungen* he stressed that Tonio's "situational pathos [Situationspathos] is obviously influenced by that of Nietzsche, who derived the cognitive value of his philosophy precisely from the fact that he was at home in *both* worlds, in the world of decadence [read: 'spirit'] as well as in that of life." [5] There is no reason to discount the significance of this statement so clearly intended to fix the new position of Tonio and to correct the impression created by Tonio's self-portrayal as "standing between two worlds and being at home in neither." [6] That portrayal had its full validity for the immature artist before he had experienced his love for the bliss of normalcy as a source of inspiration. The mature artist Tonio, in his new position—Mann would have us know—is sharing the *Situationspathos* of the philosopher, is not outside of, but "at home in *both* worlds." Mann tells us that Tonio's "admiration goes out to the proud and the cold adventurers on the paths of the great, the demonic beauty" and that he is "filled with sympathy for the tragic and comic figures and for those that are both. . . ." But, he continues, "[Tonio's] deepest and most secret love belongs to the blond and the blue-eyed, the brightly alive, the happy, the lovable, and the commonplace." [7] Mann's intention is clear. Endowing Tonio Kröger with admiration, sympathy, and love for the full spectrum of human types—with sympathy and admiration for those who represent "spirit," and with love for those who represent "life"—Mann introduces into the growing world of his fiction the first artist who has freed himself of the alienation and self-hate of the Dilettante, has left behind the "neutral" world of the litterateur Adelbert as well as the carefully cultivated "stylized [stilisierte]" seclusion of Detlev Spinell, that decadent aesthete of the *Tristan* novella. Tonio has embraced "life" with his love and now stands ready to take up the artist's highest mission—the burdens and the joys of mediation between intellect and nature, "spirit" and "life."

A comparison of Tonio Kröger with Felix Krull, the hero of the delightful *Confessions of a Confidence Man* may fur-

ther illuminate his personality and role in life as a full-fledged
artist. Like Tonio, Felix is an artist, but an artist of quite a
different sort. He is an artist of life, a *Lebenskünstler.* Felix
does not know Tonio's longing for the bliss of normalcy; he
longs to embrace "the Grand, the Whole, the Ample. . . .
This longing, from its very inception, had little of the specific about it, nor was it capable of exact definition." [8] And
Felix confesses that it was this longing for the nonspecific
which left him "all his life a child, a dreamer," [9] who was
basically indifferent to the "reality" of life, toward his
partners in life and love. These he was ever eager to change at
the enticing beckoning of the fleeting moment. "Change, rejuvenation, the stripping off of the Old Adam, the slipping
into ever new ones," [10] this was Krull's longing and joy.

Felix does not possess a definable identity, only masks; he
exists as a protean *Kostümkopf.* "The unmasked reality between the two forms of appearance [Felix as the hotel serv-
ant and Felix as the unidentified gentleman of distinction],
the ego-selfhood [das Ich-selber-sein], was not definable because it was actually nonexistent." [11] His is a purely symbolic
existance—"*Like* a soldier not *as* a soldier" [12]—in the guise of
a marquis, not as a real one—and yet, in every guise and behind every mask actually improving on nature. Felix's life is
one grand make-believe, is a game at its most free and gay, is
illusion carried to perfection, the most lifelike *Schein* but
never the reality of *Sein.*

Tonio had yearned to join the world of Hans and Ingeborg. About Felix there is an air of aloofness; his is a carefully
maintained stance of reserve. Early in his life an inner voice
had told him that companionship, friendship, a warming so-
ciability were not to be his lot. "Instead," he tells us, "I had
to make my uncommon way through life alone, withdrawn
upon myself, in a strictly maintained isolation." [13] Felix does
not know the longing for the bourgeois world of the commonplace, which we recognized as being the productive feeling in Tonio. To be sure, that longing limited the playful
freedom of Tonio's emotions, focusing them upon a definite,
invariable goal. But, conversely, this longing lent his whole

being an intensity, a constancy, that *Treue* which Felix's personality so totally lacks. It is this very constancy in love and longing that makes of Tonio a "real," a *human*, a deeply sympathetic being—and a poet. It is precisely this "reality" of being, this substance, and this "natural weight" [14] that are so conspicuously absent in the protean, mercurial, *Kostümkopf* Felix Krull. In Tonio we recognize, along with a highly developed intellect, that quality which the German likes to define as *Seele*. Krull has esprit, élan, a playful lightness, gaiety, and grace which far outshine Tonio's. And finally, Tonio *is* a poet "by the grace of God," while Krull exists *like* an artist in the spirit of *l'art pour l'art* "by the grace of his own phantasy [von Gnaden der Phantasie]." [15] Tonio, on his visit to his hometown, could be mistaken for a mountebank, but he was able to produce the manuscript to prove his identity as a writer. Could Krull's *Confessions* have established his true identity? They could not, for the simple reason that Felix does not possess identity and would not have one if he could. Had Mann been able to continue his "unfinishable" novel, perhaps he would have given us a variation on that *Tonio* scene in the hotel in Lübeck developing it in the mountebankish spirit of Felix Krull. How he loved the meaningful, witty, allusive leitmotif play across the years, linking his total *oeuvre* into an allembracing unity.

Tonio's longing for the bliss of normalcy is the spirit's longing for nature. Such a longing cannot be experienced by Felix for he himself represents the embodiment or rather the ephemeral apparition of the union of spirit and of nature in a personality that combines brilliant wit *and* beguiling beauty. Significantly, he has the blue eyes and blond hair of the Hansen type, while yet having a brunet complexion like Tonio so that "it remained uncertain, whether [he] was blond or brunet in appearance and one could speak of [him] with equal justice as being both," [16] that is, as combining in himself both Tonio and Hans, both the representative of "spirit" and of "nature."

The poetess Diana Houpflé recognized in Felix a modern-day Hermes, the god of thieves, but also the patron-god of

writing, of trade, of all sort and manner of communication
and thus—of mediation. Obviously, Felix is Mann's comic,
should we say "mountebankish," [17] treatment in the spirit of
subtle self-parody of what may well be judged the most profound and all-pervasive theme in his life and work: the artist
as mediator between self-conscious intellect and naïve life. In
this role, as mediators, Tonio and Felix are kindred spirits.
The paradox arises: Tonio whose spirit *longs for* nature, is
found to be the poet by God's grace destined to accomplish
his mediatory mission in and through his art. Felix, on the
other hand, who *represents* in his witty and handsome person
mediation accomplished, who lives before our eyes that fusion of spirit with nature, of esprit, intellect, and wit with
physical beauty, strikes us as somehow unreal, as lacking
"natural weight"; he delights us as a happy, wishful dream, a
playful figment of Mann's imagination at its most free and
gay, a *grand feu d'artifice*. This paradox is the poet's way of
reminding us of the melancholy truth that "*between spirit
and life there can be no union, but only a fleeting, intoxicat-
ing illusion of union and understanding, an eternal tension
without resolution.*" He reminds us of this truth not in pathetic tones of disillusionment, not in fanatical accents, but
in the spirit of a higher gaiety, of erotic irony, for—as he adds
with a glance at the poet, at himself—"the spirit that loves is
not fanatical; it is witty, it is politic, it woos and its wooing is
erotic irony." [18]

Let us return for a moment to our discussion of the novella *Tonio Kröger* in order to focus our attention on its
structure and style. The question arises: Has Mann been able
to achieve an aesthetically satisfying, an organic integration
between the poetic parts of the novella and its essayistic central piece, Tonio's conversation with his friend and confidante, the Russian painter Lisabeta Ivanovna? It is certain
that such a fusion and integration of apparently disparate,
antithetical elements had been Mann's avowed purpose. In
this work he consciously strove to create a "mixture of seemingly heterogeneous elements: melancholy and criticism,
soulfulness and skepticism, Theodor Storm and Nietzsche,

mood and intellect." [19] The term "mixture" obviously stands here not for a mechanical process but for organic interpenetration, for synthesis of elements that, moreover, are only seemingly heterogeneous and are, in fact, capable of being harmonized. They are harmonized in this work by an artist whose longing has reached and embraced life (melancholy, soulfulness, *Storm*, mood) while his critical faculties have remained tensely alive (criticism, skepticism, *Nietzsche*, intellect).

To appreciate fully the subtle unity of content and form that Mann has in fact achieved in *Tonio Kröger*, one must grasp the complex nature of its central character; one must realize that Tonio Kröger, much like his creator, embraces in his person, with the artist's sensibility, both seemingly antipodal spheres: "the radically literary, the intellectually disintegrating [die radikal-literarische, intellektuell-zersetzende]," on the one hand, and, on the other, the "soulful conservative [gemüthaft-konservative]." [20] In and through the poet's (Tonio-Mann's) mediatory medium, the critical lucidity and the analytical sharpness of the essayistic conversationpiece is harmonized into an organic unity with the lyricism of Tonio's homecoming to the scenes of his boyhood, with the romantic tone of Mann's evocation of Tonio's love for the sea, for the garden of his vanished boyhood, for his violin (reminiscent of the *Taugenichts*), for Storm's *Immensee* and for Hans Hansen and Ingeborg Holm.

One of the most productive insights given to Mann was his realization that a central mission of the artist was to serve as mediator between the polar spheres of spirit and nature, to strive for their fusion in the higher synthesis of the supreme creative achievement:

The *mediatory* task [*vermittelnde* Aufgabe] of the artist, art's Hermes-like magical mediatory role between the upper and the nether worlds, between idea and phenomena, between the world of spirit and that of the senses, that is, in fact, art's cosmic position, in a manner of speaking, her unique situation in this world and the only possible explanation for the playful dignity of art's doings.[21]

This profound insight derived from Mann's innermost being. Karl Kerényi, the poet's intimate friend, who had an all but uncanny insight into his makeup as man and artist, traced Mann's penchant for mediation to its mythological origins by pointing to certain Hermes-like traits in Mann's nature. He characterized Thomas Mann as "a great entelechy, compelled to move between the two sides we are accustomed to call spirit and nature, bound to neither, yet partaking in both," [22] and, we would add, enhancing both into a higher unity.

Thomas Mann himself felt this inborn role of mediation to be ordained by fate:

I am quite properly a genius of the golden mean, in which I recognize my fate: the golden mean between demonism and burgherdom, deed and conscience. It is not a bad ambience, that golden mean, and my life seems to prove that in this ambience an art can grow toward which man of humane spirit is kindly disposed [der das Menschliche sich freundlich neigt].[23]

On the other hand, Mann was also acutely conscious of the dangers inherent in this midway posture of the artist and tended to emphasize in his earlier belletristic and essayistic writings this negative aspect of the artist's role as mediator. In the *Betrachtungen* we read:

The problematical nature of the artist's midway stance, his hybrid personality composed of spirit and sensuality, these "two souls in his breast" prevent him from achieving a position of dignity. The life of an artist is not a dignified life, the way of beauty is not a way of dignity, for beauty is spiritual but it is also sensuous.[24]

Thus it was that Mann's development in the role of mediator in search of a synthesis of spirit and nature did not proceed in a straightforward, unproblematical manner. We have seen how his striving for the resolution of tensions be-

tween life and art in the higher synthesis of the liberated poet
had found expression in the novella *Tonio Kröger*. In his next
major effort, the dramatic poem *Fiorenza*, this resolution was
replaced with an unrelieved tension, this time not between
the burgher and the artist, between life and spirit, but within
the sphere of spirit itself. Here it is the fanatical Prior Girolamo Savonarola, this artist dedicated to a new morality, who
is the champion of the ascetic spirit. He looks down with
disdain and irreconcilable hatred on Lorenzo de' Medici, that
voluptuary and aesthete, and on his coterie of pseudoartists,
that band of parasites, brawlers, boasters, and clowns, leading
a life of ease and pleasure and indulging in the irresponsible
game of *l'art pour l'art*. They, in their turn, look with fear on
the Prior and despise him for his austere asceticism. Lorenzo,
to be sure, is of a conciliatory bent and would placate the
burning hatred of the fanatical monk, but his mediation is
the tired gesture of a dying man. It is ineffectual. There is no
reconciliation possible between the two antagonistic worlds
of a fanatical morality and decadent aestheticism. An abyss
yawns between the "sentimentive" artist, glorified in the figure of Savonarola, and the "naïve" practitioners of art, who
are portrayed in an all but satirical vein as the talented but
abysmally stupid dilettantes who, in their supreme unconcern
for morality and the stern imperative of the spirit, prostitute
the sacred calling of art. Thomas Mann felt the unfortunate
bias in this representation and recognized it as the ultimate
cause for his unsuccessful efforts with this play. To his
brother Heinrich he confided that he "had confused the concepts of 'spirit' and 'art' and had counterposed them as enemies in this piece. This led to the Solness* debacle, to this
fiasco in my efforts to infuse life into the intellectual con-
struct." [25]

In the novel *Royal Highness*, which followed the drama
within a year (1909), Mann's penchant for mediation reasserted itself. Here the princeling Klaus Heinrich is the representative or rather a pathetic little prisoner in the sphere of

* The tragic hero of Henrik Ibsen's drama, *The Master Builder* (*Archi-
tect Solness*, as the play is also known).

the spirit. Doctor Raoul Überbein, mentor and only confidant to Klaus Heinrich, wants to keep him in his purely formal existence, in the aristocratic seclusion of hollow representation totally divorced from the normal and commonplace, from the people. But our little prince has a healthy instinct. He escapes into life through his love of Imma Spoelmann, this far more intelligent Ingeborg Holm who anticipates, in a tentative manner, Joseph's double blessing of spirit and nature. Klaus Heinrich's love for her liberates him from his purely formal existence and unites the lovers in a "stern happiness [im strengen Glück]" that combines an aristocratic insistence on form and representation with a democratic self-dedication in service to the people. Spirit and life find each other in a symbolical marriage in this most lighthearted, gay, and playful rational fairy tale, as Mann liked to call this product of his own liberation from solitude in his love for Katja Pringsheim, who lent many a characteristic trait to the little princess, Imma Spoelmann.

Yet once again, Mann's striving for balance and synthesis proved problematical. In the novella *Death in Venice*, Aschenbach is allowed to sustain in himself only for fleeting moments a precarious balance between spirit and life. As we have seen, passion engulfs him, subverting his dedication to form and achievement and plunging him into the abyss of lassitude, erotic excess, and death. Here Mann is intent not on balance and harmony but on a dramatic demonstration of the pessimistic view that the two souls in the artist's breast prevent him from achieving a position of dignity, that the life of an artist is not a dignified life, the way of beauty not a way of dignity. Here Eros proves an unreliable guide, and the spirit highly susceptible to life's fatal fascination.

In *The Magic Mountain*, Mann resumes his role of mediator and develops the theme of balance and synthesis on a far more comprehensive scale than he was able to do in his earlier works. The young author of *Tonio Kröger* had deeply experienced the spirit's longing for nature, the maturing artist became ever more conscious that this yearning was reciprocated, that nature on its part was yearning for spirit. This insight became the central theme of the essay "Goethe and Tolstoy," the writing of which accompanied the composition of large parts of *The Magic Mountain*. Mann points out "the constant theme" of the essay as being "the yearning of the children of nature, for spirit, which is quite as 'sentimentive' as the reverse striving of the sons of the spirit for nature." [26] This insight underlies and far-reachingly determines the ideational structure of the novel as well. One important reason why *The Magic Mountain* is so infinitely more complex than *Tonio Kröger*, is precisely because the stress in the later work on spirit versus nature, on sickness versus health, and on death versus life has become so much more finely equilibrated. Tonio's yearning for the bliss of normalcy, his love for the blond and the blue-eyed, the brightly alive, and the commonplace, has become transformed into the much more subtle, more problematical, more highly differentiated attitude of Hans Castorp toward spirit and life, which permits him to keep faith with his romantic sympathy with death while dedicating himself to the service of life. It is Hans Castorp's carefully maintained midway stance between all extremes that makes him, more than any of his other traits of character, the alter ego of the mature author. Like Thomas Mann, he refuses to rush into clear-cut decisions. For him, as for his author, it is more important to distinguish than to decide; one of Castorp's favorite mottos is *audiatur et altera pars*.* Challenged by the eloquence of his mentors Settembrini and Naphta to decide between West and East, progress and reaction, freedom and tradition, justice and force, knowledge and superstition, science and faith, Castorp "sat, chin in his hand. . . . In his eyes was a certain obstinacy." [27] He was once again, as in his boyhood, down in the flat lands, the lonely boatsman on the Holstein lake, looking with dazzled eyes from the glassy daylight of the western shore to the mist and moonbeams that wrapped the eastern heavens." [28] In silence he pondered on fusion and synthesis, strove to transcend the extremes in a higher unity. This unity presented itself to him

---

* The other party should also be heard.

in palpable reality with the arrival on the mountain of the mighty personality, Mynheer Peepercorn, in whose presence the eloquent protagonists of the right and the left faded into insignificance. Thus the kingly Dutchman, far from being the ridiculous figure he might easily be mistaken for in his stammering and grandiose gesturing, proves himself a most influential mentor of our hero, under whose tutelage Castorp grows secure in his role of mediation.

Hans Eichner, in his thoughtful introduction to Thomas Mann's Works, has aptly characterized this development of Castorp. He writes:

That which had appeared before the mighty Dutchman's arrival as a mere wish, as the mere intent and desire of Castorp to avoid the unconditional surrender to either side in the ideological dispute between East and West, contemplation and action, instinct and virtue, depth and form, and instead to absorb these extremes and to enhance them into a third, higher unity, this wish and desire appeared now [with Peepercorn's arrival] as a possible achievement and thus became a task and a commitment.[29]

In any discussion of *The Magic Mountain* as a novel of education, this development of its hero in his role as mediator should weigh heavily in favor of a reading of the novel as the product not of pessimism and despair but of a positive spirit striving for the accommodation of antithetical positions in their synthesis.

Mann achieved his ultimate triumph of mediation in the *Joseph* tetralogy, and in the figure of Goethe in his novel *The Beloved Returns*, which he wrote as an extensive interlude between the third and fourth volumes of the tetralogy and which shares some of that work's central themes.

The all-embracing polarity of spirit and nature seeks and finds its transcendence in the imposing figure of Joseph the Provider: clever *and* handsome, sensitive *and* resiliently strong, endowed with a questing spirit *and* a practical mind, a thinker *and* a doer, blessed with "the double blessing from the Heavens above *and* from the depth that lieth below,"

with the double blessing of spirit and nature. Joseph personi-
fies the union of a vast array of polar opposites: of tradition
and progress, of contemplation and action, of religious reverence and sociopolitical pragmatism; he is both the active pro-
moter on the philosophical-religious plane of monotheism
and, in the mundane world of the marketplace, of the first
five-year plan in Egypt's history. In his Joseph figure, as
Mann tells us, "the Hermes motif, the moon-, rogue-, and
mediator motif" finally finds its "most detailed treatment; it
moves to the front in full instrumentation." [30] When compared with the other figure that embodied wit *and* beauty,
Felix Krull, Joseph impresses us as a much more real being, of
far greater "natural weight" and substance, not a *grand feu
d'artifice*, but firmly rooted in tradition and life. This twice-
blessed hero stands before us in all his colorful three-dimensionality as a personality capable of growth and maturing,
human in his semidivinity, divine in his vital humanity.

Peter Heller, in discussing Joseph's character and mission,
aptly defines Joseph's development:

The way toward the fullness of Spirit leads through embodiment
in Nature. Joseph does not merely naturalize the divine motifs,
he spiritualizes them as well. The man of synthesis is richer in
vitality *and* insight. Nature and Spirit yearn for each other. "Ultimately" they are one, and genius anticipates this unity which is
a timeless, not a temporal truth.[31]

Among all of Mann's mediatory figures Joseph is clearly
the least problematical; he is the most successful in uniting in
his person the upper and the nether worlds, idea and appearance, contemplation and action. Why then is the blessing
finally withdrawn from the twice-blessed Joseph and passed
on to Juda by the trembling hand of dying Jacob under the
compulsion of a higher will? Because Joseph in the very act of
achieving the harmonious balance between spirit and nature,
between the spiritual and the mundane concerns in his life,
had failed to develop that zealous single-mindedness of absolute dedication to the spiritual mission that God demands of

his elect. In becoming a ruler in the worldly sphere, Joseph irretrievably lost leadership in the realm of the spirit. His blessing, as Jacob tells him, was a worldly not a spiritual one, and therefore not the highest. Yet this discovery did not diminish Jacob's love and admiration for his favorite son. Joseph is assured by the dying patriarch of a place of honor as the future head of the tribes of Israel.[32]

This is Mann's way of saying that he, the mediator, holds in undiminished esteem the type of balanced personality that his Joseph figure represents, in spite of the fact that this very harmony and balance with their aura of a playful gaiety exclude such a person from among the spiritual élite, chosen because of their stern, unsmiling zeal in fanatical devotion to the service of God. Joseph's name, Mann tells us in Jacob's last words,

will be remembered with joy, for he succeeded where few succeed; he has gained the favor of both God and men. That is a rare blessing, for usually one has only the choice of pleasing either the world or God; but he had been favored by the spirit of gracious mediation to be pleasing to both.[33]

The figure of Goethe in the novel *The Beloved Returns*, is still another personification of the mediator. As such it exhibits many traits characteristic of the mediator Thomas Mann. In his portrayal, Mann stresses Goethe's tolerance, his conciliatory spirit, his hatred of unrestrained emotionalism and eccentric gesturing. We are reminded that Goethe felt himself born for reconciliation rather than for tragic conflict. As we hear this fictional Goethe comment on his personality and world view, we become increasingly conscious that Mann is stylizing the figure of his hero in his own image. "Are not reconciliation and compromise at the very center of all my striving," he has Goethe ask, "and are not affirmation and a productive acceptance of alternatives, are not balance and harmony my very special case?" [34] These attitudes are indeed Mann's own; they are even more deeply characteristic of him than of the historical Goethe.

While exhibiting these and many other clearly autobiographical traits, the figure of Goethe, as it appears in Mann's novel, also bears a certain resemblance to Mann's portrayal of Joseph. This fictional Goethe is, as it were, a potentiated, an enhanced, a *gesteigerte* Joseph, enhanced to the level of genius. He leaves behind the temperate humane sphere in which Joseph found his fulfillment as the provider for man's spiritual and physical needs. Goethe knows himself to be the highest possible synthesis of spirit and nature, "a résumé," as he puts it, "a *ne plus ultra* of perfection, for the achievement of which nature expended its most elaborate efforts." And he asks:

How much of tenderness and toughness, of weakness and resoluteness, of insanity and wisdom, of the impossible-made-possible, of consciousness and naïveté, of Romanticism and of a firm and active grasp on life had to be happily joined and fused [through generations] so that in the end the phenomenon of genius could make its appearance? . . . I am a feat of balance *in extremis*, a neatly equilibrated lucky stroke of nature [ein Glücksfall der Natur], a dance on the edge of a knife. . . . Genius is always the just barely possible.[35]

Mann is obviously intent on emphasizing in his portrayal of Goethe the precariousness and ambivalence of genius to show his amoral, or, to be more precise, his transmoral, nature. Especially in the reactions of those who live in the immediate presence or under the spell of Goethe, Mann confronts us with the demonic aspects of genius. Charlotte Kestner, Werther's Lotte, feels both spellbound and strangely apprehensive during her visit with her great friend. She is captivated by his ambrosial graciousness and Jovian grandeur, yet somehow ill at ease and all but horrified at the enigmatical play of his features, under the gaze of his eyes as she listens to his stories, commentaries, maxims, and reflections, which are so gracious, graceful, witty, and profound, and which, at the same time, exude icy coldness of personal noninvolvement, remoteness, and indifference.

Sitting in Goethe's box during a performance of Theodor

Körner's tragedy *Rosamunde,* Lotte is irritated by that playwright's inept definition of human greatness, and gropes in her dreamy, half-conscious way for an answer to the riddle of genius. "The outer limit of human greatness," she broods, "may well be a single one beyond which lies neither Heaven nor hell, or rather, both Heaven and hell. . . . depravity and purity fused into one." [36] Later in the spectral scene of the carriage ride, Lotte confesses to her great friend with disarming frankness that "in his house of art and in the circle of his life [she] had not felt at ease but had experienced a nightmarish feeling of oppressiveness and apprehension." And carried away by her emotions in recollection of her fate as sacrifice to Goethe's genius, she adds, "There is an odor in your presence as of sacrifice, . . . of human sacrifice . . . it is like on a battlefield . . . like in the realm of an evil emperor." [37] Intuitively she senses the ruthlessness of genius in exploiting life and offering it up in sacrifice to art. She fails to grasp the fact, however, that genius demands this sacrifice not only of others but also, inescapably, of himself as well. While inflicting suffering, he is doomed to writhe forever in the torments of guiltless guilt—torments that can be assuaged only in the cathartic act of artistic creation. Werther, Clavigo, Weislingen, Faust—they all bear witness to this anguish; they are the creatures of that suffering, their creation was the genius' act of confession, contrition, and expiation.

In speaking of the ruthlessness of genius, Lotte used the metaphor of the candle flame and the moth. Now the spectral apparition at her side explains to her, in a gesture of farewell and reconciliation, that in the change and interchange of things, genius is the *flame* in which the moth seeks and finds its immolation; but genius also is the *candle* that offers itself up in order that there be light; and, in the end, he is the *moth* as well that perishes in the candle's flame. For he is the symbol of all physical sacrifice in the act of spiritual transubstantiation. His fate is to be the immolator and the sacrifice, both in one.

If Lotte intuitively senses the paradox of genius, Riemer, Goethe's close associate, consciously probes its forbidding depths and ineluctable ambiguities. With all his senses sharpened by the torments of the contradictory emotions of love and hatred, envy and admiration, aroused by the overwhelming personality of the poet, literally carried beyond himself, Riemer is capable of comprehending the phenomenon of genius. As he pondered over it, he frequently had been reminded of that double blessing with which Joseph had been favored from the Heavens above and from the depth that lieth below. In this blessing Riemer comes to see that combination characteristic of Goethe, the paradox of "the most powerful gifts of the spirit combined with the most stupendous naïveté." [38] And he discovers another paradox: the blessing as "a curse and an apprehension." He realizes that genius embraces both the divine and the demonic; it is ambrosial and "spritelike [elbisch]"; it is spirit in its most sublime and nature in its most demonic; it is total affirmation and absolute negation, an abysmal nihilism. He explains this terrifying paradox to Lotte in his tortured conversation with her:

Since God is totality, He, of necessity, is also the devil, and evidently one does not approach the divine without approaching at the same time the demonic, so that it is as if out of one eye Heaven and love were looking at you and out of the other the hell of ice-cold negation and destructive indifference. But two eyes, my dearest, whether they lie close together or not, have but one gaze, and now I should like to ask the question: What type of gaze is it in which this frightful contradiction of the eyes is resolved? . . . It is the gaze of art, of absolute art, which is at once absolute love and the absolute destructiveness of indifference, and which represents that frightening approximation to the divine-demonic that we call greatness.[39]

This definition of greatness in its ominous ambiguity adumbrates in a striking manner the central theme of Mann's *Faustus* novel: the precarious ambivalence and final doom of modern genius. Riemer's apprehensive admiration for Goethe's greatness anticipates Serenus Zeitblom's horror-

struck admiration for the demonic genius of Adrian Leverkühn; Riemer's trembling hands as he ponders the paradox of Geothe's personality are Zeitblom's as he records in
agony and love the biography of his great doomed friend. In
that "wildest" of Mann's novels, the theme of the double
blessing does reappear, but only as its negation. In Adrian
Leverkühn's genius there is the same paradoxical cohabitation
of the divine and the demonic that Riemer had discovered in
the all-embracing totality of Goethe's genius. But here the
parallel ends. Goethe, in his epoch, in his *Zeitläufte*, could
hold the antithetical forces in a creative balance and enhance
them into a harmonious synthesis of the most powerful gifts
of the spirit with the most stupendous naïveté. As Riemer
agonizes over the torturing enigma of Goethe's greatness, he
is forced to the startling conclusion, in bemused self-contra-
diction, that in the case of Goethe, the "double blessing from
the Heavens above and from the depth that lieth below is
unblemished by any suggestion of curse, . . . it is the very
symbol of an absolute noble harmony and bliss on earth [Er-
denseligkeit]." [40] In Adrian's genius, on the other hand, in
this genius *in extremis* at a time of cultural desiccation and
disintegration, this noble harmony and bliss on earth can no
longer be attained; now spirit and nature have been torn
apart, the devil has gained unchecked power as the only force
capable of ——————— epigonous artist from sterility to renewed creativity. In Adrian's world the fusion of spirit and
nature has become unachievable. The artist finds himself
blocked in his mission as mediator between these spheres.

Thomas Mann dreamt of an ideal art of the future, "the
winged Hermes-like mediatress between life and spirit." [41] In
contrast to this ideal art, Leverkühn's represents an art that
has lost its Hermes wings. The symphonic cantata, *Dr.
Faust's Lamentation* (*Dr. Fausti Weheklag*) with its crash-
ing percussions, screaming brass, wild vocal glissandi, and unbearable silences is music born of despair, is the ultimate expression of the fierce tortures suffered by the artist deprived
of the double blessing.

In his *Lamentation*, Adrian had withdrawn, had "taken back" the message of joy, love, and friendship of Beethoven's *Ninth Symphony*; in *Doctor Faustus*, Mann withdrew the message of the double blessing that so gladdened his heart. In the figures of Joseph and Goethe he had embodied his ideal of a creative humanity; in Adrian's tragic fate he states his deeply held conviction that with the loss of this double blessing, the artist is doomed to an existence of hell on earth, burning in the flames of demonic inspiration, freezing in the icy cold of satanic cerebrality and lovelessness, unbearably tortured by fits of migraine, of that *Hauptweh* which with Adrian is but the physical symptom of the devil-induced creative impotence.

As a final example of mediation in the life and works of Thomas Mann may stand the Maya grotesque, as the poet once called the novella, *Die Vertauschten Köpfe* (*The Transposed Heads*). Mann was undecided about the nature and value of the work. First he dismissed it as a "mere divertissement and intermezzo";[42] later he came to recognize in it "well-nigh a masterpiece, an illusive being, iridescent and oscillating, refusing to yield an unambiguous meaning whenever we wish to lay hold of it." [43] On the contrary, the message and moral of this tale is all too explicit, spelled out with an all but mathematical precision that may well diminish its value as a work of art.

What is its message? Plainly, it is the lesson that the double blessing of spirit and nature is not to be had by mere manipulation, not even with the blessings of a goddess.

Sita, a beguilingly beautiful Indian maiden, is married to Schridaman, the man of the spirit. In his feeble arms she pines with longing for the beautiful body of Nanda, Schridaman's friend. Soon all three are caught in the toils of passion. In distress they make their way to the temple of Durgâ-Kâlî, the dark mother-goddess, and there, carried away by love's frustration and religious exaltation, Schridaman severs his head from his body and is followed in death by his heartbroken friend. Sita, coming upon the gory scene, flees in panic and is about to hang herself outside the temple when suddenly she hears the voice of the great world-mother reprimanding her for the disorder she has caused and instructing her sternly to put things right by going fearlessly back to the dead lovers and placing their severed heads on their bodies, thus resurrecting them with her divine assistance. Understandably distraught, Sita makes haste to follow instructions, but instead of replacing the heads, she *transposes* them. A classic Freudian slip! She now has what she yearned for— Schridaman's brainy head upon Nanda's brawny body. Alas, the double blessing proves short-lived. Schridaman's intellect soon gains domination over Nanda's body, reducing it to all but Schridamanian proportions, and Sita has once again cause for longing and pining; for in the meantime, Schridaman's body, under the influence of Nanda's head has flourished to more than Nandian beauty and draws poor Sita into the blissful embrace of its vigorous arms—and into adultery. This proves too much for all three. They choose death— Schridaman and Nanda, each by the sword of the other, and Sita as the faithful widow of both upon their funeral pyre, not, however, before giving birth to a son who is destined to be as clever as he is beautiful. Thus the double blessing of spirit and nature has once again found its embodiment, yet not by means of mechanical manipulation but through the miracle of procreation.

Surely, one might object that all this is just too pat, too didactic, too obviously and neatly calculated and manipulated for a work of art. Yet, the wittily limpid tale may well conclude, as a lighthearted coda, this discussion of the pervasiveness in Mann's work of the themes of double blessing and mediation, in a serious as well as in a playful vein. The poet himself has closed the circle; he has identified Schridaman with Tonio, Nanda and Sita with his boyhood loves, Hans Hansen and Ingeborg Holm. Speaking of his Maya-Grotesque, he wrote to Agnes Meyer in archly melancholy retrospect over the vast span of his creative work, "Yes, Tonio,

Hans, and Inge are now united in their fiery grave. Peace to their ashes." [44]

Thomas Mann experienced his own self and the world as a multifaceted set of polarities, as tension between opposites. Resolution of these antagonistic forces and polar opposites into a harmony more or less achieved, more or less stable, was a basic drive in Thomas Mann. This drive predestined him for the role of the great mediator, the *Mittler* and *Vermittler* par excellence both in the fictive world of his art and in the arena of social and political life. The polar extremes between which his genius mediated are legion: spirit and nature; art and life; tradition and progress; time and eternity; the past and the future; the romantic longing for the infinite and the classical sense of form; chaos and order; decadence and vitality; the cult of death and the affirmation of life; the aristocratic cultivation of personality and the democratic striving for a new sense of sociopolitical communality. All these the poet strives to fuse and to elevate into a higher synthesis, which he has called most aptly and all-inclusively the new humanism. We are fortunate to be able to experience this new brighter world conjured in the pages of Mann's masterworks even if we are not fated to see its realization in the world of reality.

8

World Without Transcendence?

In a life dedicated to the calling of the artist and yet bent on unflinching fulfillment of the demands of each day, Thomas Mann sought and found relief and relaxation from well-nigh overwhelming pressures under the liberating spell of his beloved sea. The sea satisfied and stilled his yearning for deep oblivion in the freedom of hovering above space and time. That it could satisfy this need of the poet explains Mann's lifelong love of the sea; he loved its soothing monotony, limitless horizons, and vast simplicity.[1] The sea was for him "not a scenic view, but the vivid experience of nothingness and death, a metaphysical dream." [2]

This yearning of the poet was also stilled in the oblivion of sweet slumber, from which he would rise, as he tells us "renewed, rejuvenated, all but reborn with the fresh innocence, high courage, and joy of youth," [3] truly a gift of Heaven, which had also been celebrated by Goethe in the immortal verses of his *Faust*.[4] And, finally, Mann satisfied and stilled this yearning most deeply perhaps in those cherished hours of his surrender to the spell of *music*.

His daughter Monika in a penetrating portrayal of her father has given us a revealing insight into Mann's complex, highly problematical relationship to this art form. She wrote:

Music is the only weakness Papa has. He regards it with a mixture of adoration, envy, and disdain. . . . Nearly always when Papa is listening to music he arouses in me the idea that he is more musical than most musicians; yet, had he chosen it or had he been chosen by it, he would have fallen into an abyss. Its inarticulateness would have corrupted him and delivered him to the devil. He is too fully and wholly the man of the word—of the prosaic, the intrinsic, the ascetic sphere—so that music for him is necessarily somehow linked to sin.[5]

Monika exaggerates her father's exclusive devotion to the word. Mann has repeatedly pointed out that he always lived close to music, that he received from it endless inspiration and artistic instruction. As a narrator he practiced the principles of musical composition and sought to recapture in the verbal medium the very essence of music:

Music and language are inseparable for me. They are essentially one. Language *is* music, and music a language; when separated, one always refers to the other and imitates it using the methods and means of the other and identifying itself as the other's substitute.[6]

Monika is right, however, about the threat that the enthralling and magical allurement of music held for her father, even if she does put it in too ominous terms, all but identifying her father with the tragic figure of Adrian Leverkühn. Still, there can be no doubt that Mann did fear to be overwhelmed by the Dionysian, romantic raptures of music. He had his doubts about its reliability as a humanizing influence. "Has the musical genius nothing whatever to do with humanism and the 'progressive society'?" he asks. "May it [music] be actually working against them?"[7] Serenus Zeitblom, the humanistic scholar in whom Mann drew a gently ironic self-portrait, echoes the doubts voiced in these questions: "Music seems to belong to a world of spirits for whose unconditional reliability in matters of rationality and human dignity I would not be quite willing to place my hand into the fire." [8]

There have been artists who felt so threatened in their creative powers by the "irrational flood" of music that they set about raising barriers against it—Stefan George and some of his followers, for instance. Their opposition to this "paradigma of all the arts" proved a weakness, not a strength, an impoverishment, not an enrichment, of their lives and works. Thomas Mann, in contrast, encompassed the enigmatical magic of music in his ample genius. "Music has always been a formative influence in my work," he tells us in his "Introduction" to *The Magic Mountain*. "I must consider myself a musician among the poets. The novel has always been for me a symphony, a work of contrapuntal structure, a texture of themes, in which ideas play the role of musical motifs." [9] And to his lifelong friend, the famous conductor Bruno Walter, he confides:

Love for that mysterious, stern, and withal rapturous art had been inborn with me. It had been my early ambition and joy to intertwine the essence and the effects of music with those of the word, to transfer music's way of "thinking," its way of weaving interlinking patterns into the word, thereby creating a narrative in the form of a web of themes [ein Themengespinst], and of a contrapuntal composition.[10]

It was this inborn love for music, for the mysterious, stern and withal rapturous art, that lent Mann's works much of their inimitable quality; it provided him central themes for *Buddenbrooks, Tristan, The Magic Mountain*, and *Doctor Faustus*; it enabled him to develop these themes with a virtuosity perfected in close study of music and musicology; it gave his compositions their uniquely musical structure and made of him the unchallenged master of the musical leitmotif; above all, this lover of music, this poet-musician was blessed with the precious gift of an unfailing sense for the basic tonality, the *Grundlaut* and specific *Sangeston,* in which the countless episodes of his immense life's work had to be "composed" to render with utmost fidelity and effectiveness their specific moods and emotional messages. It is this unique gift that magically transforms Mann's prose into a poetry which, at its best, is matched in its subtle musicality only by the verses of the great lyricists.

All these themes—"sea," "slumber," "music"—they all are interrelated in Mann's work, not only because the author has interlinked them by means of the leitmotif, as has been demonstrated repeatedly, most impressively perhaps by Hermann Weigand in his study of *The Magic Mountain,*[11] but because they all have for their common metaphysical source a central experience of the poet, his profound "sympathy with death," his *Sympathie mit dem Tode.* It is tempting to point to the poets of the Romantic school in German literature, who also favored and intertwined the themes of music, slumber, and death, and to associate Mann with this tradition. There is ample evidence of Mann's awareness of Novalis' fascination with death as a gateway to a transcendent existence; yet this was not the source of Mann's inspiration. Rather it was *World as Will and Idea* of the philosopher Arthur Schopenhauer, with its abnegation of the will to life, with its ethos of cross, death, and tomb. But even this source cannot be regarded as the ultimate wellspring of Mann's sympathy with death. For that wellspring we cannot look to literature or philosophy. Mann's sympathy with death did not originate in a *Bildungserlebnis* but represents an *Urerlebnis*—a protoexperience. It is rooted in Mann's very being. It is related to his yearning for Nirvana.

Mann's efforts at control of this romantic cult of the past, of sickness and death has found its most comprehensive artistic expression in *The Magic Mountain*. Mann has repeatedly explained that this novel is not to be considered a product of death-oriented pessimism. For instance in the essay "Vom Geist der Medizin" ("Of the spirit of Medicine"), he stresses this positive aspect of the work:

This book . . . is a book of goodwill and firm resolve, a book
that discards in the sphere of ideas much that is dear to one's
heart, many a dangerous sympathy, magical attraction, and
temptation. . . . It is a book of farewell, I repeat, of pedagogical self-mastery.[12]

Mann identifies this positive orientation as the source of the
new quality of the humor in this work. It was, he tells us, the
renunciation of many a dangerous sympathy that enabled
him to make good-natured fun of death and to present its
dignity in the tone of light-hearted irony.[13]

The Magic Mountain has its proper place, according to its
author, in the tradition of the medieval "Questing" novel.
Hans Castorp may well be seen as a modern-day Parsifal, the
guileless fool with his boyish *tumbheit* (simple-mindedness,
lack of experience) but also with a predisposition to spiritual
growth. Those who would see in him a static figure, incapable
of development are surely in error. Clearly, Hans Castorp in
his quest fails to gain permanent possession of the grail. But,
like his medieval precursors, he does reach the goal of his
quest. In the snowswept wilderness of his *Munsalväsche*, his
"wild mountain," * in the grip of death, at a moment of
heightened perception, Castorp finds the strength to break
death's fatal fascination and to dedicate himself to life, kindliness and love. The poet has underlined the importance of
this sudden illumination of his questing hero in the only italicized sentence of the thousand plus pages of the novel: *"For
the sake of kindliness and love, man should not permit death
to gain control over his thoughts."* [14] Castorp is granted the
vision of a new ideal, of a new humanism, which would hold
high the dignity of life against the dignity of death, which
would profess a steadfast faith in man's nobility, while being
deeply cognizant of the dark, mysterious depths of human
nature. This newly gained philosophy of life is the Holy Grail

---

* *Munsalväsche* is the name of "the wild mountain" (*mont sauvage*) in
Wolfram von Eschenbach's epic where the grail is kept. According to
some experts, the name derives from *Mons Salvationis* (Mount of
Salvation), an etymology which Mann would surely have found to
be most meaningful.

toward which Hans Gastorp's quest has led him. To quote the poet:

Hans Castorp does reach beyond his inborn devotion to death and arrives at an understanding [in his dream atop the mountain] of a humanity which does not, indeed, rationalistically ignore or scorn death, and all that is dark and mysterious in life, but rather takes account of it, without, however, allowing death to dominate his spirit.[15]

Hans Castorp does not ignore death, he takes account of it. His questing spirit leads him into dangerous adventures in the realm of sickness, the occult, and death. "There are," he explains to Clavdia Chauchat, "two ways to life: one is the regular, direct and upright way; the other is the 'evil way'; it leads through death, and that one is the way of genius." [16] Castorp's choice is the "evil way," the way of genius. He comes to realize that one has to go through the deep experience of sickness and death in order to arrive at higher sanity and health; in just the same way, knowledge of sin is the precondition for redemption. And, having grasped that truth, our hero "does not 'resist evil' and catches on his 'evil way' a glimpse of the 'true humanism of the future.' " [17] Mann's use here of the biblical phrase "and does not resist evil" is by no means fortuitous. It serves to underscore the fact that this new humanism is being envisaged by Mann as based on religion and colored by it. "A humanism with a religious ambience, a humanism founded on and colored by religion, a humanism that would embrace, within its tribute of honor and respect for the mystery that is man, all knowledge of the lower depths and the demonic in man's nature" [18]—such a humanism, Mann holds, could serve mankind as a guide toward a more perfect future.

Herbert Lehnert, in his searching study *Thomas Mann— Fiktion, Mythos, Religion,* rightly concludes that "religious motifs play an important role in Thomas Mann's work." He attributes "religious significance" to all the motifs we have cited above—"to the sea, as an elemental force; to music, as the overpowering art of relationship; to the thought of death as the power that annihilates individual existence in defined form, but, precisely in doing this, confers upon it its value." [19] Lehnert could have added that all these themes share the effect he assigned to sympathy with death, namely, its power of release from the individual existence in defined form, a power that, at the same time, confers upon life its metaphysical value.

There are, on the other hand, those critics who would deny to Mann's work a transcendent dimension. This is, for instance, the central argument of Hans Egon Holthusen in his tract, *Thomas Mann: Die Welt ohne Transzendenz (Thomas Mann: World Without Transcendence)*.[20] This study has for its subject Mann's novel *Doctor Faustus*, the very work which its author has repeatedly and emphatically characterized as a religious novel. Such criticism as Holthusen's disappointed Thomas Mann with its lack of empathy and perceptiveness, while proper recognition of the basic religious mood of his work pleased him greatly.[21] To Karl Kerényi he wrote:

What you wrote about the religious, Christian character of the "Faustus" affected me very much and filled me with that feeling of satisfaction which the truth always affords us. Surely, it *is* true and all but self-evident: How could so radical a book fail to reach up into religious sphere? And yet there are those who call it "godless." Such is the intelligence of people who write routinely on belles-lettres.[22]

Thomas Mann is convinced that a work which has apostasy for its central theme can never be deserving of the faithfuls' hatred. As he has Adrian Leverkühn explain, "Apostasy can never be the refutation of faith. It can happen only within faith itself. For apostasy is an act of faith, and everything exists and happens in God and quite especially the act of apostasy." [23]

The composition of *Doctor Faustus* was an altogether excruciating experience for the author. It was a confession and a life's sacrifice. The work's profound seriousness made it for Thomas Mann "a Christian work of extraordinary importance transcending everything narrowly denominational." [24] During the stirring, exhausting labors on this book of pain, Mann felt himself to be nearer than ever to God. To his friend Agnes Meyer he wrote:

I observe in myself a most serious mood. It must be that a difficult work of art [Doctor Faustus], much like battle or a storm at sea, like mortal danger, brings us closer to God by creating in us a need for blessing, help, and mercy, a religious disposition of the soul.[25]

This disposition of the poet's soul during his labors on *Faustus* was the source of the religious atmosphere that pervades the work. Its basic tonality is best characterized as numinous in Mann's definition of that term as "divinely demonic." Even in the earliest stages of composition Mann knew that this novel would have to be written in that tonality. From the very beginning he "had in mind something satanically religious, demonically pious." [26] With this work Mann made his closest approach to the apocalyptic sphere of holy criminality and criminal holiness given such overwhelming reality in Dostoevsky's works.

It is this numinous aura emanating from the emotion-charged scenes of *Doctor Faustus* that lends this novel its transcending power. How masterfully has Mann succeeded in suggesting the devil's authorship of every event, has made us sense the demonic presence long before the evil one finally appears *in propria persona* to seal the pact with his victim. His presence chills the waters of the Kuhmulde and the Klammweiher, those ponds, or rather, *that* pond, on the Leverkühn-Schweigestill estates and colors their depths a mysterious black; *he* peers out at us from Adrian's frightening gaze; *his* laughter echoes threateningly in Leverkühn's haughty, derisive laugh charged with cold cynicism. As we examine, together with young Adrian and his friend Serenus, Jonathan Leverkühn's collections of butterflies and shells, as we watch the old man's experiments with the osmotic plants and hear his speculations, we sense the presence of the evil tempter, while at the same time we are conscious of the profound piety in the Melanchton-like features of Jonathan's face. It is impossible to decide whether we have entered the realm of black or white magic, the divine or the demonic sphere; we are caught up in the satanically pious ambience of this enigmatical work. For its symbol and signature we may well take Jonathan's description of his seashells: They are the traditional accessories of the witch's kitchen and the alchemist's den, and at the same time they are ornaments in the temple of God, fashioned into splendorous reliquaries and used as sacred chalices at the rite of the Last Supper. "How much is conjoined here," observes the wise old man, "poison and beauty, poison and magic, but also magic and liturgy." [27]

In his article "The Devil Secularized," Erich Kahler speaks of "life's ambiguity, life's paradox" which he finds revealed in *Doctor Faustus:* "The Devil resides in God and God in the Devil. Sublimest chastity becomes the easiest prey of the whore." [28] He speaks, of course, of Adrian, the sublimely chaste who succumbs to the evil tempter's emissary, the whore Haetera Esmeralda.

While Kahler's central thesis, the "Secularization of the Devil," is open to argument, his formulation of life's paradox is certainly a most apt characterization of Adrian's ambiguous nature. In him the divine and the devilish do indeed interpenetrate inextricably. He is the doubter, the cynic with the devil's cold sneer; yet he partakes of God's spirit, is not without piety: *"Ein Spötter, dabei aber 'ein Gottgeistiger Mensch.'"* [29] Adrian's haughtiness delivers him to the devil, while yet his spirit yearns for beauty divine. Furtively he makes forbidden contact with the celestial sphere in the angelic messenger, the elfin child Nepomuk, little Echo. When Adrian resolves to withdraw and annul the message of love and kindness, of joy, hope, and friendship proclaimed so triumphantly in Beethoven's *Ninth Symphony*, he does it in a fit of demonic fury, in the depths of despair over the unbearable loss of little Echo. If ever Mann's feeling for the reli-

gious was active in molding his work, it was in the scenes of
Echo's advent, suffering, and death. The poet confides his
feelings:

I intensified a tenderness of my heart to a degree that was no
longer altogether rational and raised it to a loveliness in the figure
of Echo that caused the people in their hearts to believe in divin-
ity, in the advent of a messenger from afar and above, to believe
in Epiphany.[30]

Comparing Mann's deliberately objective, distanced description of Hanno's death in the *Buddenbrooks* with Echo's
heartrending end, one gains a sense of the full measure of
emotional intensity that created this scene of "redemptive
sacrifice" in the *Faustus* novel. Mann wrote of his change of
mood and of the development of his creative powers over the
long years between the two compositions to Frank Hirschbach: "At twenty-five, I was able to give living reality to the
decadent princeling Hanno Buddenbrook. But describe an
epiphany, that I could do only at seventy." [31]

Yet one cannot deny a religious disposition to *young*
Thomas Mann. To a marked degree, he had this always. In a
comparison of himself with his brother Heinrich, the author
singled it out as a salient characteristic of his make-up, which
differentiated him from his brother. He characterized it as "a
preponderance of the Nordic-Protestant element." [32] This
Nordic-Protestant element is present in Mann's creations
more pervasively than would appear on superficial contact. It
is recognizable in the pages of so early a work as the novella
Gladius Dei, though it is couched there in humorous or
ironic tones. It reappears, this time in elevated style, in the
drama *Fiorenza* to rescue Savonarola's religious fervor from
mere theatrical make-believe and pathetic gesturing.[33] It lends
a basic tone of sincerity to those pages of the *Betrachtungen*
in which Mann expressed his admiration for the gesture of
prayer and drew the portrait of man kneeling before God in
dignity and humility, in *Würde und Demut*.[34] Another in-

stance of this religious sensibility in the same work is Mann's homage to Hans Pfitzner's musical legend, the opera *Palestrina*. This masterpiece moved him deeply with its ethos of cross, death and tomb; its metaphysical mood satisfied his deepest, most personal needs. It "offered me consolation and succor [in days of political strife] . . . and corresponded exactly with my concept of humanism." [35] The pages of the *Betrachtungen* also record one of Mann's earliest attempts at defining the complex nature of his belief:

I dare not say that I believe in God. I dare not boast that I am a religious man. But if we may understand *religiosity* as that freedom which is a way and not a goal; if we take religiosity to mean open-mindedness, sensitivity, questing, doubting, and erring; if we recognize in it a way . . . to God or, for that matter, even to the devil . . . then, perhaps, I would be prepared to call such freedom and such religiosity my own.[36]

With advancing years, Mann's interest in legend, myth, and religious history grew apace. In his *Studien* Hans Wysling reported a conversation Mann had in 1926 with Oskar Maurus Fontane on a planned novelistic triptych—"Joseph in Egypt, a Spanish-Dutch theme, and Erasmus–Luther." Growing enthusiastic, Mann exclaimed:

How I am attracted to the religious in these novellas! Hitherto I had looked upon the religious only with the naïve awe of an earthling before the unfathomable. Now it attracts me with infinite intensity, and this happens to me, I believe, not incidentally, but of necessity. The religious will determine our entire near-range future. The aesthetic in all its aspects is definitely of the past.

First I came to these three plots [*Joseph, Philip II, Luther,* and *Erasmus*] . . . drawn to them by amateurish fancy. . . . But the more I became preoccupied with them, the more I realized that this fancy had a secret significance, that it had something to do with a powerful attraction: the religious.[37]

Such reorientation toward the metaphysical, toward myth and religion, Mann found linked with a person's growing maturity:

It is probably normal that with advancing years a person gradually loses his former taste for everything merely individual and special. . . . Instead, the typical, the always human, the always returning, the eternal, in short, the mythical, takes the center of the stage.[38]

With Thomas Mann the typical, the eternal, the mythical certainly did move to center stage. It is a matter of general knowledge among readers of Thomas Mann, that Goethe's reference in his autobiography *Dichtung und Wahrheit* (*Poetry and Truth*) to the biblical Joseph story as being all too brief served the author as a challenge to undertake his narrative expansion of the Old Testament tale. Less well-known may be the fact that a central passage of the biblical story furnished the "seed-bud [Keim]," as Mann called it, of his *Joseph* tetralogy and provided him with ever fresh inspiration during the long years—nearly a decade—of its composition. To Ernst Bertram Mann explained:

It [the seed-bud] is the dying Jacob's blessing of Joseph: "You have been blessed by the Almighty *with the blessing from Heaven above and with the blessing from the depth that lieth below.*" In order for me to undertake a work, its plot must offer somewhere in its scope a "productive point" that can gladden our heart whenever we come in contact with it. The double blessing is such a productive point.[39]

Mann developed this theme of the double blessing into a central leitmotif of the tetralogy.

The indebtedness of the tetralogy's plot to the Testaments, Old and New, and to biblical apocrypha is too obvious to need elaboration. That fact in itself, however, would not have vouchsafed the religious atmosphere of the work. The author could well have assumed a cynical attitude toward his materials. He could have related the story in a satirical vein, in sardonic and mocking tones that would have transformed the religious message into one of atheistic nihilism. This was not Mann's approach. To be sure, he did not treat his materials in the spirit of rigid orthodoxy. He shaped them with the light touch of humor, infused them with a higher gaiety. But, as the author remarks, "a humorous game with the sacred can well be a form of modesty and a cautious manner of approaching the holy." [40]

The basic dialectic of the *Joseph* tetralogy embraces Heaven *and* earth, religion *and* history, myth *and* psychology, revelation *and* Freud. To the mundane and terrestrial is subtly imparted an aura of transcendence. "The revolving sphere [die rollende Sphäre]," the tetralogy's central leitmotif, links events in Heaven with those on earth and mirrors terrestrial happenings in the Heavens above: Joseph, enacting in the human sphere the mythical sacrificial role of Tamuz-Adonis-Osiris, is at the same time foreshadowing the role of Christ on earth and in Heaven, His sacrificial death, His descent into hell, and His resurrection. The dialectic interchange and interaction of the Heavenly and the earthly spheres is the pervasive rhythm of this grand song of humanity, this *Menschheitslied* that strives to bring mankind a "higher gaiety in God [Eine höhere Heiterkeit in Gott]."

"The idea of progress which is central in the *Joseph* novels and determines the form of [their] composition," is according to Thomas Mann "most precisely defined with the phrase, 'moving forward together with God.'" [41] The image of man created by the poet in his vast epic is the image of *homo dei* laboring to conceptualize the one, almighty God, invisible, omniscient, ubiquitous, in order with His help, in a mutually enhancing interaction with Him, to move forward toward a nobler future, to break out of obsolete traditions, and to approach the truth. There had been conventions which, in their times, were sound and acceptable; but at a certain point in mankind's history they ceased to be rational and deteriorated into what Mann calls *Gottesdummheit* (stupidity-in-God). Humanity must move beyond these. True religiosity for Thomas Mann consists in our ability to recognize God's purpose with the human race and to assist Him actively in creating the new image of truth. Those who are capable of such attentiveness and active collaboration partake of *Gottesklugheit* (wisdom-in-God); those, on the other hand, who are blind and deaf to the will of God and remain caught up in their old ways become the hapless victims of *Gottesdummheit*. Such hapless victims were Huij and Tuij, the benighted sibling-parents of poor Potiphar. They had failed to grasp God's intent when they emasculated their son, offering up his manhood in a sacrifice no longer acceptable to the Almighty at that advanced hour in world history.

In this tetralogy's humanism, theology and history, myth and psychology, the Bible and Freud are all drawn into a harmony, the common source of which is the author's feeling for the religious. A believer, rigid in his orthodoxy, will surely question the authenticity of such a religiosity. In fact, the Catholic Church and many a devout Lutheran did take umbrage, accusing Mann of having perverted the absolute authority of the Christian dogma to a relative value. Thomas Mann would not deny the justice of this accusation. He frankly admitted that his faith was never, in any sense, a rigid orthodoxy. "Religiosity, which I do not consider to be at all alien to my heart, is, to be sure, something other than an orthodox, denominationally circumscribed religion." [42] Mann's faith is characterized by an unshakable conviction "that the divine—if it is not above us—must be undeniably, inalienably, irrevocably within the human being." [43]

Mann was quite prepared to concede that the tetralogy does, in fact, humanize the Christian religion, just as it humanizes the myths that appear in it fusing them into the harmony and unity of a work of art. For Mann religion was always something very human, but by the same token his humanism was not such as would make of him a disbeliever. Serenus Zeitblom surely is speaking for Thomas Mann himself when he says of his religiosity:

It would displease me if people considered me a thoroughly irreligious man. This I am not; rather I agree with Schleiermacher

. . . who defined religion as the "predisposition and taste for the infinite" and who called it a condition and an attitude peculiar to man.[44]

The quotation determines Mann's position with great precision as being at the point where theology and humanism meet and penetrate each other in romantic thought. We can be all the more certain that Serenus is indeed speaking for Mann since on another occasion the author uses a variation of Zeitblom's words with direct reference to himself in a nonfictive context: "To be sure," he writes here, "I do see in the religious sphere something thoroughly human and in theology a science of man and not—of God." And playing on the word *Wissenschaft*, which in German has both the meaning of "science" and of "knowledge," he adds with a smile: "How could one, after all, have a 'science' of Him." Then, in a serious vein again, he concludes, echoing Zeitblom's words: "Despite this my attitude toward religion, in the book [the *Joseph* tetralogy] as elsewhere, is not one I should like to hear defined as the attitude of a decided unbeliever." [45]

Another central religious theme that runs as a leitmotif through Mann's works is the theme of divine grace and mercy. It links the *Joseph* tetralogy to *Doctor Faustus* and to the novella *The Holy Sinner*. In each work God's grace ultimately is bestowed on a great sinner: In the tetralogy, at its very end, it is Juda who gains God's mercy and receives dying Jacob's blessing despite his carnal transgressions. He receives it because of the fervent, questing radicalism of his spirit. For his fierce struggle against the tyranny of his sinful flesh, for his yearning after purity, he is chosen to be the bearer of God's message, to champion and to enhance it. Bestowing the blessing, Jacob conjures up a vision of Juda as Dionysus, the god of rejuvenation and fertility who, in his mythical constellation is, at the same time, Zagreus, the dismembered one. Thus, by the grace of God, the sinner Juda receives in Mann's great song of man his part in the cosmic orbiting image, in the *Kreislaufbild* of birth, sacrifice, and resurrection.

In *Doctor Faustus* the mercy of God finds its truly celestial symbol in the high G of the cello in Adrian's final work, in his heartrending oratorio, *Dr. Fausti Lamentation.* That transcending sound shines forth like a light in the night of Adrian's and Germany's agony, offering a faint hope, ever so tentatively, of divine forgiveness for the tortured victims of the hellish fiend.

Finally, in *The Holy Sinner* divine mercy becomes the central serious concern of the author. Mann had come across the legend of Saint Gregorious in the course of his wide-ranging readings for *Doctor Faustus.* While browsing in the famous collection of legends and secular tales, the *Gesta Romanorum,* he was attracted by the Saint's miraculous fate because it extolled the wondrous workings of God's grace and forgiveness. He decided to retell the story in a humorous vein, humanizing the legend much as he had humanized the biblical tale of Joseph. He would play his humorous game with the sacred here too, but the central theme would be a serious concern to him. "Amidst all the jests, I am in dead earnest about the religious core of the legend, about the idea of sin and mercy. For a very long time my life and my thinking have been influenced by this idea." [46] On another occasion, varying the wording in his leitmotif fashion, Mann reemphasized his serious intent: "The playful novel, that late form of the legend, indulges in many a jest. But with sincere earnestness it preserves the legend's religious core, its Christianity, the idea of sin and mercy." [47] Hermann Hesse, in a letter to Thomas Mann, expressed his misgivings about the reader's ability to penetrate to the religious core of the novella; "Most readers," he thought, "would have sufficient insight to be aware of the irony in this delightful composition," but he had his serious doubts, that "all would be able to sense the earnestness and the piety which underlie these ironies and lend them their true, lofty gaiety." [48] The text certainly justifies Hesse's doubts. Only the most empathetic reader, suspending disbelief, will be able to detect the poet's serious intent with the religious core of the legend so effectively disguised by the wittily ironic, gaily parodistic style even of those passages which deal with the theme of sin and divine mercy. Yet in his justification we might recall Mann's words: "A humorous game with the sacred can well be a form of modesty and a cautious manner of approaching the holy."

In the last years of his life, while working on the *Confessions of Felix Krull, Confidence Man,* Mann's thoughts often turned to his early plans of a religious triptych. Portraits of Erasmus and Luther were to form the middle part, and scenes and characters from the Spanish Counter Reformation, linked with the German Humanism and Reformation, the third, while the Joseph story was to open the series, as had been his plan from the very beginning. At this time his interest centered on the periods of Reformation, Counter Reformation and Humanism:

That whole business with Spirituali, Bernardo Ochino, with the onrush of the Counter Reformation sparked by Pope Paul's Bull, with Ochino's flight, his meeting with Calvin and Luther . . . this entire story that would also include the lives of Zwingli and especially of Erasmus, attracts me infinitely and represents a dream that has never been realized and can probably no longer be accomplished.[49]

While despairing of writing the work, Mann yet felt strongly that labors on such a theme or a similar one would be far more appropriate and dignified for a man of his age than his preoccupation with the *Confessions of a Confidence Man.* To his daughter Erika he confided:

While I am working on *Krull* I keep asking myself, "What is the purpose of this nonsense." It all seems to lack proper background —though I might be mistaken. As of the moment, I have another chapter planned. But in case I do not know how to continue, I will write a dignified and masterly [würdig-meisterhafte] historical novella about Erasmus, Luther, and Ulrich von Hutten.[50]

As Herbert Lehnert has shown, Mann's final literary studies centered on the Protestant sixteenth century and were just beginning to crystallize into "a play of serious import," with the tentative title "Luther's Marriage" when death intervened.[51] The manner in which the Nordic-Protestant element in Mann's personality reasserted itself in this final phase of his artistic career is highly characteristic of the organic unity in Mann's life and art. It is salient proof against the theory of a break in his intellectual development, which certain critics claim took place at the end of World War I when Mann renounced Germany's romantic, aristocratic past and turned his interest and his sympathies toward a rational, democratic future. As will be shown in the last chapter, Mann did develop a far more lively sense of social responsibility and did integrate the political realm into the sphere of art as a proper concern of the poet. Nevertheless, his highest ideal of art remained amazingly consistent. He aptly characterized it as a resounding ethos, as *tönende Ethik*, as "a structure without profane intent and aim, where every part fuses with the other without the need of mortar, joined and sustained by the 'hand of God.'" This kind of art he always strove for, while being conscious that he had never been able to achieve it: "This *l'art pour l'art* is truly my ideal of art, which I in no way represent, but toward which I shall always be striving." [52] In one of his last letters, barely a year before his death, he told his correspondent that the most appropriate motto for his entire work would be the words of his Gregorius, the holy sinner: "I did it to offer God entertainment [Ich tat es um Gott eine Unterhaltung zu bereiten]." [53] Then he added these cautious words so characteristic of the man and the artist: "One is used to saying that art strives for perfection. But is such striving really altogether an earthly effort?" [54]

In an epilogue to Mann's letters, his daughter Erika told of her father's increasing preoccupation, "What concerned him ever more insistently was the resonance of his name in the hereafter—not on earth and with reference to his books, but in the ethico-religious sphere and in the transcendental." [55] For his *Doctor Faustus* Mann had been reading the *Apocalypse* of Saint John. He pointed out to Erika the passage that had gripped him most profoundly. It was God's praise of the saint for his steadfastness in His service: "Yours was a small power, and yet, you have held high My word and have not betrayed My name! . . . Blessed be," he told his daughter, "who deserves these words for his epitaph. *Wohl dem, der das als Epitaph verdient.*" [56]

9

Champion of Humanism

In his early years Thomas Mann had been critical of the modern artist and all his works. He saw in him a charlatan and a gypsy, "unfit for any serious business, intent on nothing but nonsense and trivia [Allotria], of no use to society, in fact a constant thorn in its side." [1] This sharply critical view was soon to mellow. Yet a certain suspicion of the artist's role in life did linger. Mann never joined in celebration of the poet as the God-inspired seer and charismatic leader of humanity without fail or flaw. He remained ever conscious of the artist's problem-beset way through life. This consciousness did much to stiffen Mann's resolve to gain and to maintain an unchallengeable social position and to attain to the acclaim and dignity of exemplary achievement. Mann's life and work bear impressive witness to his success in demonstrating the artist's capacity of remaining faithful to the freedom and high gaiety of the creative spirit while carrying on a responsible and socially productive life as a staunch champion of humanism in its time of crisis.

When, under the pressures of World War I and its aftermath, Mann abandoned his attitude of nonengagement and entered the political arena, he found himself attacked from left and right. There were those who resented his conservative and Germanophile stance, his suspicion of the Allied cause, which were characteristic of him in his *Betrachtungen*. When Mann took up a more liberal, democratic, and cosmopolitan position, voices from the conservative right accused him of political opportunism. His opponents claimed that he had sensed Germany's move toward democracy in the wake of the debacle of the monarchical system and opportunistically hastened to jump on the bandwagon of the Weimar Republic.

The fact is, Mann did change his sociopolitical views in the turbulent postwar years, but representing the writer's intellectual growth and maturation as political opportunism is a distortion of the fact caused either by ignorance or by premeditation or outright malice. The record calls for fair statement and emphasis.

During the fateful years of World War I the poet supported his fatherland, not with patriotic fervor which was not in his nature, but in a spirit of solidarity growing out of a genuine love and admiration of Germany.[2] In his *Betrachtungen* written in the years of conflict, 1916–1918, he fought to prevent what he called "the politization of the spirit [Politisierung des Geistes]," [3] and to preserve the cultural values he believed in and which he felt his country's struggle against the Allies served to protect. He was convinced in those war years that a German victory would be a blessing to humanity as the triumph of culture over soulless civilization. He believed it would be the victory of German "inwardness [Innerlichkeit]" over facile, unprincipled intellectualism, of metaphysics over empiricism, of irony over radicalism, of the world of music and Romanticism over the materialistic world of effete pleasure-seeking and political opportunism, of the *Dichter* over the Francophile *Zivilisationsliterat*, whom he had recognized and come to hate in his brother Heinrich. Undeniably, there are pages in the *Betrachtungen* that make it clear that Mann was very conscious of his part in the spiritual sphere of Heinrich by dint of his Romance heritage from his mother's side. He realized that he could not but share the litterateur's point of view. He knew its value and was conscious of its proper claim to the future. Yet, in loyalty to his native land, he was determined to stand against the Allies, would not permit his knowledge to subvert his faith. He steadfastly clung to his convictions, all the more successfully since his love for Germany and its culture was deep indeed, for Germany's music, its Romanticism, its "soul."

Gradually, however, Thomas Mann came to realize that his cherished values were not basically threatened, that they were, in fact, protected and furthered by the West's democratic ideals of equality and fraternity and by its legal system. He recognized that freedom and human dignity were vouchsafed by the political principles and processes, which the Allies upheld. To state it bluntly: Mann grasped the truth that soul and intellect were not irreconcilable enemies, a disastrous text preached, for example, by Ludwig Klages in his paradigmatic book, *Der Geist als Widersacher der Seele* (*Intellect as the Antagonist of the Soul*), and that politics was indeed a proper concern for a poet.[4] Such insights could not be gained by opportunistically jumping on the Republican bandwagon; they had to be developed in a process of growth in which Mann did not lose his faith in the past while keeping pace with the present. He wrote:

Certainly when I put down the last words of the *Betrachtungen* I no longer had the attitude with which I wrote the first. I progressed, as is proper and fitting for any spirit that keeps alive; however, in my special way I did not drop anything from my life, but rather carried along my earlier thoughts and insights, fusing them into the later, so that they could at any time become productive again.[5]

Mann could rightly claim to have experienced, "more intensely perhaps and more personally than anyone else, in a violent struggle of conscience, the pressure of the times for a change from metaphysical individualism to social awareness." [6]

It is important, in fairness to the poet, to emphasize that

he fought at all times for the world of truth and beauty, poetry and music, for the great cultural heritage of the West. He was fighting for this ideal even while he was siding with conservative Germany. He always stood for the ideal of tolerance and mutual respect and defended the humanistic mean [die humanistische Mitte] against all fanatics, whether they carried their attack from the extreme left or the extreme right. Looking back upon the fight he had waged in the *Betrachtungen* he could, in all sincerity, ask the question, "And was it not this very element, the element of Humanism, that I defended in that work, both against the right and the left? . . . Yes, under the heaviest of pressures, more even against the left than the right?" [7] Mann had early recognized the overzealous ideologist as his real enemy. He characterized and criticized him in the neo-Gothic man of the *Betrachtungen*,[8] and gave him his fictional reality in the figure of Naphta of *The Magic Mountain*. The fanatic's prejudicial aggressiveness, his self-righteousness, his total lack of humor, irony, and intellectual charity, those were the qualities that repelled Thomas Mann perhaps most violently in the character of the *Zivilisationsliterat*.

It was certainly no exaggeration or distortion of his central mission both as an artist and as a champion of humanism in the political arena when, at a press conference in 1952, Mann pointed out, in retrospect upon his life's work, that all his efforts were proof of his constant striving to contribute, within the limits of his ability, to the great heritage of the West. And he asked, "Is there anyone who has really read even one of my books, who could deny that terror, brute force, untruth, and injustice are abhorrent to me?" [9] In all his creative efforts, be it in the world of art or in the world of politics, Mann had consistently been motivated by an inborn yearning for an enlightened, humane life, "a life in the spirit [ein Leben im Geiste]," as he called it. This is the main reason why Thomas Mann was able to raise his voice, as one of the very first, in warning against the onrush of the neo-barbarians, the National Socialists in the Germany of the late twenties and early thirties. That is also the reason why he could recognize the values of democracy and advocate this form of government as the best hope for Germany's citizenship in a world of tolerance and respect for man's dignity and freedom.

On October 15, 1922, on the occasion of Gerhart Hauptmann's sixtieth birthday, Thomas Mann, the nonpolitical, held his first political speech. He delivered his manifesto "Von deutscher Republik" ("The German Republic"), proclaiming the identity of humanism and democracy and linking "the divine name of Goethe with the name of the thunderer of Manhattan"—Walt Whitman. Mann was motivated to juxtapose the paragon of humanism with the champion of democracy by the realization that "humanism was but the classicistic, old-fashioned name for democracy." [10] For one who had considered faith in democracy as outright obscurantism[11] and had criticized politics as the evil despoiler of spirit and the soul, this meant indeed a long step forward in his progress toward the role as champion of a new humanism. In his speech Mann called upon the great Romantic poet Novalis as a witness to the fact that German Romanticism was by no means irrevocably bound to a reactionary, aristocratic past, but that the movement did carry within it the seeds of democracy. He spoke of Novalis' dream of a great state formed by all the people embracing all separate national states in the idea of a universal humanity. He reminded his listeners "that all the nations had grown old and wise and that the epic-heroic period in their developments had been long left behind each and every one of them and that any attempt to revert to that early stage would be tantamount to a dissolute rebellion against the law of our times." [12] He warned his fellow citizens: "If the idea of nationalism is not to fall into complete disrepute, if it is not to become altogether a curse, then it will be imperative to recognize in it not the quintessence of militarism and aggression but rather the object of *a cult of peace.*" [13] It is amazing to see with what instinctive certainty this nonpolitical man foresaw, in those early days of the Weimar Republic, the grave danger posed by Germany's nationalism, which was soon to be perverted into a crassly aggressive chauvinism—into a dissolute rebellion against the law of our times.

Thomas Mann's speech was immediately attacked as a betrayal of Germany and of the convictions that Mann had professed in his *Betrachtungen*. As a matter of fact, this speech was the organic product of Mann's consistent spiritual growth, and thus the direct continuation of the earlier work.[14] As Thomas Mann wrote to Felix Bertaux:

My essay "Von deutscher Republik," in which I sought to furnish information on my idea of humanism, has now been held against me as a betrayal of Germany and as a contradiction of the *Betrachtungen*, while, as a matter of fact, in its innermost thought, it is their direct continuation.[15]

Thomas Mann did not enter the political arena for some years following this manifesto of his faith in humanism and democracy. Nevertheless, he remained as ever acutely aware of the gathering storm of Fascism and Nazism. This awareness and apprehension found their expression in many a letter, in many a statement he wrote in response to the demands of the day, and in the fictive disguise of the novels and novellas created during those years.

It is easy to forget that *The Magic Mountain*, the inception of which, to be sure, dates back to the years preceding World War I, is nevertheless, in large part, the product of developments on the European scene and in Mann's life during the war and during the first crucial years of the struggling Weimar Republic. The novel was finished late in 1923. From the point of plot-chronology, the "peal of thunder" of the outbreak of war that casts Hans Castorp down upon the flaming battlefields of the *Flachland* (the lowlands) in August of the fateful year, 1914, is a most deceptive finale to a narrative which, in significant measure, records and analyzes the author's impressions and thoughts that postdate the war, and are the *result* of the apocalyptic cataclysm.* The protagonists

---

* In the Preface [Vorsatz] to his novel Mann has fixed its chronology as antedating the war, thus compounding the confusion. It must be realized that Mann speaks here as the epic poet, the conjurer of the

in the pages of this novel are portrayed by a poet matured beyond the emotional and intellectual stance that had been his at the beginning of the war or even at its end. Thus, Settembrini is clearly the product of Mann's greatly mellowed view of the once hated *Zivilisationsliterat* and generally of Mann's progress toward a democratic, cosmopolitan stance. This figure is drawn with an eye not focused on the past but on the future. And so is his antagonist, the Jesuit Jew Naphta. In him Mann created a figure not, primarily, typical of bourgeois prewar society but rather of the postwar scene. In Naphta's world view the author sounds his warning of an ideological development which, though rooted in war and revolution, had grown beyond these, to threaten in the form of modern totalitarianism the very foundations of Western civilization with a ruthless and insidious force more devastating than even the brutality of war. Naphta is Mann's portrayal of the modern ideologue ready to sacrifice man on the altar of utopia, enjoying his dialectical triumphs but ending in self-destruction.

It has been suggested that the Marxist literary and social historian, Georg Lukács, has furnished some traits for the figure of Naphta. That may well be. However, Lukács' Marxian thoughts had little if any influence on Naphta's basic philosophy. That philosophy is far more the anticipation of the type of Fascist reactionary neo-barbarism which Mann was to present, some two decades later, in its full-blown form in the racist rantings of Dr. Chaim Braisacher in his *Faustus* novel. Braisacher was drawn in retrospect, after the dread event. With Naphta, however, Mann furnished in the early twenties striking proof of his uncommon skill at sociopolitical and cultural diagnosis and even prognosis.

The Magic Mountain presents an extensive record of Mann's growing awareness of the poet's responsibilities in the

---

past. Yet even here, Mann hastens to point out that the "past" of his narrative continues into the future: "Sie spielt . . . vor dem grossen Krieg, mit dessen Beginn so vieles begann, *was zu beginnen wohl kaum schon aufgehört hat.*" (III, 9–10. Italics mine.)

social and political life of his time. It reveals this development at least as impressively as Mann's voluminous correspondence of those years or his seminal essay "Goethe and Tolstoy," which he subtitled "Fragments Toward the Problem of Humanism." Written in 1921, this essay is an apt companion piece to the novel, which in its own way is also a great fragment toward the solution of the problem of humanism. Interpreters who seek to establish the *locus classicus* in the work of Mann's rejection of his former conservative stance in favor of a democratic dedication in the service of life generally focus on the chapter "Snow." Without denying its central importance, we would draw the readers' attention to another statement of Mann's painful liberation from a seductively alluring Romanticism and dedication in the service to humanity. We find it in the chapter *"Fülle des Wohllauts"* ("Plenitude of Euphony"). Here Hans Castorp muses on the meaning of Franz Schubert's famous song of the "Linden Tree" ("Am Brunnen vor dem Tore"). Through the "alchemical enhancement [alchemische Steigerung]" experienced by Hans Castorp in the Hermetic, pedagogical sphere of the mountain, he is enabled to penetrate to the morbid essence of that magical song which had held him spellbound. In his state of "illumination" he realizes that this beloved melody, despite its enchantment, or rather precisely by the very power of its spell, was a

. . . life-fruit begotten of death and pregnant with death. It was a miracle of the soul—the loftiest perhaps in the sight of a beauty devoid of conscience. . . . And yet a miracle viewed with distrust by a responsible sense of friendship to life . . . and this for good reasons.

In the final judgment of conscience, Castorp now finds this miracle of a song "standing condemned as an allurement that had to be overcome in an act of self-conquest." This is a most painful truth that has dawned on our humble hero, for it amounts to the sacrifice of a part of his very self. "Yes," Castorp muses, "self-conquest might well be the essence of this renunciation of my 'love,' of that soul-magic fraught with such ominous consequences." [16]

In distant retrospect, in a letter to his friend and confidante Agnes Meyer, written in 1943, two decades after the novel's completion, Mann makes it abundantly clear that Castorp's musings on the enchanting song and his painful self-conquest in its renunciation were Mann's very own. "This song," he explains to his friend, "had become a symbol for me of all that is lovable, but also of all that is seductive, of all that harbors the secret seed of corruption." Mann still admits, at this late date, that "Romanticism is far more attractive, even richer, spiritually, than humanism." But he knows now beyond a doubt that "intellect has no right to devote itself to the 'attractive' at a time when it is so emphatically a matter of serving *mankind* as it is today. And," he concludes, "for me that 'today' was even then," [17] even in those early years when he was composing the linden tree scene, lending artistic form to his painful self-conquest in service to mankind.

Another central scene in the novel, expressive of Mann's basic reorientation, is Hans Castorp's conversation with Madame Chauchat, which takes place shortly after the reappearance of Castorp's paramour in the company of Mynheer Peeperkorn. In this scene we have a splendid example of the author's extraordinary ability to enhance the meticulously detailed portrayal of his characters into a significance that transcends the individual and imbues the specific with a paradigmatical importance. In the richly delineated personality of Clavdia Chauchat, Mann succeeds admirably to present, literally to embody, his conception of Russian national characteristics. The exchange between Clavdia and Castorp reveals impressively his dream of a creative interaction of the aristocratic Western spirit with Russia's democracy-of-the-heart to create Mann's fervently hoped for ideal of an aristo-democratic society of the future.

No doubt the poet used both Clavdia Chauchat and Hans Castorp as his spokesmen to deliver an urgent message, a warning to his fellow-Germans, his fellow-Westerners. And yet, in using his figures for this openly ideological purpose, the poet did not abuse their integrity as fictional personae. The message springs organically from the medium; Mann's thoughts are quite naturally those of the protagonists of his novel, who remain true to their basic character throughout the work.

Clavdia's Slavic personality and Castorp's German, Western make-up are effectively counterposed to one another as antithetical world views. Chauchat accuses her conversation partner of selfishness and of egocentricity, arguing that his is a way of life totally devoid of *passion*. She remarks with biting irony:

I am extraordinarily relieved to hear that you are not a passionate man. But how could you be passionate? You would have to become estranged from your kin and kind. To be passionate means living for the sake of life. But it is well known that you, all of you, live for the sake of experience. Passion is self-forgetfulness. But what you all want is self-enrichment. *C'est ça.* You don't realize what revolting egoism it is, and that one day this egoism will turn you into an enemy of the human race! [18]

In this significant passage, with its various strata of implication, Thomas Mann placed his finger squarely on the central weakness, not of the German character alone, but of the make-up of humanism in all Western countries. It is the inherent individualistic egocentricity and aristocratic exclusiveness of humanism which Mann exposed here, significantly, through the medium of the Slav's differently conditioned and oriented psyche. To be sure, Mann was not the first to discover this fateful shortcoming in humanism. Goethe in the wisdom of his old age became very conscious of it and sought to correct it in *Wilhelm Meisters Wanderjahre* as well as in the second part of *Faust*, where, all too abruptly, perhaps, Faust, that highest incarnation of man bent on self-perfection and self-enrichment, seeks his salvation in altruistic social activity. Yet it was Mann's contribution to have shown in the Slavic temperament a possible cure to the West's malady of solipsism and to have called for the fusion of the East's passionate antiegocentricity with the West's conscious glorification and cultivation of the great personality, its dignity and inviolability. Mann was to emphasize this thought by frequent repetition. Years later, in 1941, he still considered the reconciliation and fusion of these two world views a central concern of the day:

The reconciliation of two principles, *intra muros et extra,* is an urgent matter: The "sovereign" individual must make social concessions to the collective, Socialism and Democracy, "Russia" and "America" must be fused in union.[19]

In 1929 appeared Mann's novella *Mario und der Zauberer* (*Mario and the Magician*). Henry Hatfield in a perceptive interpretation[20] was one of the first to point out its political message as being basic to its structural unity. The political theme does, in fact, relate the extensive introductory part (which depicts the effect of nascent Fascism on the life of the tourists, among them Mann and his family at the Italian sea-side resort, Forte dei Marmi) to the central part of the narrative, the vivid description of an evening's macabre entertainment staged by the most powerful hypnotist the narrator had ever encountered.

Cipolla's powers over members of his audience whom he chooses as victims for his mesmeric feats are indeed prodigious. With a steady stream of suggestive comments, with commands and exhortations, with invective and cajolery, with his hypnotic gaze and gestures and with the crack of a claw-handled whip, he subdues the people's will, deprives them completely of self-determination, and degrades them to puppets and dupes of his diabolically dominating presence.

Cipolla's demonic tyranny over his victims seems complete in the grotesque moment when Mario, helpless under the magician's evil spell, kisses the disgusting flesh of the seducer's pallid cheek in the delusion of kissing the ruby lips of his beloved, Silvestra. It is indeed a moment of abject surrender, but that moment is brief. In a most unexpected denoue-

ment, our simple little waiter, this common man and salt of
the earth, waking from his trance, thoroughly avenges his humiliation by shooting his tormentor dead, casting him down
"in a chaotic heap of rags and bones." The novella ends with
grotesque horror.

Yet for Thomas Mann it was "a liberating ending." In his
closing words the narrator tells us that he "could not and still
cannot to this day feel otherwise about it." [21] This concluding
comment points to the tale's moral and political message,
which remains as timely today as it was at the work's first
appearance. What is this message? Now, in retrospect, it is
not difficult to recognize in the magician Cipolla the Fascist
Duce and in the simple waiter Mario the representative of
the people under the spell of the megalomaniac demagogue.
But the poet was able to perceive the ominous symbolical
meaning of the macabre happening he witnessed before Mus-
solini had achieved complete domination over his people, and
long before he was shot by the partisans, the Marios of
Mann's prophetic story.

In the novella, the author delved to the ultimate cause of
the hypnotist's terrible power over his victims. He traced it to
a paralysis of their will not only because of the hypnotic spell
cast by the evil magician, but also because of the absence of a
positive goal or ideal toward which the victims could have
directed their will, thus activating it. As the narrator of the
tale explains:

It is impossible for man to live in a spiritual attitude of nonvoli-
tion. Not to will a specific act cannot in the long run amount to a
meaningful content for one's life; merely not to want a thing and
the complete surrender of one's will . . . these are attitudes
probably too closely related as not to result in the subversion of
the idea of freedom.[22]

Mario finds the strength of will to challenge the demagogue's
tyrannical domination. He breaks the spell and avenges his
humiliation. His act of brutal murder is a horrible ending to
the tale; yet when perceived as the act of a strong will which

reasserts its freedom and rehabilitates personal dignity, then it can be experienced as a liberating ending to the oppressive nightmare of tyranny.

A short year after the appearance of the novella, Mann was again engaged in a direct confrontation with the rising Nazi power. In the *Reichstag* elections of September 1930, the party of Hitler had received alarming support. Mann's reaction was his now famous "Deutsche Ansprache, ein Appell an die Vernunft" ("An Appeal to Reason") delivered in Berlin's Beethoven hall on October 17 of that year. In that speech Mann traced Hitler's successes to the ill-conceived Treaty of Versailles and to constitutional and economic difficulties encountered by the young and inexperienced Weimar Republic. He begged his audience not to discard thoughtlessly the state-form of parliamentary democracy, arguing that this form of government, though new to Germany, was yet far more acceptable to the German temperament and spiritual orientation than its alternatives, "the dictatorship of a class [Communism] or the dictatorship of a Caesar-like adventurer [Hitler] brought to power by democratic processes which the dictator despises and would promptly discard." [23] But the main reason for Hitler's success and the appeal he held for large segments of the German nation, Thomas Mann discovered in the cultural realm. He linked it to the spiritual reorientation of a whole generation "which turned away from such bourgeois ideals as freedom, justice, education, and a belief in progress" and "acclaimed as the only vital, life-instilling powers, the irrational, the dynamic drives." This young generation, Mann warned his listeners, "celebrates as the only existential truths the dark depths of the soul, the maternal-chthonic [das Mütterlich-Chthonische], and the sacred procreative nether world [die heilig-gebärerische Unterwelt]." [24] Of this nature-religion with its orgiastic excesses much had entered into the neo-nationalism of those days, creating a movement very different in its spiritual and ideological orientation from the Nationalism of the nineteenth century. That Nationalism had contained balancing cosmopolitan and humanistic elements. Hitler's brand of nationalism frowned on these and gloried in "nature-cult, in a radical anti-humanism, in dynamistic auto-intoxication, and in a total lack of rational self-control." [25] The central theme of Mann's "Appeal to Reason" was his appeal to the German people not to fall prey to the blandishments of the "new barbarians" and their "New Order," that witches' brew of "political mysticism."

This "Call" was Thomas Mann's declaration of total war against the forces of darkness. He carried on this war under heavy personal sacrifices—in his exile in Switzerland and the United States with a hatred of which, as he admits, he would not have thought himself capable, "a hatred that burst out of us unexpected, burning, unconditional, implacable." [26] Mann would concede to Hitler only one virtue, that of having "brought about a great simplification in my feelings, of having roused in me an unequivocal 'no,' a clear and deadly hatred against the neo-barbarians." [27]

Agnes Meyer had expressed concern over Mann's political interests and activities, in which she thought she recognized a lamentable diversion of Mann's energies from his main task, from his creative efforts. Thomas Mann strongly disagreed:

Je fais la guerre—and you wish to see me *au dessus de la mêlée*. . . . But this *mêlée* is mankind's battle of decision and, truly, everything is being decided in it, *including* the fate of my life's work. . . . Have I borne up poorly in these years, have I let hatred degrade and paralyze me? I have written "Joseph in Egypt" and "The Beloved Returns" and "The Transposed Heads" in evidence of my superiority over the barbarians. I am quite proud of the fact that instead of joining the pathological and the downhearted I was able to accomplish all this, and I believe that my friends ought to recognize a sign of strength and not of weakness in my ability to carry on the good fight while continuing my work as a creative writer.[28]

During those hectic, heartrending years of the Nazi's rise to power, during his American exile and World War II, Thomas Mann found the strength to fashion, line upon patient line, his *Joseph* tetralogy with its promise of a humane future in its symbolic hero Joseph the Provider. In the years of the Nazis' death throes, their final collapse and the subsequent turmoil in Germany, he created in his *Doctor Faustus* a monumental record of these truly apocalyptic events, giving his profound interpretation of the underlying causes of Nazidom's rise and fall.

These works, together with his *Goethe* novel, *The Beloved Returns* and the short story *Das Gesetz* (*The Tables of the Law*) were certainly no escape or refuge for the poet from the political events of the day. *The Tables* are once again, this time in fictional form, an appeal to reason to hold high the Ten Commandments against the neo-barbarians who would defile and despoil them.

The *Goethe* narrative, in many a passage, gives such an obviously autobiographical expression to Mann's insight into and his suffering because of the destructive elements in the German character that criticism leveled against the author for having anachronistically distorted the historical image of Goethe was not without foundation. The poet defended himself by frankly admitting that the political message was as important to him as the portrayal of the exemplary figure of Goethe which was to remind the German people of the nation's former greatness that had been defiled and perverted by the Nazi barbarians. Mann derived great satisfaction from the knowledge that excerpts from the novel were clandestinely circulating among grateful readers in Hitler's beleaguered Reich.*

One brief excerpt from Mann's message as delivered by his fictional hero must suffice here. The author has Goethe characterize his fellow Germans in these bitter words of censure and disavowal:

But that they hate clarity—that is not right of them. That they do not know the inspiration of truth is to be lamented; that they cherish every sort of humbug and intoxication and berserk-like excess is revolting. It is miserable to see them follow in blind

* Under the camouflaging title, "Aus Goethes Gesprächen mit Riemer" ("From Goethe's Conversations with Riemer").

faith every ecstatic scoundrel who appeals to their lowest instincts, confirms them in their vices, and teaches them to miscon-
ceive nationality as isolation and brutality. . . . I don't even
care to appease them. So they don't like me—all right! I am not
exactly fond of them either, and so I am quits with them. . . .
They think they are Germany. As a matter of fact, it is I who
represent that nation, and if the ship of the nation goes down
with all hands, Germany will live on in me . . . because Germany represents freedom, culture, universality, and love! That
they have no idea of this fact does not change the truth.[29]

We have no evidence that the historical Goethe ever spoke
or wrote these words, though in a milder form they are not
incompatible with Goethe's critical attitude toward certain
manifestations of chauvinism and martial fervor among the
freedom fighters in Germany's War of Liberation in 1813.
Yet, obviously these words are meant to be Mann's curse of
the ecstatic scoundrel Hitler; they are Mann's judgment of
his deluded compatriots; they are a ringing declaration of his
indomitable faith in an ideal Germany of cosmopolitanism,
freedom, tolerance, and love. Not that Mann accepted the
theory of a good versus a bad Germany. In his speech
"Deutschland und die Deutschen" ("Germany and the Germans") he rejected that theory outright. But he lived in the
faith that the bad Germany contained the good, and thus
carried within its soul its own redemption.

Mann's thoughts and reactions regarding the sociopolitical developments in Germany are also subtly woven into the
higher gaiety of the fictional fabric of the *Joseph* tetralogy.
The obscurantism and chauvinism of the Nazi regime find
many an echo in the attitude and pronouncements of the
reactionary Beknechon, the High Priest of the archaic god
Amun; the chauvinism and pride of the master race, the *Her-
renvolk*, in its exaggerated manliness is archly parodied in the
grotesquely comical figure of the dwarf Dûdû—that proto-
Egyptian swollen with ethnic pride and strutting his sexual
potency. Mut-em-enet's harangue of her servants and slaves,
seeking to rouse their hatred toward the foreigner Joseph, is a
wonderfully effective takeoff on Nazi demagoguery with its

total perversion of truth, its *grosse Lüge*, its hypocritical flat-
tery of the underlings, and its shrewd appeal to the ethnic
pride of the "Egyptian brethren, the children of Kheme
(Cham), the sons of the stream and the black earth!" [30]
One actually seems to hear the blood and soil rantings of
Göbbels and his *Führer*.

On the other hand, the optimism that pervades this work
reflects Mann's hopes sparked by Roosevelt's experiment of
the New Deal. Joseph's appealing figure bears recognizable
traits of the President whose charm, wit, and experimental
boldness the author greatly admired. At a meeting with Roosevelt in the White House, Mann was impressed with "the
Hermes-like nature of the man, blessed with the gift of skill-
ful and gaily artful mediation between spirit and life, idea
and reality, the desirable and the necessary, between conscience and deed, morality and power." [31] This characterization of the President surely applies with equal if not with
even greater felicity to the gaily artful mediator between
spirit and nature, between idea and reality, to Joseph, the
twice blessed Provider.

Mann's central aim in the *Joseph* novels—to humanize
myth—was an avowedly political action. In his speech on the
tetralogy which he delivered in the Coolidge Auditorium of
the Library of Congress, he dwelt with special emphasis on
this political aspect of the work:

In the last decades myth has been so often misused as an instrument of obscurantist counter revolution that a mythical novel
like *Joseph*, when it first appeared, necessarily stirred up the suspicion that its author was swimming in this muddy stream. The
public has had to give up this suspicion, for on closer examination it perceived a reversal of the function of myth of which one
would not have thought myth capable. Readers observed an event
comparable to capturing a cannon in battle, turning it around,
and aiming it at the enemy.[32]

Mann felt engaged in a life and death struggle. Myth had
to be wrung from the hands of the Fascist demagogues and
propagandists who, under the leadership of the evil genius,

Alfred Rosenberg, the perpetrator of *The Myth of the Twentieth Century*, wielded that dangerous weapon with disastrous effect. To Karl Kerényi, Mann wrote in those critical days: "One must take myth away from the intellectual fascists and tranpose it into the humane." [33] This transposition Mann did accomplish in his tetralogy. He did wrest "myth from the hands of the fascists, humanized it to the last linguistic detail," [34] and enlisted it in the cause of mankind's progress.

In the vast scope of his work, Mann represents human history not as a fatalistically predetermined closed circle in the nihilistic spirit of Oswald Spengler,[35] but as an ever rising spiral of limitless possibilities, as a meaningful development raising mankind from the dark depths of its totemistic beginnings to a state of clear self-awareness as autonomous personalities, from childish self-centeredness in narcissistic solipsism to social consciousness and commitment. Joseph's

artist-ego . . . finds its way, as it matures, into the social sphere; he becomes the benefactor and provider of foreign peoples as well as his own. Joseph's ego frees itself from its insolent self-centeredness and reenters the collective; thus, in this fairy tale, are resolved the antitheses of the artist and the bourgeois, of isolation and communality, of the individual and of society. It is our hope and heartfelt wish that, just as in our fairy tale, these antitheses would be resolved in the democracy of the future, in the cooperation of free and diverse nations under the scepter of equality and justice.[36]

Mann called his *Joseph* tetralogy a "book of the beginning," the beginning of a freer and a nobler humanity. His *Doctor Faustus* he called "the book of the end," of the tragic end of a nation and an artist. Adrian Leverkühn, that tragic hero of our times, has lost all contact with the people; his art, he feels, hovers suspended in a vacuum without proper foundation in tradition or a claim to the future. Isolated as a person and as an artist, alienated from his very self and from his fellow men, Adrian yearns for a new sense of communality. He would gladly sacrifice his deeply problematical, torturing freedom for the shelter of rooted, integrated, and cohesive culture, being quite ready to argue that submission to rule need not result in loss of freedom. As an artist, he may safely believe in the Goethian maxim that law and order are the highest forms of freedom. However, Adrian falls into fatal error when he refuses to heed his friend's, Zeitblom's, insistent warnings that law and order—ideals in the realm of art—when raised to overriding principles in the sociopolitical life of a nation, turn into dire threats to individualism and freedom and tend to deteriorate into the hideous coercion of totalitarianism.

Here is the vantage point from which to view the interrelation of Adrian's and Germany's fates. Though never identical, each is intensified through subtle reference to the other. Adrian's disillusionment with the ideals of individualism and freedom was shared by many Germans, especially by German intellectuals and artists. Having experienced his autonomy and freedom as unbearable isolation and alienation, many a German, like Adrian, had come to yearn for natural ties to his fellow man and to nature, for *naturale Lebensbezüge* and for religious and ethnic affiliations, for *theonome oder völkische Bindungen*—dangerous slogans, which Mann has the young students of theology at the University of Halle espouse with fervent conviction even before World War I.[37] Mann wants us to recognize that in the life of the German nation, more radically than in the life of Adrian, there occurred that fateful dialectic reversal [dialektischer Umschwung] from alienated individualism to mystical collectivism, from dangerously devitalized rationality to an even more dangerous emotionalism, from skepticism and cynicism to blind faith and unquestioning obedience, from sublimated intellectualism and aestheticism to primitivism and a neo-barbarism of calculated brutality and cerebrated bestiality. The central metaphor for this dialectical reversal in the structure of Mann's novel is Adrian's (and Germany's) Faustian pact with the devil.

Thomas Mann has given a superbly vivid characterization of the forces that set the stage for the German tragedy. We

meet in the pages of *Doctor Faustus* His Excellency Baron
von Riedesel, influential patron of the arts, who in his naïveté
and ignorance supports everything "traditional," "ancient,"
and "historical," vaguely sensing therein a bulwark against
the feared and hated liberal and radical ideas and ideals in art
and politics. The really dangerous saboteurs of progress, de-
cency, and common sense, however, Mann finds among the
"brilliant" minds. They are the leaders in this strangest of
revolutions, this revolution in the form of crass reaction and
rebarbarization. They are excellently chosen types, attesting
to the author's perceptive observation of, and prodigious experience in, the cultural life of his times. There is the con-
sumptive intellectual, Dr. Helmut Institoris, aesthetician and
historian, who derives vicarious satisfaction from his blind
worship of the ruthless Renaissance supermen of Nietzschean
extraction. There is the brilliant Dr. Chaim Breisacher, disciple of Sorel and Spengler, sophistic critic of culture as a
symptom of decadence, a most eloquent champion of man's
rebarbarization. Jacob Taubes, in an informative essay, "From
Cult to Culture," [38] has shown that the figure of Breisacher is
based on Oskar Goldberg, a violently antirational interpreter
of myths, whose theories both fascinated and repelled
Thomas Mann. There were other brilliant minds that helped
to pervert Germany's rational stance and to lure the nation
into emotional excesses: Professor Georg Vogler, for instance,
champion of an ethnic interpretation of culture and author
of a history of literature written from the point of view of
tribal membership [Stammeszugehörigkeit], is unmistakably
Mann's fictional portrayal of the literary historian Joseph
Nadler; then there is an equally unmistakable Georgianer,
Daniel zur Höhe (Ludwig Derleth),[39] the author of a high-
sounding Proclamation that calls for poverty, chastity, and
unquestioned obedience to "Christus Imperator Maximus,"
and concludes with the grandiloquently macabre boast: "Sol-
diers, I place the world into your hands for pillage and plun-
der." [40] Thomas Mann makes amply clear how this brilliant
avant-garde, mostly quite unaware of their messages' dread
effect, eagerly prepared their own and Germany's dooms,

rousing the racial, the martial, the irrational and mystic, the truly demonic passions latent in the German nation—and not in it alone.

These, then, were the intellectual—or rather, antiintellectual—attitudes Mann recognized as the forces laboring to destroy man's hard-won heritage of spiritual enlightenment and cultural refinement, of his freedom and dignity in mutual tolerance and respect. Wherein lay Mann's hope for a tolerable future? What was his positive message to his fellow-men? He was the advocate of a world economy in which the importance of political boundaries would gradually diminish and a certain denationalization of the states would take place. He hoped that humanity would at long last awaken to the realization of its unity, if only for practical reasons, and would finally organize a world state. Mann came to see, more clearly than ever, the need for a productive interaction between the aristocratic principle of the cult of personality and the modern gospel of democratic sociality which would ultimately result in the ideal state, for which he coined the term "Aristo-Democracy." Mann knew that in the relationship of freedom and equality the center of gravity had shifted perceptibly toward the side of equality and economic justice, away from the individual and toward the social.[41] "If democracy is to hold its own," he admonished his listeners in a wartime lecture in 1942, "it must be done through a socially established freedom that rescues individual values by friendly and willing concession to equality." This would require the humane adjustment between freedom and equality, the reconciliation of individual values and the demands of society—an adjustment that would "never completely and finally be attained but would always remain a problem humanity would have to solve again and again." [42] This passage stands here not only as a summary of Mann's political faith but also as an expression of Mann's creative dialectic, which sees, in the spirit of a modern-day Lessing, the eternal search and striving for perfection, not its possession, as the divine gift to mankind, as its truly creative stance.

Thomas Mann was firmly convinced of the viability of a

productive interaction between seemingly irreconcilable extremes in the hard-bitten sociopolitical reality of his times, the
rapprochement between East and West. It was this conviction that gave him the strength to carry forward with startling
determination and tenacity his efforts of breaching the wall,
of building the bridges of understanding between Russia and
Germany, Russia and the United States, efforts that were to
expose him to violent attacks from ideological zealots. Especially after his trip to Weimar in the Goethe bicentennial
year 1949, Mann found himself the target of repeated accusations of betrayal of the democratic West, of hidden or even
open sympathies with communism. In his defense Mann
stressed his profound faith in the importance of his mission
as an intermediary between the hostile camps, a mission that
he held to be the overriding obligation of all men of goodwill
and of a truly enlightened spirit. In a letter to Paul Olberg,
Mann explains the purpose of his trip to Weimar: "I traveled
to Weimar because I lament the deep rift . . . that runs
through Germany, and because I am convinced that one
should not deepen this rift but should, whenever possible,
bridge it, even if only on festive occasions." [43] And to a young
Japanese who inquired about Mann's political orientation, he
sent a most revealing reply:

No, I am not a communist; I am as far from being one as you
are. Totalitarianism and all its practices are alien to me and ter-
rify me to the very core of my being, and with horror do I look
forward to a world in which human beings will be forced to lead
an existence of extreme intellectual impoverishment, bent under
the yoke of rigid dogmas, estranged from the thought of freedom.
Still, I cannot but grant communism a certain moral justification
in its revolt against a social and economic order which, because of
excessive symptoms of corruption and inner decay, is progres-
sively forfeiting its right to be called an "order" and does indeed
appear to this observer condemned in the judgment of history.[44]

Mann knew that with such convictions and attitudes he
was standing between the camps and playing the difficult role

of an intermediary. Yet this awareness could not discourage him in the free exercise of his critical judgment with the intent of alleviating tensions and benefiting both sides. He liked to quote Erasmus, that great Humanist in whom he recognized a kindred spirit bent on mediation between extremes. "It is, as I see it, my fate to be stoned by both parties, while I am intent on aiding both." These words of Erasmus Thomas Mann would have us apply to himself.

Looking back upon a life heavy with responsible toil and rich in accomplishments, Mann recognized it for what it had been—an artist's life devoted *not* to nonsense and trivia, but, on the contrary, to the steadfast defense and cultivation of the great humanistic heritage, all the more precious to Mann for being desperately endangered both from within and without. In a speech entitled "Meine Zeit" ("My Time") delivered in 1950, he emphasized, in retrospect, this lifelong devotion and dedication and pointed to their central cause and motivation: "It was the antihumanism of the times that made it clear to me that I had never done anything other—or that I had, at any rate, never intended to do anything else— but to defend humanism. And I shall never do anything other than that!" [45]

Of all the many honors that were showered upon the poet, including the Nobel Prize in 1929, there was none that touched him more deeply and that made him more proud and happy than the award of the Officers' Cross of the French Legion of Honor, and this primarily, as Mann points out, because of the accompanying citation, which read:

*Cette distinction est un hommage rendu par la France à l'exceptionnelle valeur et à la signification mondiale de votre oeuvre littéraire ainsi qu'à la lutte que vous n'avez cessé de mener dans l'intérêt de la liberté et de la dignité humaine.**

This theme echoes and reechoes significantly in the

---

* "France bestows on you this distinction in recognition of the exceptional valor and the worldwide significance of your literary work as well as for the good fight which you have never ceased to wage in the interest of human liberty and dignity." (Letter to Agnes Meyer. Feb. 8, 1953. Br. III, 289.)

chorus of praise from North and South, East and West. Bestowing upon him the honorary citizenship of Weimar, the East German government acclaimed Thomas Mann as the worthiest representative of humanism in our time, while Italy's Accademia Nazionale dei Lincei extolled him as "that paragon of a living humanism which transcends the spiritual schism of our times, offering guidance to all creative men." [46]

While championing the cause of humanism, Mann became deeply conscious of its inherent weakness, which he recognized as springing, paradoxically, from its very strength. He recognized this weakness to be intimately connected with humanism's disdain of fanaticism, with its spirit of tolerance and with its love of doubt. Mann knew from bitter experience that it could, under certain conditions, spell humanism's doom. To avert this tragic development, Mann called for a "new humanism," a "militant humanism" which would have shed its sentimentalism, its easy optimism, its naïveté and would no longer shrink from facing up to the terrors lurking in the demonic depths of human nature, but would confront them unflinchingly, unmask them for what they are, and thus keep them in check. He warned that our "sense of freedom would have to grow strong with a faith in its right to self-defense," that it would have to grow into a "freedom with authority, a manly freedom that would not let itself be seduced by intellect into doubt of its right to exist here on earth, a freedom that would know how to defend itself against a treachery that would ever and again misuse freedom in order to destroy it." [47]

Thomas Mann had no illusions about his time. He knew it to be a time when men of good will had to stand united against the forces of evil, a time of decision when "one had to deliver proof of one's character and convictions, a time," as he put it, "when one has to declare oneself in unmistakable terms: *wo man mit klaren Worten Farbe bekennen muss*." [48] Thomas Mann found that strength of character; he had those firm convictions. As the champion of humanism he took his unequivocal stand on the side of freedom and human dignity, on the side of spirit against brute force. He believed in peace as in the highest law and the foremost necessity. He warned that mankind would be ill-served in the end by hatred and war between nations and between ideologies. He urged that "time be given a chance to work its magic of conciliation, of the transformation of antagonisms into a higher harmony," and called on every one of us "to fill our time, this precious gift, with work in self-improvement." [49]

APPENDICES

APPENDIX 1:
TWO UNPUBLISHED LETTERS OF
THOMAS MANN TO THE AUTHOR
IN THE ORIGINAL WITH
ENGLISH PARAPHRASES

Lake Mohonk Mountain House
Mohonk Lake. New York

19. VI. '45

Sehr geehrter Herr Professor,

ich werde mit der Abtragung der Dankespflichten, mit denen eine gutmütige Welt mich in diesen Tagen belastet hat, *nie* zu Rande kommen, aber Ihnen möchte ich gleich zu Anfang für das wertvolle, mich wahrhaft interessierende literarische Geschenk danken, mit dem Sie mich erfreuten. Mein Verhältnis zur russischen Welt, in seiner Intensität und Ambivalenz einmal so übersichtlich und umsichtig dargestellt zu sehen, war mir ein wirkliches Vergnügen, und ganz objektiv glaube ich Sie zu der kritisch-psychologisch verdienstlichen Arbeit beglückwünschen zu dürfen.[1] Was im "Zauberberg" Russisches vorkommt, ist ja etwas vexatorisch gefärbt durch den immer halb komischen Mittelmeer-Dünkel des Herrn Settembrini; aber meine tiefe Bewunderung für das russische Schrifttum ist hoffentlich jederzeit eindeutig geblieben, und was das Politische betrifft, so erinnere ich mich immer wieder an das Wort, das im Jahre 1938, gleich nach meiner Ankunft in Princeton, der kluge alte Abraham Flexner zu mir sprach: "Die Zukunft und Hoffnung der Welt beruht auf zwei Ländern: Amerika und Russland." Ich finde, dies Wort wird immer wahrer, und wenn Sorge einen beschleicht, dass

eines der beiden Länder may not live up zu dieser Prophezeiung
—so ist es—nicht Russland, dem sie gilt.

Ihr ergebener

Thomas Mann.

My dear Professor,

I shall never be able to settle all debts of gratitude with which
a kindly world has burdened me in these days, but I do wish to
thank you, without delay, for the valuable literary gift with
which you delighted me, and which truly was of great interest to
me. It was a real pleasure to see my relationship to the Russian
world, in all its intensity and ambivalence, for once presented so
lucidly and with such insight. I feel objectively justified in con-
gratulating you on this meritorious work of psychological interpretation. What there is of the Russian theme in *The Magic
Mountain* is, to be sure, somewhat illusively colored by the consistently semihumorous Mediterranean arrogance of Mr. Settembrini; but I do hope that my profound admiration for Russian
literature has always remained unambiguous. And as for politics,
I shall always remember the words of wise old Abraham Flexner
when he spoke to me in 1938, right after my arrival in Princeton:
"The future and the hope of the world rest with two nations:
America and Russia." I find these words become ever more true
as time goes on, and when doubts assail me—doubts that one of
these two nations may not live up to this prophecy—then it is
not Russia that causes such doubts.

Your devoted

Thomas Mann

Thomas Mann
150 San Remo Drive
Pacific Palisades,
California

20. XI. '48

Sehr verehrter Herr von Gronicka,

das ist freilich etwas anderes[2] als das träge, fühllose, manchmal auch einfach boshafte Zeug, das ich hierzulande (mit einigen
wohltuenden Ausnahmen) über den 'Faustus" zu lesen bekom-
men habe. Ich danke Ihnen recht herzlich für Ihre intensive
Beschäftigung mit einem Werk, das mir teuer ist, weil es mich
viel gekostet hat. Es ist ihm eine Erregung eingeboren, die
mir Stumpfheit im Verhalten dazu fast unnatürlich erscheinen
lässt. . . .

Zeitbloms Aeusserung "Dies ist kein Roman" sollte nicht
ganz ernst genommen werden. Es ist ja doch einer—d.h. es ist
keiner, weil es eine Biographie ist, mit allen Merkmalen einer
solchen; aber da diese Biographie Fiktion ist, was ist sie denn
dann? Von dem "plot," das sogar einen Eifersuchtsmord in der
Trambahn mit sich bringt, und davon, dass doch beständig Son-
derbares und Romanhaftes los ist in dem Buch, rede ich nicht.
Auch widerspreche ich garnicht [!], wenn man sagt: "Es ist kein
Roman mehr." Das ist wohl die Situation des Romans über-
haupt heute. Schon von Joyce schrieb Einer:[3] "He has enor-
mously increased the difficulty of writing a novel." Der Faustus
ist ein End-Buch in jeder Beziehung, ein Buch des Endes und,
mag sein, ein endendes Buch.

Sie haben recht, zu sagen, dass Zeitblom aus seiner ursprüng-
lichen Rolle fällt, oder, wenn nicht fällt, ihr doch zuweilen ein
bisschen entgleitet. Und doch ist eigentlich nicht zu sagen, wo er
seine Linie verlässt, und wenn er auf ihr zu weit gelangt—könnte
man nicht zur Rechtfertigung an eine Art von fieberhafter "Steig-
erung" denken, die ihn im Lauf seines Buches über sich selbst in
Furcht und Zittern hinausführt?

Sehr schön und klug ist, unter anderem, Ihre Bemerkung,
dass die persönliche und die nationale Sphäre niemals identisch
sind, sich aber durchdringen und wechselseitig intensivieren. Die
"deutsche" Allegorie wird oft überbetont. Adrian ist weit mehr

"ein Held unserer Zeit," [4] ein Mensch, der das Leid der Epoche trägt, als der Repräsentant Deutschlands.

Wie fein sind Ihre Worte über die erhöhte Problematik und Leidensfähigkeit seit den Tagen des alten Faust, über Adrans [!] archaische Modernität! Auch ist es wahr, dass ich die Beschreibungen seiner Werke nicht gemacht habe, um mit Virtuosität und Kenntnissen zu glänzen. Sondern ich war mir von vornherein klar darüber, dass man heute keinen "Künstler-Roman" mehr schreiben kann, in dem das Genie des Helden nur behauptet wird. Ich hatte es zu beweisen, zu realisieren, hatte Exaktheit von mir zu verlangen—um jeden Preis, auch um den, mir dabei von Fachleuten[5] helfen zu lassen, damit alles unangreifbar sei. Uebrigens [!] habe ich eine Entstehungsgeschichte des Buches geschrieben, ein die Jahre 1943 bis '47 umfassendes Stück Autobiographie. Ich weiss noch nicht, ob, wann und wie ich diese Confessionen herausgebe.[6]

Nochmals, Sie haben mir eine wirkliche Freude gemacht mit Ihrer Interpretation. Manchmal wünsche ich mir, es noch zu erleben, dass man die besten Aeusserungen über den Roman (vielleicht zusammen mit den absprechendsten) in einem Bande vereinigt. Die Ihre dürfte darin nicht fehlen.

Ihr sehr ergebener
Thomas Mann.

Dear Mr. von Gronicka,

This is, indeed, something very different from the idle, insensitive, at times even outright malicious stuff I had to read about the *Faustus* novel in this country (with some comforting exceptions). I thank you most cordially for your intensive preoccupation with a work that is very dear to me because it cost me so much. Inherent in it is an excitement that makes indifference toward it seem to me downright unnatural. . . .

Zeitblom's words, "This is not a novel," should not be taken too seriously. It most certainly is a novel—that is, it is not one because it is a biography, with all the earmarks of such a work; but since this biography is fiction, what, then, is it [if not a novel]? I am not speaking of the plot, which even offers a murder in a streetcar committed from jealousy, nor am I speaking of the fact that, after all, much that is unusual and novelistic constantly occurs in this book. Nor would I disagree at all with the statement, "This is no longer a novel." That, apparently, is the situation in which the novel as a genre finds itself today. Of Joyce a critic has already written, "He enormou˰ly increased the difficulty of writing a novel." The *Faustus*-novel is an end-book in every respect, a book of the end, and, it may well be, a final book.

You are right in saying that Zeitblom steps out of his original role, or, if he does not exactly step out of it, that he eludes it slightly at times. And yet, one cannot really say where he departs from his line; and when he does go too far—can one not think in his justification of a sort of feverish "enhancement" that, in the course of the book, carries him beyond himself in terror and trembling?

Your observation, among others, that the personal and the national spheres are never identical, even though they constantly interpenetrate and intensify one another, is very fine and clever. The "German" allegory has often been stressed excessively. Adrian is far more "a hero of our time," a human being bearing the sorrows of the time than a representative of Germany.

How fitting are your words about the increased complexity of contemporary problems and the increased capacity for suffering since the days of the old Faustus, and about Adrian's archaic modernity. It is also true that I did not give descriptions of his works in order to shine with virtuosity and knowledge. Rather it was clear to me from the very beginning that one can no longer write an "artist-novel" in which the genius of the hero is merely asserted. I had to prove it, had to make it real; I had to demand exactness from myself—at any cost, even at the price of obtaining help from specialists, so that every detail would be unassailable. By the way, I have written a history of the book's development, an autobiography covering the years 1943 to 1947. But I do not know yet if, when, and how I shall publish these confessions.

Let me tell you once more that you have given me great pleasure with your interpretation. Sometimes I wish I could live to see the best comments on my book (perhaps together with the most critical) collected in one volume. Your interpretation should not be missing in such a volume.

Very sincerely yours
Thomas Mann

APPENDIX 2:
CHRONOLOGICAL LIST OF
IMPORTANT EVENTS

June 6, 1875   Paul Thomas Mann born in Lübeck.

1882–1889   Studies at Progymnasium of Dr. Bussenius, private school.

1889   Enters Katharineum Gymnasium in Lübeck.

1891   Death of his father, Senator Thomas Johann Heinrich Mann, at 51 (October 13).

1894   Leaves school and joins his mother in Munich. Works as volunteer at Süddeutsche Feuerversicherungsgesellschaft. During office hours secretly writes his first novella *Gefallen* (*The Fallen One*). Gives up his job. As unmatriculated student attends lectures at the Technische Hochschule, planning to become a journalist.

1895   First trip to Italy with brother Heinrich Mann: Palestrina and Rome.

1896   Second Italian trip: Venice, Ancona, Rome, Naples. First volume of novellas containing *Der kleine Herr Friedemann* (*The Little Herr Friedemann*) in preparation. Works on novellas *Der Tod* (*Death*), *Bajazzo* (*The Dilettante*), *Tobias Mindernickel*, *Luischen* (*Little Lizzie*).

1897   Begins to write *Buddenbrooks* in Rome, Via Torre Argentina.

1898   Returns to Munich.

1898–1900   Reader for the journal *Simplicissimus*.

1899   Vacation trip to Denmark. Visits Lübeck, is almost arrested there as a confidence man. Stays nine days at Aalsgard am Sund where he plans the novella *Tonio Kröger*. First acquaintance with the philosophy of Arthur Schopenhauer.

1900   *Buddenbrooks* completed. First plans for

verse drama *Fiorenza*. Works on novella *Tristan*.

1901   *Buddenbrooks* appears.

1903   Publication of volume of novellas *Tristan* containing *Tonio Kröger*. Mann, introduced to Munich's society, becomes a frequent visitor at the home of Alfred Pringsheim, mathematics professor at the University of Munich. Courts daughter Katja Pringsheim (born July 24, 1883 in Munich.) Meets Gerhart Hauptmann at the home of Samuel Fischer, Mann's publisher and lifelong friend. Writes novella *Das Wunderkind* (*The Prodigy*), continues work on *Fiorenza*, and plans novel *Königliche Hoheit* (*Royal Highness*).

1904   Engaged to Katja Pringsheim.

1905   Marries Katja. Birth of Erika Julia Hedwig Mann (November 9).

1906   Birth of Klaus Heinrich Mann (November 18).

1908   Trip to Vienna. Acquaintance with Arthur Schnitzler and Hugo von Hofmannsthal.

1909   *Royal Highness* completed. Sets up basic plan for *Bekenntnisse des Hochstaplers Felix Krull* (*Confessions of Felix Krull, Confidence Man*).

1910   Birth of Monika Mann (June 7). Suicide of his youngest sister, actress Carla Mann (July 30). Meets Max Reinhardt and Gustav Mahler after premiere of the composer's Eighth Symphony.

1911   Vacations on the Lido near Venice. Situations and impressions there are to result in *Tod in Venedig* (*Death in Venice*). Begins work on *Death in Venice* at Bad Tölz, Bavaria.

1912   Joins Katja Mann in Davos sanatorium of Dr. Jessen for three weeks. Collects impressions for novella [!] *The Magic Mountain*, which he plans as interpolation in his work on *Confessions of Felix Krull. Death in Venice* completed.

1913   Lecture tour to Budapest. Meets Ernst Bertram. Beginning of friendship that is to find its end with the rise of Nazism championed by Bertram. Begins work on *Der Zauberberg* (*The Magic Mountain*).

1914   Outbreak of World War I.

1915   Interrupts work on *The Magic Mountain.* Begins writing *Betrachtungen eines Unpolitischen* (*Contemplations of a Nonpolitical Man*).

1916   Reads his brother Heinrich's essay on Émile Zola, is deeply hurt by the hidden attack. His hostility finds expression in the chapters "Zivilisationsliterat" and "Gegen Recht und Wahrheit" of *Betrachtungen.*

1917   Beginning of lifelong friendship with conductor Bruno Walter.

1918   Finishes *Betrachtungen.* Birth of Elisabeth Veronika Mann (April 24).

1919   Revolution in Munich. Murder of Ministerpräsident Kurt Eisner. Mann's villa is spared ransacking through the personal intervention of Ernst Toller. Birth of Michael Thomas Mann (April 21). Resumes work on *The Magic Mountain.* Receives honorary doctorate from Rheinische Friedrich Wilhelm Universität at Bonn on the occasion of the centennial celebration of the university.

1921   Begins work on essay, first planned as a lecture, "Goethe and Tolstoy."

1922   Lectures about "Goethe and Tolstoy" in Prague, Brno, Vienna, Budapest. Meets the literary historian Georg Lukács. Uses some traits of Lukács for portrait of Naphta in *The Magic Mountain.* Reconciles himself with brother Heinrich at his sickbed. Begins work on speech "Von deutscher Republik" ("The German Republic"). Plans it as manifesto addressed to the conscience of the young generation. Delivers speech in the Beethoven hall in Berlin on October 15.

1923 Death of his mother Julia, neé da Silva-Bruhns, at 73 (March 11). Trip to Spain, lectures on "Goethe and Tolstoy" at the University of Madrid, is received by Infanta Isabella. Vacations in Bolzano, meets Gerhart Hauptmann, who furnishes Mann certain traits for Mynheer Peeperkorn of *The Magic Mountain*. This "theft" for a time strained the relations between the two authors. Visits painter Hermann Ebers, whose illustrations for a Joseph story incite Mann to write on the *Joseph* theme. Plans a novella as first part of triptych of historical narratives.

1924 Trip to Holland and England. Guest of honor at PEN-Club; is welcomed with a speech by its president, John Galsworthy, and entertained at Galsworthy's home in Hendon. Publication of *The Magic Mountain*. Tours Denmark, lecturing on "Goethe and Tolstoy."

1925 Guest of the Stinnes steamship line, takes a cruise through the Mediterranean; visits Venice, Port Said, Cairo, Luxor, Karnak, Constantinople, Athens, Naples. In Egypt gets further inspiration for *Joseph* novel. Celebrates his fiftieth birthday; acclaimed throughout the European press; personal greetings from Stefan Zweig, Gerhart Hauptmann, Jakob Wassermann, Hugo von Hofmannsthal, among many others.

1926 Trip to Paris; dines in the Paris PEN-Club, the "Cercle Littéraire Internationale," with Edmond Jaloux, Jules Romains, François Mauriac, Charles du Bos, Felix Bertaux, and other prominent French men of letters; meets Russian literary historian, Dmitri Merezhkovsky, author of the studies *Tolstoy and Dostoevsky* and *Gogol*, both of which notably influenced his views on Russian literature.

On his return to Germany guest of honor at celebration of Lübeck's 700th anniversary; delivers the lecture "Lübeck als geistige Lebensform" ("Lübeck as a Form of Spiritual Life"). Starts work on novel *Joseph in Ägypten*. Vacations in Forte dei Marmi; attends a performance by a hypnotist that furnishes him impressions for novella *Mario und der Zauberer* (*Mario and the Magician*).

1927   Invitation by the Polish section of the PEN-Club to Warsaw; lectures on "Freiheit und Vornehmheit" ("Freedom and Distinction"); meets prominent men of letters, among them Stanislaus Przybyszewski; takes part in E.T.A. Hoffmann celebration at the restaurant Weinstube Fugger. After lectures in Danzig, Essen, and Heidelberg, and a vacation on the island of Sylt (Kampen, Haus Kliffende), returns to Munich. Immersion in Kleist's comedy *Amphitryon* leads to composition of "Amphitryon" essay. Lecture tour through Karlsruhe, Wiesbaden, Aachen, Düsseldorf.

1928   Trip to Vienna; reception in the Rathaus; reads from *Joseph* to members of the Kulturbund. Speaks at the centennial celebration of Reclam publishing house in the Alte Theater in Leipzig; meets Gerhart Hauptmann, Borries Freiherr von Münchhausen, Josef Ponten, Jakob Schaffner. Lecture tour through Austria and Switzerland; reads from *Joseph*. Visits Hamburg and Lübeck; lectures and reads from *Joseph* in Magdeburg, Liegnitz, Berlin.

1929   Trip to Stockholm with Mrs. Mann; is awarded the Nobel Prize for Literature. Text of Mann's diploma reads: "Thomas Mann, recipient of the literary Nobel Prize of the year 1929, awarded especially for his great novel *Buddenbrooks*, which has enjoyed, over the years, an ever more secure recognition as a classical work of the present."

1930   Trip to Egypt and Palestine; aboard the Nile
steamer *Assuan-Wadi-Halfa* to Nubia; return
trip by way of Assuan, Luxor, and Cairo.
Reichstag elections: Mann is worried about the
great increase of National-Socialist strength;
delivers speech "Deutsche Ansprache: Ein
Appell an die Vernunft" ("An Appeal to
Reason") in the Beethovenhall in Berlin,
amidst turmoil instigated by the Nazis. Completion of the first volume of *Joseph* tetralogy,
Die Geschichten Jaakobs (*The Stories of Jacob*).

1931   Beginning of lasting friendship with the historian and philosopher Erich Kahler. Lectures
on Sigmund Freud at the Germanic Institute
of Sorbonne University. Meets Felix Bertaux
and André Gide. After his return to Munich
is visited by Gide. Summer months in Nid-
den.

1932   Works on the lecture "Goethe als Representant des bürgerlichen Zeitalters" ("Goethe
as the Representative of the Bourgeois Epoch"). Holds lecture at Prussian Academy
of Arts, Berlin, on March 18, 1932, on the
occasion of the centennial of Goethe's death.
Receives Goethe medal for "important collaboration on the Goethe Centennial." Holds
lecture "Goethes Laufbahn als Schriftsteller"
("Goethe's Career as a Writer") on March
21 at City Hall in Weimar. Completes second *Joseph* volume, *Der junge Joseph* (*Young
Joseph*). Works on the third. Growing hatred
of the Nazis.

1933   Reads essay "Leiden und Grösse Richard
Wagners" ("The Sufferings and Greatness
of Richard Wagner") at the University of
Munich in commemoration of the fiftieth
anniversary of Wagner's death. This essay
was to be the immediate cause of Mann's
exile. With Mrs. Mann leaves for Holland
without realizing that this was to be his last

contact with Germany for many years to come. After the burning of the Reichstag, receives warnings from Germany not to return. Settles in Küsnacht near Zurich.

1934 Correspondence with the Hungarian mythologist and historian of religious thought, Karl Kerényi, who was to become Mann's trusted adviser, especially on the *Joseph* novels (volumes 3 and 4). First trip to America on invitation of publisher Alfred A. Knopf; reception by the New York PEN-Club; Goethe lecture at Yale; testimonial dinner at the Plaza Hotel, New York, with a speech of welcome by Mayor La Guardia. Back in Küsnacht (June 18). Death of publisher Samuel Fischer (October 15), "the representative of an epoch" which Mann knew to be his own. Great personal loss.

1935 Celebration of Mann's sixtieth birthday. Lecture tour to Prague, Brno, Vienna, Budapest with the Wagner essay. In Budapest, meets Karl Kerényi. Essay volume "Leiden und Grösse der Meister" ("Sufferings and Greatness of the Masters") appears as his last work to be published in Germany until 1946. Second trip to the United States; receives honorary doctorate from Harvard together with Albert Einstein; is President and Mrs. Roosevelt's guest at a private dinner in the White House. Back in Küsnacht (July 13), continues work on the third volume of *Joseph*.

1936 Lecture tour to Vienna, Brno, and Prague. In Vienna, visits Sigmund Freud. Third volume of *Joseph* (*Joseph in Egypt*) completed. Plans *Lotte in Weimar* (*The Beloved Returns*) as an interlude between the third and fourth volumes of *Joseph*. Receives Czechoslovak citizenship. Loses German citizenship on grounds of "subversive attacks on, and the gravest insults to, the Reich." (*Völkischer Beobachter*, December 12, 1936). After Bonn

University withdraws its honorary doctorate,
Mann writes to the Dean of the Philosophical
faculty, Professor Karl Justus Obenauer, a
letter that gains wide circulation in America
and Europe as his manifesto against the Nazi
regime.

1937   In Arosa, works on *The Beloved Returns*.
Decides to publish journal *Mass und Wert*.
Third trip to the United States on the invitation of the New School for Social Research,
New York; guest of Eugene Meyer, editor of
the *Washington Post*, and wife, Agnes Meyer,
who becomes Mann's benefactress and confidante; acquaintance with Caroline Newton,
devoted admirer of Mann and collector of his
works; seriously considers emigration to America. Receives Herder-Prize of Czechoslovakia
for exiled writers.

1938   Fourth trip to America; tours New York,
Philadelphia, Chicago, San Francisco, and
Los Angeles among other cities lecturing on
"The Coming Victory of Democracy." Emigration to the United States. "Where I am
there is Germany." Accepts position as lec-
turer in the humanities offered him by Harold
W. Dodd, President of Princeton University.
Receives honorary doctorate from Columbia
University. After brief stay in Küsnacht, arrival in New York on the S.S. Nieuw Amsterdam. Czechoslovakia surrendered; dismayed,
Mann writes the essay, "This Peace." Assumes his duties at Princeton. Resumes work
on *The Beloved Returns*.

1939   Tours Boston, New York, Detroit, Cincin-
nati, Chicago, St. Louis, Fort Worth, and
Seattle with the lecture "The Problem of
Freedom." Receives honorary doctorates from
Rutgers University and Princeton University.
Holds first seminar on *The Magic Mountain*
entitled "Einführung in den *Zauberberg* für
Studenten der Universität Princeton" ("In-

troduction to *The Magic Mountain* for the Students of Princeton University"). First trip to Europe (avoiding Germany) with his wife; vacations in Noordwijk aan Zee; visits Paris, Zürich, London; as German delegate attends the PEN-Club meeting in Stockholm. With the outbreak of World War II, returns to the United States on the S. S. Washington, in a throng of 2000 people who escape the war. Completes *The Beloved Returns*.

1940 Begins work on *The Transposed Heads*. Tours Canada, the Midwest, and the southern United States with the lecture "The Problem of Freedom." Returns to Princeton; lectures on "Goethe's Werther," "Die Kunst des Romans," ("The Art of the Novel"); in Professor Hans Jaeger's seminar gives two lectures "On Myself." Completes *The Transposed Heads*. Starts work on the fourth volume of the *Joseph* tetralogy. Begins broadcasts to Germany over BBC under the title "Deutsche Hörer!" ("German Listeners!").

1941 Guest of President Roosevelt, who makes a strong impression on Mann. Imparts some traits of Roosevelt's personality to Joseph the provider. Dissolves household in Princeton. Moves to California. Receives honorary doctorate from the University of California in Berkeley. Induction into the Phi Beta Kappa Honorary Society. Moves temporarily to Pacific Palisades, 740 Amalfi Drive. Own house, 1550 San Remo Drive, completed in February 1942. Visit of Michael Mann and family with grandchild Fridolin, who, as Nepomuk Schneidewein, as Little Echo, was destined to play important role in novel *Doctor Faustus*. Tour through South, East, and Midwest of the United States with the lecture "The War and the Future." In Washington, D.C., visits the Meyers. Thanks to Agnes Meyer is appointed to a three-year "Consultantship in Germanic Literature" at the Library of Congress (1941–1944). Japan attacks Pearl Harbor; Germany and Italy declare war on the United States. Mann, not yet a U.S. citizen, becomes an "enemy alien."

1942 First mention of *Doctor Faustus*. "Buddenbrook" house destroyed during night air attack on Lübeck. In Lotte Lehmann's Santa Barbara home, Mann enjoys German *Lieder* sung by the great soprano accompanied by Bruno Walter. Trip to the East, to Washington and New York; lectures on "The Theme of the Joseph-novels" at the Library of Congress; is introduced by Vice President Henry A. Wallace. On visit to Princeton meets old friends, among them his translator Helen Lowe-Porter and Erich Kahler. Back in Pacific Palisades, after a brief visit with the family of son Michael (Fridolin!) in San Francisco.

1943 *Joseph the Provider* completed. Begins writing the novella *Das Gesetz* (*The Tables of the Law*). Completed by end of February. Begins work on *Doctor Faustus*, using old notes that date back some forty-two years. Dr. Theodor Wiesengrund-Adorno becomes the poet's expert adviser on musical problems in *Doctor Faustus*. Mann makes lecture trip to the East Coast and to Canada; lectures on "The War and the Future" at the Library of Congress; is introduced by Chief Librarian and poet Archibald MacLeish; repeats the lecture at Hunter College, New York, then in Boston, there under the title "The Order of the Day"; in Montreal, before the Canadian Women's Club, delivers speech on "The New Humanism"; causes a near-riot with hundreds of people unable to enter the overcrowded auditorium. On return trip to the West, lectures at Columbia University, in Cincinnati, St. Louis, Chicago, and Kansas City.

1944   Is impressed with coincidence of his sixty-ninth birthday and D-Day, June 6, sees it as another aptness (*Stimmigkeit*) in his life. Mr. and Mrs. Mann become citizens of the United States.

1945   Writes lecture "Deutschland und die Deutschen" ("Germany and the Germans"). Death of President Roosevelt (April 12). "We were distraught, feeling that all around us the world was holding its breath." Germany capitulates. Mann shows first symptoms of deteriorating health. Nevertheless, carries through the yearly tour of the East Coast. Delivers lecture on "Germany and the Germans" at the Library of Congress. The free world celebrates Mann on his seventieth birthday; is honored with testimonial dinner at the Waldorf-Astoria Hotel in New York; attending, as toastmaster, Robert Sherwood and, among other prominent guests, Associate Justice of the Supreme Court Felix Frankfurter, the former Spanish Premier Juan Negrín, and the Secretary of the Interior Harold Ickes. Returns to Pacific Palisades. Composes essay "Dostojewski—mit Massen" ("Dostoevsky—in Moderation"). First mention of *Der Erwählte* (*The Holy Sinner*.)

1946   Serious lung infection. Is successfully operated on by the famous lung specialist Dr. Adams at the Billings Hospital in Chicago. Recovers rapidly. Returns to Pacific Palisades.

1947   Bonn University reinstates Mann as honorary doctor. Completes *Doctor Faustus* after working on it for almost four years. Writes "Nietzsches Philosophie im Lichte unserer Erfahrung" ("Nietzsche's Philosophy in the Light of Contemporary Events"). Departs for the East Coast and Europe. Delivers

speech "Nietzsche's Philosophy in the Light
of Contemporary Events" at the Library of
Congress and at Hunter College, New York.
Embarks on the H.M.S. *Queen Elizabeth*
(May 11). Delivers Nietzsche lecture at
King's College of London University; is in-
terviewed at BBC. In Zurich, delivers Nietzsche lecture on the occasion of the Fourteenth
International PEN-Congress; reads from *Doctor Faustus* in the Zurich Schauspielhaus.
Vacations in Nordwijk aan Zee, Huis ter
Duin. Returns to America on the Dutch
steamer *Westerdam*. Back in Pacific Palisades
(on September 14). Is elected member to
the Academia dei Lincei, Rome. Begins to
write *The Holy Sinner*, "a medieval legend-
novella which, together with the *Vertauschte
Köpfe* and the Moses story, could well form
Trois Contes; thoughts on the further development of the *Felix Krull* fragment into
a modern rogue's novel."

1949   Elected honorary president of the Bayer-
ische Akademie der schönen Künste. Receives
the Medal of Merit of the Academy of Arts
and Letters. In the Goethe year delivers
lecture on "Goethe and Democracy" at the
Library of Congress, then at Hunter College,
New York. Flies to London; is awarded a honorary doctorate by Oxford University; holds
lecture on "Goethe und die Demokratie"
("Goethe and Democracy") in German before a capacity audience in the *Taylorian
Institute*; repeats the lecture in English under
the auspices of the English Goethe Society in
the Senate House of London University. Lecture tour to Sweden and Denmark. Honorary
doctorate of the University of Lund. Suicide
of Mann's eldest son Klaus (May 21). Flies
to Zurich. From there takes the first trip to
Germany after his emigration. Honored guest
of the city of Frankfurt; speaks in Paulskirche

at the Goethe Celebration. Delivers "Ansprache im Goethejahr" ("Speech in the Goethe Year") at the Nationaltheater in Weimar; receives the Goethe Prize in the amount of 20,000 East Mark, which he donates for the restoration of Herder Church in Weimar. Returns to America on the S.S. *Nieuw Amsterdam*. Is awarded the Goethe Prize of the City of Frankfurt and the honorary citizenship of the City of Weimar *in absentia*. Repeats the "Speech in the Goethe Year" at the University of California, Berkeley.

1950   Death of brother Heinrich (March 12). In New York, lectures on "Meine Zeit" ("My Times") under the auspices of the German newspaper *Der Aufbau*. Departs for Stockholm. Is given a reception in the Börsensaal of the Swedish Academy on invitation of Prinz Wilhelm of Sweden and the Swedish PEN-Club; delivers lecture "My Times." By way of Paris ("My Times" delivered at Sorbonne) to Zurich. Visits Hermann Hesse in Montagnola. On the eve of his seventyfifth birthday, is given a reception in his honor under the auspices of the International PEN-Club and the Zurich Schauspielhaus (June 5). Flies to Los Angeles by way of London and New York. Returns to Pacific Palisades. Completes *The Holy Sinner*.

1951   Resumes work on *Felix Krull*. First considerations of a possible return to Europe for permanent residency, partly because of political developments in the United States. In Europe, visits Zurich, Lugano, and Salzburg. Back in Pacific Palisades. Membership in the American Academy of Arts and Letters.

1952   Works on novella *Die Betrogene* (*The Black Swan*). Is awarded Literature Prize by the Academia Nazionale dei Lincei, Rome. Departure from Pacific Palisades. Last stay in

Chicago and New York. "With advancing years . . . the wish for a homecoming to the old soil in which at long last I want to rest has grown ever more insistent." Arrival in Zurich. After brief visits to Salzburg (lectures: "Der Künstler und die Gesellschaft" ["The Artist and Society"]), Munich, Frankfurt (November 9, celebration of Hauptmann's ninetieth birthday in the Schauspielhaus), Vienna. Rents a house in Erlenbach near Zurich. Receives Officer's Cross of the Legion of Honor.

1953   Completes novella *The Black Swan.* Returns to manuscript of *Krull.* Trip to Rome to express in person his gratitude to the Academia Nazionale dei Lincei for the Literature Prize; sees Pope Pius XII in private audience; visits Palestrina, which bears rich memories for him. Flies to London to receive honorary doctorate from Cambridge University (June 4). Flies to Hamburg; reads from *Felix Krull* at Hamburg University; stays briefly in Travemünde and Lübeck, for the first time since 1931. Is deeply moved by his boyhood surroundings. Elected honorary member of the Gerhart Hauptmann Society.

1954   Buys house in Kilchberg, Alte Landstrasse 39, as his last home. Finishes first volume of *Felix Krull* after forty-five years, begun in November 1909. Vacations at "Waldhaus Sils Maria"; frequently meets Hermann Hesse and wife, who live in the same hotel. Works on "Versuch über Tschechow" ("Essay on Chekhov"). Works on Schiller speech for 150th anniversary celebration of Schiller's death in Stuttgart and Weimar.

1955   Honorary membership in the Deutsche Akademie der Künste. At Stuttgarter Landestheater, delivers main speech on the occasion of the 150th anniversary of Schiller's death. Other speakers are Bundespräsident Heuss,

Ministerpräsident Gerhard Müller, and the
president of the Schillergesellschaft, W. Hoffmann. At Schiller festivities at the Nationaltheater in Weimar, Mann again is the main
speaker, introduced by Johannes R. Becher.
Receives honorary doctorate of Friedrich
Schiller University in Jena. Is made honorary
president of the Deutsche Schillergesellschaft
in Weimar. Spends final week in his native
city of Lübeck and his beloved Travemünde;
is awarded the honorary citizenship of Lübeck
in the city's Rathaus. Is awarded an honorary
doctorate of Natural Sciences by the Eid-
genössische Technische Hochschule of Zurich, which pleased him particularly as a most
unusual distinction for a writer. Celebration
of Mann's eightieth birthday at Zurich
Schauspielhaus; Bruno Walter conducts Mo-
zart's *Eine Kleine Nachtmusik*; congratula-
tions and gifts from all over the world;
numerous guests at Kilchberg House; is presented a "Thomas Mann Gift" in the
amount of DM 50,000 in support of ailing
and impecunious German writers, the twelve-
volume edition of Mann's *Collected Works*
by Aufbau Publishing House, Berlin, and a
Festschrift, Homage de la France, with con-
gratulatory greetings from the President of
the Republic, Vincent Auriol, the honorary
President of the National Assembly, Edouard
Herriot, the Minister of the Exterior, Robert
Schumann, from Albert Camus, André Mal-
raux, Pablo Picasso, Albert Schweitzer, and
many other notables—an honor that pleased
Mann all the more as it came from much-
admired France. Delivers Schiller speech at
the University of Amsterdam; receives the
Great Cross of Orange-Nassau presented to
him by the Queen. Vacations at favorite
summer place, Noordwijk aan Zee, Huis ter
Duin. Is received by the Queen at her sum-

mer residence, Castle Soesdijk near Amsterdam. Sudden indisposition with severe pains and swelling of left leg. Is flown to Kantonspital, Zurich, for special treatment of his ailment. Recovers very slowly. Informed by the Hessian Minister of Education, Arno Hennig, of the award of the "Pour le Mérit."

August 12, 1955   Sudden total collapse. Blood pressure drops to zero. Transfusions and injections prove futile. At eight in the evening Thomas Mann's heart stops beating. Buried, as was his wish, in the cemetery of Kilchberg, not far from the grave of Conrad Ferdinand Meyer (August 16). Countless eulogies, among them a heartfelt farewell from Mann's lifelong friend Hermann Hesse, which echoes the suffering endured by these great men caused by Germany and the chaotic times:

> In deep sorrow, farewell to Thomas Mann, to the dear friend and great colleague, to the master of German prose, to a man who, despite success and honors heaped upon him, has been much misunderstood. All that lies hidden behind his irony and virtuosity, his great heart, his faithfulness, a sense of responsibility and the capacity for love—qualities unrecognized for decades by the German public—all these will keep Mann's work and memory alive far beyond our chaotic times.

NOTES

The following editions have been used as the main sources of
Thomas Mann quotations:
1. Hans Bürgin (ed.). *Thomas Mann. Gesammelte Werke in
   zwölf Bänden.* Frankfurt am Main: S. Fischer Verlag, 1960.
   Roman and arabic numerals refer to volume and page of this
   edition, unless otherwise indicated.
2. Erika Mann (ed.). *Thomas Mann. Gesammelte Briefe.* Frank-
   furt am Main: S. Fischer Verlag, 1961–1965:
   Volume I: Briefe 1889–1936. Abbr.: Br. I
   Volume II: Briefe 1937–1947. Abbr.: Br. II
   Volume III: Briefe 1948–1955 and Nachlese. Abbr.: Br. III
English translations, unless otherwise indicated, are my own.
For other available renderings see, Bibliography I.

1   The Artist's Enigma

1. "Lebensabriss." XI, 98.
2. "Lübeck als geistige Lebensform." XI, 386.
3. *Loc. cit.*
4. "Süsser Schlaf." XI, 333–339.
5. *Ibid.,* 336.
6. *Loc. cit.*
7. *Ibid.,* 338.
8. Anton Ehrenzweig in his book *The Hidden Order of Art,*
   (London: Weidenfeld, 1968) arrives at a similar definition
   of the nature of genius: "The overall picture," he writes, "is
   of a creative ego-rhythm that swings between focused *gestalt*
   and oceanic undifferentiation." (p. 57). Hans Wysling, one
   of the foremost Thomas Mann scholars, characterizes the
   make-up of Mann, the artist, as follows in striking corrobora-
   tion of our view: "A dreamy meditativeness is watched over
   by a combinative intelligence . . . A half dreamy, half syn-
   thetic and analysable art-world." Paul Scherrer and Hans

Wysling, *Thomas Mann Studien. Bd. I. Quellenkritische Studien zum Werk Thomas Manns.* (Berne and Munich: Francke Verlag, 1967), p. 280. (Henceforth: *Studien.*)

9. *Death in Venice and Seven Other Stories,* trans. H. T. Lowe-Porter (New York: Knopf, 1930), p. 75. (Parenthetical page numbers in the text refer to this work.)

10. See for example *Betrachtungen eines Unpolitischen.* XII, 28, 517. (Henceforth: *Betrachtungen.*)

11. *Death in Venice.* Lowe-Porter renders it imprecisely as "cold fury," cf. p. 44.

12. *Blätter der Thomas Mann Gesellschaft,* No. 6. Zurich, (1966), p. 15.

13. *Doktor Faustus. Das Leben des deutschen Tonsetzers Adrian Leverkühn erzählt von einem Freunde.* VI, 345. (Henceforth: *Doktor Faustus.*) Cf. also letter to Bruno Walter. March 1, 1945. Br. II, 416.

14. *Doktor Faustus.* VI, 410.

15. *Ibid.,* 646–647.

16. *Ibid.,* 647.

17. *Die Entstehung des Doktor Faustus. Roman eines Romans.* XI, 203: (Henceforth: *Entstehung.*)

18. *Doktor Faustus.* VI, 428.

19. See for example, Hans Eichner, *Thomas Mann. Eine Einführung in sein Werk.* (Berne: Francke Verlag, 1953), p. 99.

20. *Entstehung.* XI, 291.

21. *Loc. cit.*

22. *Ibid.,* 291–292.

23. *Ibid.,* 292.

2   Heritage

NIETZSCHE, WAGNER, AND SCHOPENHAUER

1. "Lebensabriss." XI, 139.

2. Letter of June 23, 1950. Br. III, 152–153. Italics Mann's.

3. "Richard Wagner und der 'Ring des Nibelungen.'" IX, 502–503 (Henceforth: "Ring.") Italics mine.

4. Letter to Felix Bertaux. Dec. 28, 1924. Br. I, 221.

5. Letter to Kurt Martens. March 28, 1906. Br. I, 62.

6. "Lebensabriss." XI, 109.

7. *Betrachtungen.* XII, 22.
8. Letter to Ernst Fischer. May 25, 1926. Br. I, 255–256.
9. *Betrachtungen.* XII, 79.
10. *Loc. cit.*
11. *Loc. cit.* Italics Mann's.
12. "Yes, in years when one is not as yet versed in disdaining, I was forced to disdain the pseudo-aesthetic Renaissance-Nietzscheanism, because I had recognized it for what it was, a boyishly-misconceived imitation of the real Nietzsche." *Betrachtungen.* XII, 539.
13. *Ibid.,* 538–539.
14. *Ibid.,* 87–88.
15. "Nietzsches Philosophie im Lichte unserer Erfahrung." IX, 696. (Henceforth: "Nietzsches Philosophie.")
16. *Loc. cit.*
17. *Ibid.,* 700.
18. "Nietzsche's Philosophy in the Light of Contemporary Events. An Address Delivered in the Coolidge Auditorium in the Library of Congress on May 29, 1945." (Washington, D.C.: 1945).
19. "Nietzsches Philosophie." IX, 707–708.
20. *Betrachtungen.* XII, 74.
21. Letter of Feb. 18, 1942. Br. II, 239.
22. Perhaps the most severe criticism of Wagner is found in Mann's notes to a planned but never written essay, "Geist und Kunst." Now published in *Studien,* 203.
23. *Betrachtungen.* XII, 73.
24. *Ibid.,* 79–80.
25. *Ibid.,* 80–81.
26. The most important interpretations are "Leiden und Grösse Richard Wagners," and "Richard Wagner und der 'Ring des Nibelungen,'" translated into English in *Past Masters and Other Papers* and in *Essays of Three Decades,* respectively. I quote from the German originals in my translation.
27. "Ring." IX, 515.
28. Letter of April 1, 1910. Br. III, "Nachlese," p. 457. Italics Mann's.
29. "Leiden und Grösse Richard Wagners." IX, 371. (Henceforth: "Leiden.")
30. Cf. Chapter 6 for the discussion of "Myth plus Psychology" in Mann's life and work.

31. "Ring." IX, 516. Italics Mann's.
32. "Leiden." IX, 363–364
33. *Ibid.*, 365.
34. *Ibid.*, 408.
35. *Ibid.*, 422.
36. "Lebensabriss." XI, 111.
37. *Betrachtungen.* XII, 72.
38. Cf. Chapter 1.
39. "Schopenhauer." IX, 559.
40. Arthur Schopenhauer, "Über den Tod und sein Verhältnis zur Unzerstörbarkeit unseres Wesens an sich," *Die Welt als Wille und Vorstellung.* II (Leipzig: Inselverlag, n.d.), 1240–1298.
41. *Buddenbrooks.* I, 657–658. Italics Mann's.
42. "Schopenhauer." IX, 561.
43. *Ibid.*, 556–557
44. *Loc. cit.*
45. *Betrachtungen.* XII, 73.
46. "Schopenhauer." IX, 569.
47. *Ibid.*, 580.

THE HOLY RUSSIAN LITERATURE

1. Cf. A. von Gronicka, "Thomas Mann and Russia," *Germanic Review*, 20 (April, 1945), 105–137. Also Lilli Venohr, *Manns Verhältnis zur russischen Literatur*, (London: Hain, Glan, 1959), and, most recently with considerable Marxist bias, Alois Hofman, *Thomas Mann und die Welt der russischen Literatur*, (Berlin: Akademie-Verlag, 1967).
2. Klaus Schröter, *Thomas Mann*, (Hamburg: Rowohlt Verlag, 1964), pp. 34*ff.*
3. Letter of April 27, 1933. Br., I, 331. Italics mine.
4. For a succinct statement on these, see Henry C. Hatfield, *Thomas Mann.* (Norfolk, Conn.: New Directions Press, 1951), pp. 34–35.
5. All this reading was done in German translation. Mann knew no Russian. To J. T. Gömöri Mann wrote: "I know not a word of Russian, and the German translations of the great Russian authors of the nineteenth century which I read as a young man were poor indeed. Nevertheless, I must

count this reading among my greatest educational experiences. [Bildungserlebnisse]." Letter of Nov. 15, 1951. Br. III, 230.

6. "Russische Anthologie." X, 592–593. See also letter to Agnes Meyer of Dec. 3, 1940. Br. II, 170.

7. "I have greatly admired Merezhkovsky, the critic, especially his book on Tolstoy and Dostoevsky and that on Gogol. His novels . . . had no influence on me whatever." Letter to Anna Jacobson. Feb. 22, 1945, Br. II, 413.

8. "Russische Anthologie." X, 597.

9. *Loc. cit.*

10. "Goethe und Tolstoi. Fragmente zum Problem der Humanität." IX, 126. (Henceforth: "Goethe und Tolstoi.")

11. *Ibid.*, 87.

12. *Ibid.*, 129.

13. *Vospominania o L've Nikolaeviche Tolstom.* (Berlin: Lazhnikov, 1921), p. 8.

14. "Goethe und Tolstoi." IX, 64.

15. *Ibid.*, 116.

16. *Loc. cit.*

17. *Ibid.*, 118.

18. *Ibid.*, 91.

19. Letter to Albrecht Goes. Br. III, 263. Italics Mann's.

20. Letter to Stefan Zweig of July 28, 1920. Br. I, 181.

21. "Goethe und Tolstoi." IX, 64.

22. Letter to Stefan Zweig, Br. I, 181.

23. *Loc. cit.* See also *Betrachtungen.* XII, 519.

24. "Dostojewski—mit Massen." IX, 661. The portrait Mann draws of Dostoevsky in this late essay differs little from his portrayal of the Russian writer in his study "Goethe und Tolstoi."

25. *Loc. cit.* Italics Mann's.

26. *Ibid.*, 673.

27. "Russische Anthologie." X, 594–595. Mann is heavily indebted to Merezhkovsky in his view of Gogol. Cf. D. Merezhkovsky, *Gogol, Sein Leben und Sein Werk.* (Munich and Leipzig: Georg Müller, 1914.)

28. Letter to Korfiz Holm. June 7, 1898: "I have read *The Duel* with enormous interest. Those Russians know how to tell a tale! . . . And for once an excellent translation." Br. I, 9.

29. "Russische Anthologie." X, 592.

30. "Versuch über Tschechow." IX, 846.
31. *Betrachtungen.* XII, 437.
32. "Russische Anthologie." X, 600.
33. *Loc. cit.* In so late an essay as "Meine Zeit," (1950) Mann still holds the same view of Russia and its literature: "Who would want to deny Russia, eternal Russia, its humaneness. There has never and nowhere been a deeper humaneness than in Russian literature, in the *holy* Russian literature." XI, 320. Italics Mann's.

FRIEDRICH SCHILLER AND
JOHANN WOLFGANG VON GOETHE

1. Letter to Albrecht Goes. Dec. 11, 1950. Br. III, 177.
2. Letter of August 6, 1918. *Thomas Mann an Ernst Bertram. Briefe aus den Jahren 1910–1955.* Inge Jens, ed. (Pfullingen: Neske Verlag, 1960), p. 72.
3. Letter of Nov. 27, 1945. Br. II, 458.
4. Letter to Max Stefl. May 16, 1954. Br. III, 340.
5. Letter to Erich Kahler. May 15, 1946. Br. II, 489.
6. *Betrachtungen.* XII, 541. Italics Mann's. Thomas Mann's guide to Meyer was the aesthetician and literary historian Franz Ferdinand Baumgarten, the author of *Das Werk Conrad Ferdinand Meyers: Renaissance-Empfinden und Stilkunst* (Munich: 1917).
7. "Rede über Lessing." IX, 229–246.
8. "Kleists Amphitryon." IX, 187–229. In the "Lebensabriss" Mann recalls the weeks of "loving immersion in the comedy and the wonders of his [Kleist's] metaphysical wit." XI, 139. See also "Heinrich von Kleists Erzählungen." IX, 823–843.
9. *Betrachtungen.* XII, 375–428.
10. "Chamisso." IX, 35–58.
11. "Der alte Fontane." IX, 9–35.
12. This admiration was to be lifelong. In 1942, more than forty years after his first acquaintance with the author, Mann still wrote to Agnes Meyer that he was "reading him [Fontane] again with indescribable pleasure." Letter of May 12, 1942. Br. II, 255.
13. "Versuch über Schiller." IX, 929.
14. *Ibid.,* 892.
15. "Schwere Stunde." VIII, 371–380.

16. The most drastic expression of this passing attitude we find in the Schiller-parodies from the *Bilderbuch für artige Kinder* (*Picturebook for Well-Behaved Children*), now lost, on which Thomas collaborated with his brother Heinrich in those early years and which have been reproduced (from memory) by the youngest brother, Victor, in his biographical account of the Mann family, *Wir Waren Fünf* (Constance: Südverlag, 1949), p. 53.

17. "Goethe und Tolstoi." IX, 79. Italics Mann's.

18. *Ibid.*, 97. Italics Mann's.

19. *Ibid.*, 138.

20. Bernhard Blume, *Thomas Mann und Goethe* (Berne; Francke Verlag, 1949). Herbert Lehnert has recently brought proof of Mann's early interest in Goethe. Nevertheless, we would agree with Blume that "Mann's development does not begin under the influence of Goethe. . . . The young Thomas Mann recognized himself in Schiller, not in Goethe." p. 25.

21. *Ibid.*, 24.

22. See "Über Goethe's 'Faust.'" IX, 581–622. To Hermann Hesse, Mann wrote: "I have busied myself once again with *Faust II*. . . . Once again I was completely transporté and *encouraged*. . . . How splendid it is in all its parts, how brilliant and full of humor in its treatment of myth and the mystery of Helena! How *aptly is everything expressed* with the witty, wise, lyrical word!" Letter of Nov. 25, 1947. Italics Mann's. Br. II, 569. Following is Mann's characterization of Goethe's style: "This style is not elevated, pompous, priestly or pathetic . . . instead everything is uttered in the middle register and with moderate strength of voice, prosaically *spoken*, even in his lyrics; yet everything is marked by a strange gay boldness. The word appears recreated, unique, as if lifted for the first time from the womb of language, newly discovered, imbued with new meaning—and this is achieved in such a way that this new meaning takes on a strange transcendency, producing something gayly spectral, something both *goldig*—as one says in West Germany—and sublime, civilly-bold, in that special meaning of Goethe's statement that in every artist 'there is a seed of audacity' without which talent is unthinkable." "Goethe als Representant des bürgerlichen Zeitalters." IX, 312. Italics Mann's. See also

"Phantasie über Goethe." IX, 713–755; "Goethe's Werther." IX, 640–655; and "Zu Goethe's Wahlverwandt- schaften," IX, 174–186.

23. "Zu Goethe's Wahlverwandtschaften." IX, 186.

24. Letter to Agnes Meyer. Jan. 12, 1943. Br. II, 290.

25. See letter to Ferdinand Lion. Dec. 15, 1938: "I am slowly writing the chapter [of *The Beloved Returns*] and am enjoy- ing indescribably the intimacy [with Goethe], not to say the *unio mystica* with him." Br. II, 72.

26. Letter of Oct. 10, 1932. Br. I, 323.

27. Letter to Fritz Kaufmann. Feb. 3, 1943. Br. II, 296.

28. Letter to G. W. Zimmermann. Undated, probably written in December, 1949. Br. III, 117.

29. See especially, "Goethe und die Demokratie." IX, 755–783.

30. "Geist und Wesen der deutschen Republik." XI, 855–856. Cf. "Phantasie über Goethe." IX, 752–753.

31. Letter to Josef Ponten. Jan. 21, 1925. Br. I, 229.

32. "Versuch über Schiller." IX, 911.

33. *Ibid.*, 909.

34. *Ibid.*, 905.

35. *Ibid.*, 934.

36. *Ibid.*, 935.

37. The problem of Mann's relation to Schiller and especially to Schiller's aesthetics awaits comprehensive treatment. Horst Daemmrich has made a competent beginning with his study, "Friedrich Schiller and Thomas Mann: Parallels in Aesthetics," *Journal of Aesthetics and Art Criticism*, 24 (December 1965), 227–249.

38. "Goethe und Tolstoi." IX, 61.

39. "Versuch über Schiller." IX, 946.

40. *Ibid.*, 947.

41. Letter of Feb. 19, 1955 to Agnes Meyer. Br. III, 380.

42 "Versuch über Schiller." IX, 939. Mann reproduces Schil- ler's italics.

43. Cf. Letter to Agnes Meyer, Feb. 9, 1955. Br. III, 375–376.

44. "Versuch über Schiller." IX, 940.

45. *Lotte in Weimar.* II, 662.

46. *Studien*, 211. Note 110 to "Geist und Kunst." Italics Mann's.

47. "Vorwort zu 'Altes und Neues.' " XI, 695.

3 *Thomas Mann and His Contemporaries*

THE NATURALISTS

1. *Betrachtungen.* XII, 140. See also letter to Julius Bab. April 23, 1925. Br. I, 238.
2. "Ein Werk des Naturalismus." X, 556.
3. "Anna Karenina." IX, 627.
4. "Einführung in den *Zauberberg.*" XI, 612. (Henceforth: "Einführung.")
5. See for instance "Lübeck als geistige Lebensform." XI, 385.
6. "Gerhart Hauptmann." IX, 806.
7. Letter of May 27, 1914. Br. I, 108.
8. *Betrachtungen.* XII, 167–168.
9. *Ibid.,* 153.
10. Hans Wysling offers the following survey of these interests: "Thomas Mann caught hold of everything in newspapers and periodicals which at that time aroused his interest. He wanted to grasp all cultural tendencies of the times, partly because he was in need of targets for his polemics. Thus, his discussions of Wagner, Mahler, Strauss, and Pfitzner, his dialogues with Hauptmann, Hofmannsthal, George, Klinger, Stuck, and the other great were accompanied by minor sallies against Richard Schaukal and Alexander von Bernus. . . . Thomas Mann was familiar with the thoughts of all the important writers of the day." (*Studien,* 126–127.) Wysling enumerates Jentsch, Scheffler, Dora Luisa Frost, Harden, Lamprecht, Hofmiller, Frau Neumann, Gundolf, and Wolfskehl as examples. "Mann read the 'Neue Rundschau' ('Freie Bühne'), the 'Zwiebelfisch,' and, of course, the 'Simplicissimus.' In addition to all this there were [the newspapers]—the 'Münchner Neuesten Nachrichten,' the 'Berliner Tageblatt,' the 'Wiener Neue Freie Presse'—from all of which Thomas Mann excerpted liberally for ready reference. There was nothing that did not stimulate him! The range was enormous, from art exhibits to evening dances, from Kothe's 'Volksliederbuch' to Count Zeppelin. When the Count was made a national hero in 1909, Thomas Mann collected everything on him that he could get hold of in order to be better able to polemicize against this

type of spiritualization [Vergeistigung] of the nation. Certainly there was enough of the merely ephemeral. Yet Thomas Mann always succeeded in detecting the important tendencies of the day and the hour in the chaotic mass of the timebound. He knew very well that whatever most fascinated and most repelled him always involved his own self. 'Criticism of the times is, basically, criticism of oneself.' " (*Loc. cit.*)

SIGMUND FREUD

1. *Internationale Zeitschrift für Psychoanalyse*, XI (April 1925), 58.
2. Wolfgang Michael, "Thomas Mann auf dem Wege zu Freud," *Modern Language Notes*, 65 (March 1950), 169–170. Quoted from Fr. J. Hoffmann, *Freudianism and the Literary Mind* (Baton Rouge: 1945), p. 211.
3. For Mann's characterization of Krokowski's role in *Der Zauberberg*, see his essay "Mein Verhältnis zur Psychoanalyse," XI, 748–749.
4. *Ibid.*, 748.
5. "Schopenhauer." IX, 578.
6. "Freud und die Zukunft." IX, 500.
7. *Loc. cit.*
8. "Religion in Thomas Mann's *Joseph and His Brothers*." *Boston University Graduate Journal* XV, (Fall, 1967), 19.

THE NEOCLASSICISTS

1. Letter of Dec. 6, 1908. Br. III, "Nachlese," 455.
2. "Zu Goethe's Wahlverwandtschaften." IX, 179.
3. *Death in Venice and Seven Other Stories*, trans. H. T. Lowe-Porter, pp. 12f.
4. *Betrachtungen.* XII, 517. Italics mine.
5. *Ibid.*, 28. Italics mine.
6. *Loc cit.*
7. *Loc. cit.*
8. *Ibid.*, 96.
9. "Versuch über das Theater." X, 60.
10. "Über die Kunst Richard Wagners." X, 842.

THE EXPRESSIONISTS

1. *Betrachtungen.* XII, 212.
2. *Betrachtungen.* XII, 212–213.
3. *Ibid.,* 213.
4. Letter of Dec. 25, 1917. *Thomas Mann an Ernst Bertram, op. cit.,* p. 55.
5. "Über eine Szene von Wedekind." X, 70–76.
6. Mann recognized in Kafka "the secret king of contemporary writers." Letter to James Laughlin. Nov. 4, 1940. Br. II, 167.
7. "Should *Demian,* a work I very much love, be really by Hesse?" Letter to Philipp Witkop. June 23, 1920. Br. I, 175.
8. *Studien,* 230. Thomas Mann's admiration of Hesse developed over the years into mutual friendship. Cf. Mann's gratulatory message to Hesse on the occasion of the poet's seventieth birthday. Anni Carlsson, ed. *Hesse/Mann. Briefwechsel* (Frankfurt: Suhrkamp/Fischer, 1968), pp. 130–134. (Henceforth: *Briefwechsel.*)
9. Letter to Maximilian Harden. Aug. 30, 1910. Br. I, 86. Italics Mann's.

4   *The Hallmark of the Artist*

1. *Berliner Tageblatt,* September 23, 1902.
2. Cf. Chapter 1.
3. Letter of June 1, 1902. Br. III, "Nachlese," 436.
4. *Tristan.* VIII, 251.
5. Letter to Victor Polzer. March 23, 1940. Br. II, 137–138.
6. "Einführung." XI, 607.
7. "Sometimes my thoughts range beyond the *Joseph* novels which need only finishing touches, and reach out toward an artist-novella [Künstler-Novelle, *Doktor Faustus*], which may well turn out to be the most daring and weird of all my works." Letter to Agnes Meyer, Feb. 2, 1942. Br. II, 241.
8. Letter to Victor Polzer. *Op. cit.*
9. "Joseph und seine Brüder. Ein Vortrag." XI, 661.
10. "Legitimacy, that is what is most important and decisive. And thus, these dreams [the *Joseph* novels] had their roots in my childhood [Kindheit]." "Lebensabriss." XI, 138.

11. *Entstehung.* XI, 155–156.
12. Letter to Kurt Martens. March 28, 1906. Br. I, 63. See also *Betrachtungen.* XII, 144–145.
13. *Death in Venice and Seven Other Stories,* trans. H. T. Lowe-Porter, *op. cit.* p. 11. This phrase was originally coined by Samuel Lublinski with reference to Thomas Mann in his *Die Bilanz der Moderne* (Berlin: S. Fischer Verlag, 1904). Cf. K. Schröter, *Thomas Mann im Urteil seiner Zeit.* (Hamburg: Christian Wegener Verlag, 1969), p. 29.
14. *Fiorenza.* VIII, 1018.
15. *Der Erwählte.* VII, 92.
16. *Ibid.,* 144.
17. Letter of Oct. 19, 1938. Br. II, 58.
18. "Mitteilungen an die Literaturhistorische Gesellschaft in Bonn." XI, 716.
19. *Loc. cit.*
20. Letter to Ida Herz. March 21, 1954. Br. III, 332.
21. *Loc. cit.*
22. "Vladimir Nabokov on Nabokov and Things," *New York Times Book Review* (May 12, 1968).
23. "Erziehung zur Sprache." X, 863.
24. Peter Heller, *Dialectics and Nihilism. Essays on Lessing, Nietzsche, Mann and Kafka* (Amherst, Mass.: University of Massachusetts Press, 1966), p. 169.
25. "Die Kunst des Romans." X, 356–357.
26. "Bilse und Ich." X, 20.
27. *Ibid.,* 15.
28. Herbert Lehnert, *Thomas Mann—Fiktion, Mythos, Religion* (Cologne: Kohlhammer Verlag, 1965), p. 193.
29. "Humor und Ironie." XI, 802.
30. Letter to Agnes Meyer. June 2, 1943. Br. II, 320–321.
31. Letter to Agnes Meyer. Oct. 10, 1947. Br. II, 557.
32. Mark van Doren, "Joseph and his Brothers: A Comedy in Four Parts," in H. Hatfield (ed.), *Thomas Mann: A Collection of Critical Essays* (Englewood Cliffs, N.J.: Prentice Hall, 1964), pp. 98ff.
33. *Loc. cit.*
34. *Loc. cit.*
35. Gotthold Ephraim Lessing, *Minna von Barnhelm.* Act IV, Scene 2.
36. Victor Mann, *Wir Waren Fünf, op. cit.,* p. 53. Here are

some of the lines as recorded by Victor Mann from memory: *Ha, den Busen presst die Lotterfaust/ Während du in Jovis Auge schaust,/ Der im Kreise der Olympier schmaust,/ Schorke, ha, dem vor sich selbst nun graust,/ Eine Laus, ein Wurm nur stehst du da,/ Seelen fordert Philadelphia.* Following is an approximate rendering in prose of the nonsense verses: Ha, the fist of the hugger-mugger presses the bosom while you gaze into the eyes of Jove feasting in the company of the Olympians. Villain, ha, now horrified by your own self, there you stand, a mere louse, a worm; souls are claimed by Philadelphia.

37. "Einführung." XI, 606.
38. *Doktor Faustus.* VI, 322.
39. Letter of Jan. 31, 1948. Br. III, 17.
40. Herman Meyer has made a comprehensive study of this device in *Das Zitat in der Erzählkunst. Zur Geschichte und Poetik des Europäischen Romans.* (Stuttgart: Metzler Verlag, 1961). On pp. 207–245 he treats the device in Mann's *Zauberberg* and *Lotte in Weimar*. Meyer finds Mann's use of quotations becoming "ever more cryptic" in the late works, in *Lotte in Weimar, Doktor Faustus* and the *Erwählte. Ibid.,* 228.
41. "Bemerkungen zu dem Roman *Der Erwählte.*" XI, 690.
42. *Betrachtungen.* XII, 144.
43. "Die Kunst des Romans." X, 353.
44. "Der Schriftsteller und die Gesellschaft." X, 399.
45. Klaus-Jürgen Rothenberg, *Das Problem des Realismus bei Thomas Mann. Literatur und Leben,* Vol. 11. (Cologne and Vienna: Böhlau Verlag, 1969).
46. *Ibid.,* 179.
47. *Ibid.,* 178.
48. Letter to Frank Hirschbach of June 14, 1952. Br. III, 263.
49. Reinhard Baumgart, *Das Ironische und die Ironie in den Werken Thomas Manns* (Munich: Karl Hauser Verlag, 1964).
50. *Ibid.,* 85.
51. *Goethes Sämtliche Werke. Jubiläums Ausgabe,* Eduard von der Hellen, (ed.) 21 (Stuttgart and Berlin: Cotta Buchhandlung, 1901), 191.

5   *Progressive Universal Poesy*

1. Erich Heller, *The Ironic German: A Study of Thomas Mann* (Boston and Toronto: Little, Brown, 1958), p. 202. I acknowledge herewith, gratefully, my indebtedness in this chapter to this highly stimulating study.
2. A term which resists exact translation. The English term "poetry" restricts the meaning to lyrics. "Literature," on the other hand, is too inclusive a term. I have therefore chosen "poesy" as the closest approximation to the German.
3. Friedrich Schlegel, *Kritische Schriften*, W. Rasch, ed. (Munich: 1956), pp. 37 *et passim*.
4. *Thomas Mann–Karl Kerényi: Gespräch in Briefen.* Karl Kerény, ed. (Zurich: Rhein Verlag, 1960), p. 157. (Henceforth: *Gespräch.*)
5. *Entstehung*, p. 41.
6. Appendix 1, pp. 182–183.
7. Letter of Aug. 28, 1951. Br. III, 218–219.
8. *Betrachtungen.* XII, 229.
9. "Bilse und ich." X, 16.
10. For a typical example of such a reply in selfdefense, see "Vom Geist der Medizin. Offner Brief an den Herausgeber der *Deutschen Medizinischen Wochenschrift.*" XI, 591–596. Also see letter to Arnold Schoenberg of Dec. 19, 1949. Br. III, 121–122, and the "Open letter to the *Saturday Review of Literature.*" Dec. 10, 1948. Br. III, 60–62.
11. Käte Hamburger, *Thomas Manns Roman "Joseph und seine Brüder"* (Stockholm: Bermann Fischer Verlag, 1945), pp. 63–64f.
12. Hermann Weigand, *Thomas Mann's Novel "Der Zauberberg": A Study* (New York: Appleton, 1933), p. 159.
13. Erich Heller, *op. cit.*, 189f.
14. Friedrich Schlegel, *op. cit.*, 37.
15. See Ronald Peacock, *Das Leitmotiv bei Thomas Mann* (Bonn: Haupt Verlag, 1934) and Peter Heller, "Some Functions of the 'Leitmotiv' in Thomas Mann's *Joseph* Tetralogy," *Germanic Review*, XXII (1947), pp. 126–141.
16. "Lebensabriss." XI, 116.
17. "The book [*The Magic Mountain*] strives by its artistic means [especially the leitmotif] to eliminate time, to lend

to its musical-ideational totality complete presence at any and every instant and thus to achieve a magical *nunc stans.*" "Einführung." XI, 612. This observation on the leitmotif function in *The Magic Mountain* holds equally true with reference to Mann's entire output in the period of his artistic maturity.

18. See *Germanic Review,* XXIII (April, 1948), 125–130.
19. Herman Hesse put his finger on the questionable aspect of this technique when he wrote, "To the sublime esoteric aspect of the book there corresponds an exoteric, an outer form which is achieved by almost any means, also by such means as are forbidden to the less great." *Briefwechsel,* p. 148.
20. *Entstehung.* XI, 165–166.
21. *Ibid.,* 166.
22. Letter of Jan. 31, 1948. Br. III, 16.
23. *Entstehung.* XI, 175.
24. Gunilla Bergsten, *Thomas Manns Doktor Faustus. Untersuchungen zu den Quellen und zur Struktur des Romans* (Stockholm: Bonnier Verlag, 1963) and Hans Wysling, "Die Technik der Montage: Zu Thomas Manns *Erwähltem,*" *Euphorion,* LVII (January/February 1963), 156–199.
25. Schlegel, *op. cit.,* 270.
26. Erich Heller, *op. cit.,* 181.
27. Schlegel, *op. cit.,* 12.
28. *Ibid.,* 37.
29. "Pariser Rechenschaft." XI, 77.
30. Letter of May 6, 1934. Br. II, 360.
31. "Leiden." IX, 373–374. Italics Mann's.

6 *Poet and Writer—Myth Plus Psychology*

1. *Betrachtungen.* XII, 87–88.
2. Letter of March 2, 1910. Br. I, 82.
3. "Rede Über Lessing." IX, 232–233. For other very strong statements see "Zum sechzigsten Geburtstag Ricarda Huchs." X, 429–435, especially pp. 432–433, and two letters to Josef Ponten of January 21 and April 22, 1925. Br. I, 226–229 and 236–238, written partly in answer to Ponten's "Open Letter," in which he emphasized the dichotomy of *Dichter* vs. *Schriftsteller.* Cf. Schröter, *Thomas Mann im*

Urteil seiner Zeit (Hamburg: Christian Wegener Verlag, 1969), pp. 110–118.

4. "Rede über Lessing." IX, 232. Italics mine.
5. *Death in Venice and Seven Other Stories*, trans. H. T. Lowe-Porter, *op. cit.*, p. 46.
6. Letter to Fr. H. Weber. March 28, 1954. Br. III, 334.
7. *Studien*, 149.
8. Letter to Kuno Fiedler. June 19, 1955. Br. III, 406.
9. Letter to Hermann Lange. March 19, 1955. Br. III, 387. Italics Mann's.
10. *Gespräch*, p. 98.
11. "Leiden." IX, 368. Italics Mann's.
12. See André von Gronicka, "Myth Plus Psychology: A Stylistic Analysis of Thomas Mann's *Death in Venice*," *Germanic Review*, XXXI (October, 1956), 206–214.
13. A term coined by Nietzsche in reference to Wagner's art.
14. *Death in Venice and Seven Other Stories*, trans. H. T. Lowe-Porter, *op. cit.*, p. 33.
15. *Loc. cit.*
16. *Ibid.*, 29.
17. *Ibid.*, 31. Lowe-Porter's translation is slightly edited in order to approximate the German original more closely.
18. *Ibid.*, 75. Italics mine.
19. *Ibid.*, 42. Compare the following passage from Homer's *Odyssey* in which Proteus is speaking to the demigod Menelaos: "It is not ordained that thou should die . . . in horse-pasturing Argos; but to the Elysian plain and to the bounds of the earth will the immortals convey thee."
20. *Thomas Mann/Heinrich Mann. Briefwechsel, 1900–1949.* Hans Wysling, ed. (Frankfurt: S. Fischer Verlag, 1968), pp. 150–151.
21. *Loc. cit.*
22. "Lebensabriss." XI, 124.
23. *Loc. cit.*

7 *The Mediator*

1. Cf. Chapter 1, p. 5.
2. *Tonio Kröger.* VIII, 338.
3. Reinhard Baumgart, *op. cit.*, p. 116.

4. *Tonio Kröger.* VIII, 338.
5. *Betrachtungen.* XII, 92. Italics Mann's.
6. *Tonio Kröger.* VIII, 337.
7. *Ibid.,* 338.
8. *Bekenntnisse des Hochstaplers Felix Krull.* VII, 315. (Henceforth: *Felix Krull.*)
9. *Loc. cit.*
10. *Ibid.,* 528.
11. *Ibid.,* 498.
12. *Ibid.,* 372.
13. *Loc. cit.*
14. Mann liked to speak of the "natural weight [ein natürliches Schwergewicht]" which he felt was his, both as a person and as an artist. See, for example, his letter to Josef Ponten. Oct. 1, 1924. Br. I, 217.
15. *Felix Krull,* 489.
16. *Ibid.,* 273.
17. With reference to the *Joseph* novels Mann wrote: "What I busy myself with, is a kind of harmless mountebankery." This holds true for his work on *Felix Krull* afortiori. Letter to Agnes Meyer. July 12, 1942. Br. II, 267.
18. Letter to Carl Maria Weber. July 4, 1920. Br. I, 179. Italics Mann's. Cf. also *Betrachtungen.* XII, 569.
19. *Betrachtungen.* XII, 92.
20. *Loc. cit.*
21. "Schopenhauer." IX, 534. Italics Mann's.
22. *Gespräch,* p. 18.
23. Letter to Stefan Zweig. July 26, 1925. Br. I, 245.
24. *Betrachtungen.* XII, 573.
25. *Thomas Mann/Heinrich Mann. Briefwechsel, op. cit.,* pp. 34–35.
26. "Goethe und Tolstoi." IX, 124–125. See also p. 138.
27. *Zauberberg.* III, 714–715.
28. *Ibid.,* 226.
29. Eichner, *op. cit.,* p. 58.
30. Letter to Agnes Meyer. May 2, 1941. Br. II, 186–187.
31. Peter Heller, *op. cit.,* p. 211. Italics Heller's.
32. *Joseph der Ernährer.* V, 1745.
33. *Ibid.,* 1804.
34. *Lotte in Weimar.* II, 658.
35. *Ibid.,* 653–654.

36. *Ibid.*, 754.
37. *Ibid.*, 763.
38. *Ibid.*, 440.
39. *Ibid.*, 439–440.
40. *Ibid.*, 441.
41. "Bruder Hitler." XII, 852.
42. Letter to Agnes Meyer. July 27, 1940. Br. II, 152.
43. Letter to Agnes Meyer. June 18, 1941. Br. II, 198.
44. *Loc. cit.*

8 *World Without Transcendence?*

1. See, for example, the letter to Kurt Martens of March 3, 1899. Br. I, 12.
2. "Lübeck als geistige Lebensform." XI, 394.
3. "Süsser Schlaf." XI, 333.
4. Johann Wolfgang von Goethe, *Faust*, Part II. Act. I, "Anmutige Gegend."
5. Monika Mann, "Papa," in Charles Neider (ed.), *The Stature of Thomas Mann* (New York: New Directions Press, 1947), p. 80.
6. *Doktor Faustus.* VI, 217.
7. *Entstehung.* XI, 289–290.
8. *Doktor Faustus.* VI, 16–17. Settembrini in *The Magic Mountain* had far sharper words of criticism: "Music . . . is the semi-articulate, the irresponsible, the indifferent. . . . Music by itself does nothing to further the progress of the world." *Zauberberg.* III, 160–161. This position is, of course, not to be taken for Mann's own.
9. "Einführung." XI, 611.
10. "Für Bruno Walter." X, 479.
11. Weigand, *op. cit., passim.*
12. "Vom Geist der Medizin." XI, 595.
13. *Loc. cit.*
14. *Zauberberg.* III, 686.
15. "Einführung." XI, 613. Mann has indicated the importance which this positive interpretation of his "hero's" development has for him by frequent repetition. Cf., for example, the letter to Josef Ponten: "He [Hans Castorp] is physically and intellectually in love with death (with mysticism, Ro-

manticism); but this evil love is purified at least in moments of heightened perception into a prescience of a new humanism, which he bears as a seed corn in his heart." Letter of Feb. 5, 1925. Br. I, 232.

16. *Zauberberg.* III, 827.
17. "Einführung." XI, 613.
18. "Nietzsches Philosophie." IX, 711.
19. Lehnert, *op. cit.*, 188–189.
20. Hans Egon Holthusen, *Die Welt ohne Transzendenz: Eine Studie zu Thomas Manns "Doktor Faustus" und seine Nebenschriften* (Hamburg: Ellerman Verlag, 1949).
21. See, for example, Mann's letter to Agnes Meyer of Dec. 25, 1943. Br. II, 343, among others.
22. *Gespräch*, p. 167. Italics Mann's.
23. *Doktor Faustus.* VI, 176.
24. *Gespräch*, p. 164.
25. Letter of Dec. 25, 1943. Br. II, 343.
26. *Entstehung.* XI, 246.
27. *Doktor Faustus.* VI, 26.
28. Erich Kahler, "The Devil Secularized: Thomas Mann's *Faust*," in H. Hatfield, ed., *Thomas Mann: A Collection of Critical Essays.* (Englewood Cliffs, N.J.: Prentice-Hall, 1964), p. 121.
29. *Doktor Faustus.* VI, 350. Italics mine.
30. *Entstehung.* XI, 291.
31. Letter of June 14, 1952. Br. III, 263.
32. *Betrachtungen.* XII, 541. Mann calls the "Protestant-Romantic realm" one "dear and near to his heart"; he was determined to defend it against the Allies' "Jacobinic, Puritanical virtue propaganda." Cf. letter to Hermann Hesse. Feb. 8, 1947. *Briefwechsel*, 123.
33. "This rivalry for the highest prize, this contest between the aesthetic principle [personified in Lorenzo] and the *religious impulse* [personified in Savonarola], between the idea of the eternal feast and the *sanctifying spiritualization of life* for the possession of power and the right to rule," that is, according to Mann, the central theme of the play. In Savonarola Mann sought to portray "an artist . . . who, however, would, at the same time, *be a saint* who would 'make morality possible once again.'" Letter to Karl Bachler. July 8, 1955. Br. III, 408. Italics mine.

34. *Betrachtungen.* XII, 480.
35. *Ibid.,* 407. See also letter to Bruno Walter. July 24, 1917: "With its metaphysical mood, its ethos of 'cross, death, and crypt,' with its combination of music, pessimism, and humor . . . it [the opera *Palestrina*] satisfies my deepest personal needs." Br. I, 137.
36. *Betrachtungen.* XII, 536.
37. *Studien,* 245. See also *Thomas Mann/Heinrich Mann. Briefwechsel, op. cit.,* p. 210.
38. "Joseph und seine Brüder." XI, 656.
39. Letter of Dec. 28, 1926. Br. I, 263. Italics Mann's.
40. Letter to Jonas Lesser. Jan. 23, 1945. Br. II, 410.
41. Letter to Anni Löwenstein. Oct. 27, 1945. Br. II, 455. Italics Mann's.
42. *Loc. cit.*
43. Letter to Gerhard Seger. June 4, 1940. Br. II, 143. In the *Betrachtungen* Mann sets up a definition of his belief, which is certainly not inconsistent with his "religious humanism" of the later years. Here he asks, "What is God? Is He not comprehensiveness, the plastic principle, the omniscient justice, all-embracing love?" and concludes, "Faith in God, that is faith in love, life and in art." *Betrachtungen.* XII, 504.
44. *Doktor Faustus.* VI, 120.
45. Letter to Jonas Lesser. Jan. 23, 1945. Br. II, 410.
46. Letter to Julius Bab. May 30, 1951. Br. III, 210.
47. Letter to Werner Weber. April 6, 1951. Br. III, 201.
48. Letter of November 8, 1950. *Briefwechsel,* 168.
49. Letter to Hans Mühlenstein. Dec. 21, 1950. Br. III, 181.
50. Letter of May 20, 1951. Br. III, 206–207. See also letter of June 7, 1954. Br. III, 345.
51. Lehnert, "Dritter Abschnitt, Lutherstudien," *op. cit.* See also Mann's letter to Agnes Meyer of March 16, 1955. Br. III, 385.
52. *Betrachtungen.* XII, 319.
53. Letter to Siegfried Marck. May 23, 1954. Br. III, 342.
54. *Loc. cit.*
55. "Epilogue," Br. II, 586.
56. *Loc. cit.* As quoted by Erika Mann.

9   *Champion of Humanism*

1. "Im Spiegel." XII, 332.
2. "Deeply shaken, aroused, challenged by shrill voices, I threw myself into the tumult and defended what I felt to be my own in heated debate. But, God is my witness, I shall feel much better again when my soul, cleansed of politics, will once again be free to contemplate life and humanity." *Betrachtungen.* XII, 489.
3. "It is this 'politization of the spirit,' that perversion of the concept of spirit into a meliorative enlightenment [besserische Aufklärung], into a revolutionary philanthropy, that affects me like poison and opiates." *Ibid.,* 31.
4. The position occupied by Mann during the war years is best expressed in the *Betrachtungen:* "From the obvious fact that spirit, philosophy, and truly valuable thinking have no place in politics, there follows the need to *separate* the spiritual life from the political, to send politics on its questionable way and to elevate the life of the spirit to a gay independence of everything political." XII, 269. Italics Mann's. Over against this attitude we have the stance of the mature author succinctly indicated in the following passage from a letter to Hermann Hesse of April 8, 1945: "It is my firm belief that nothing really alive and vital can get around politics in our day and age." *Briefwechsel,* p. 105. See also Br. II, 245. We would single out "Kultur und Politik" (XII, 853–861) as the essay which most faithfully traces Mann's development and defines most precisely his newly acquired attitude as a socially conscious and politically engaged artist. See also *Thomas Mann/Heinrich Mann Briefwechsel,* esp. pp. 206–208.
5. Letter to G. W. Zimmermann. Dec. 7, 1949. Br. III, 118.
6. "Lebensabriss." XI, 136.
7. "Von deutscher Republik." XI, 830–831.
8. *Betrachtungen.* XII, 496f.
9. Pressekonferenz vom 18. November, 1952, "Bekenntnis zur westlichen Welt." XII, 971–972.
10. "Von deutscher Republik." XI, 831.
11. *Betrachtungen.* XII, 494.
12. "Von deutscher Republik." XI, 816.

13. *Loc. cit.* Italics Mann's.

14. "This republican admonition ["Von deutscher Republik"] continues exactly and without a break the line of the *Betrachtungen;* its intellectual convictions are those of that earlier book [*Betrachtungen*], unchanged and unbetrayed." "Von deutscher Republik. Vorwort." XI, 810. Max Rychner had been one of the first to recognize the consistency in Mann's political development. Alfred Andersch has given the analysis of this development, which Mann has singled out as being "of such an amusing and, at the same time, painful truth and insight as [he] had never before experienced and did not hope to experience again." Letter to Andersch of March 23, 1955. Br. III, 388. The essay Mann refers to is Alfred Andersch, "Thomas Mann und die Politik," *Die Blindheit des Kunstwerks und andere Aufsätze* (Frankfurt: Suhrkamp Verlag, 1966).

15. Letter of March 1, 1923. Br. I, 207.

16. *Zauberberg.* III, 906–907.

17. Letter of Jan. 12, 1943. Br. II, 291. Italics Mann's.

18. *Zauberberg.* III, 824.

19. Letter to Franz Silberstein. Dec. 28, 1941. Br. II, 228.

20. Henry Hatfield, "Thomas Mann's *Mario und der Zauberer.* An Introduction," *Germanic Review,* XXI (1946), 306–312.

21. *Mario und der Zauberer.* VIII, 711.

22. *Ibid.,* 702.

23. "Deutsche Ansprache. Ein Appell an die Vernunft." XI, 876.

24. *Ibid.,* 877.

25. *Loc. cit.*

26. Letter to Berthold Viertel. April 2, 1945. Br. II, 423.

27. *Loc. cit.* For an unique instance of Mann's "embarrassed and guilt-ridden" and yet determined effort to discover even in Hitler a "species of the artist [eine Erscheinungsform des Künstlers]" and thus—*sit venia verbo*—a " 'brother,' " see "Bruder Hitler." XII, 845–861.

28. Letter of Jan. 24, 1941. Br. II, 175. Italics Mann's.

29. *Lotte in Weimar.* II, 657–658.

30. *Joseph in Ägypten.* V, 1262–1263.

31. "Franklin Roosevelt." XII, 942.

32. "Joseph und seine Brüder. Ein Vortrag." XI, 658.

33. Letter of Sept. 7, 1941. *Gespräch,* 100.

34. "Joseph und seine Brüder. Ein Vortrag." XI, 658.
35. For Mann's attack on Spengler and his *Decline of the West* (*Untergang des Abendlandes*), see "Über die Lehre Spenglers." X, 172–180.
36. "Joseph und seine Brüder. Ein Vortrag." XI, 667.
37. *Doktor Faustus.* VI, 162.
38. Jacob Taubes, "From Cult to Culture," *Partisan Review,* XXI (July 1954), 387–400.
39. W. F. Michael was the first to point out the identity of Daniel zur Höhe in "Thomas Mann, Ludwig Derleth, Stefan George," *Modern Language Forum,* XXXV (March–June 1950), 35–38.
40. *Doktor Faustus.* VI, 483.
41. "Dieser Krieg." XII, 887.
42. Thomas Mann, "How to Win the Peace." *Atlantic Monthly* (February 1942).
43. Letter of Aug. 27, 1949. Br. III, 95.
44. "An einen jungen Japaner." XII, 969–970. See also "Schicksal und Aufgabe." XII, 934–935.
45. "Meine Zeit." XI, 314.
46. Letter to Agnes Meyer. June 20, 1952. Br. III, 264.
47. "Achtung Europa!" XII, 778–779. See also "Schicksal und Aufgabe." XII, 920. Here Mann calls for "a new humanism which would have the courage to distinguish between right and wrong, and would not be bogged down in the morass of a spiritless relativism."
48. Letter to Hermann Hesse. Feb. 9, 1936. *Briefwechsel,* 63.
49. Letter to Emil Belzner. May 24, 1950. Br. III, 146–147.

Appendix 1

1. Mann's reference is to the author's article "Thomas Mann and Russia." See Bibliography 3.
2. Mann is referring to the author's article "Thomas Mann's *Doctor Faustus:* Prolegomena to an Interpretation." See Bibliography 3.
3. Harry Levin, Professor of Comparative Literature at Harvard University.
4. Mann alludes here to the title of M. Y. Lermontov's famous novel, *A Hero of Our Time.*

5. Theodor W. Adorno, philosopher, sociologist, musicologist, and composer, was of special help to Mann during the work on the novel.
6. *Die Entstehung des Doktor Faustus. Roman eines Romans* (Frankfurt am Main: Bermann-Fischer Verlag, 1949).

SELECTED BIBLIOGRAPHY

The most comprehensive bibliography of Thomas Mann's works to date is Hans Bürgin, *Das Werk Thomas Manns*. Frankfurt am Main: S. Fischer Verlag, 1959.

The two most complete editions of Thomas Mann's works to date are:

1. Hans Bürgin (ed.). *Gesammelte Werke in zwölf Bänden*. Frankfurt am Main: S. Fischer Verlag, 1960.
2. *Gesammelte Werke in zwölf Bänden*. Berlin: Aufbau Verlag, 1955.

BIBLIOGRAPHY 1:
THOMAS MANN'S WORKS IN ENGLISH
TRANSLATION

Novels and Novellas*

Buddenbrooks. Translated by H. T. Lowe-Porter. New York: Knopf, 1924.

Death in Venice. Translated by H. T. Lowe-Porter. London: Martin Secker, 1928.

Royal Highness. A Novel of German Court-Life. Translated by A. Cecil Curts. New York: Knopf, 1916.

Baushan and I. Translated by H. G. Scheffauer. New York: H. Holt, 1923.

The Magic Mountain. Translated by H. T. Lowe-Porter. New York: Knopf, 1927.

Mario and the Magician. Translated by H. T. Lowe-Porter. New York: Knopf, 1931.

Stories of Three Decades. Translated by H. T. Lowe-Porter. London: Secker and Warburg, 1936.

The Tales of Jacob. Translated by H. T. Lowe-Porter. London: Martin Secker, 1934.

* Arranged in order of their appearance in German.

The Young Joseph. Translated by H. T. Lowe-Porter. New York: Knopf, 1935.

Joseph in Egypt. Translated by H. T. Lowe-Porter. New York: Knopf, 1938.

Joseph the Provider. Translated by H. T. Lowe-Porter. New York: Knopf, 1944.

The Tables of the Law. Translated by H. T. Lowe-Porter. New York: Knopf, 1945.

The Beloved Returns. Translated by H. T. Lowe-Porter. New York: Knopf, 1940.

The Transposed Heads. A Legend of India. Translated by H. T. Lowe-Porter. New York: Knopf, 1941.

Doctor Faustus. The Life of the German Composer Adrian Leverkühn as told by a Friend. Translated by H. T. Lowe-Porter. New York: Knopf, 1948.

The Holy Sinner. Translated by H. T. Lowe-Porter. New York: Knopf, 1951.

The Black Swan. Translated by Willard R. Trask. New York: Knopf, 1954.

Confessions of Felix Krull, Confidence Man. Memoirs. Part I. Translated by Denver Linley. New York: Knopf, 1955.

Essays and Speeches*

Three Essays. Translated by H. T. Lowe-Porter. London: Martin Secker, 1932. Contents: "Goethe and Tolstoy"; "Frederick and the Great Alliance"; "Occult Experiences."

Past Masters and Other Papers. Translated by H. T. Lowe-Porter. New York: Knopf, 1932. Contents: "The Sufferings and Greatness of Richard Wagner"; "Epilogue to Goethe's *Elective Affinities*"; "Speech on Lessing"; "Nietzsche and Music"; "Dürer"; "Tolstoy"; "Freud's Position in the Modern History of Ideas"; "Culture and Socialism"; "On the Teachings of Spengler"; "Preface to Joseph Conrad's 'Secret Agent' "; "Cosmopolitanism"; "On the Film"; "Sleep, Sweet Sleep."

Freud, Goethe, Wagner. Three Essays. Translated by H. T. Lowe-Porter and Rita Mathias-Reil. New York: Knopf, 1937.

* Arranged in order of their appearance in English translation.

Order of the Day. Political Essays and Speeches of Two Decades. Translated by H. T. Lowe-Porter, A. E. Meyer, and E. Sutton. New York: Knopf, 1942. Contents: "The German Republic"; "An Appeal to Reason"; "Europe Beware!"; "I Stand with the Spanish People"; "Mass und Wert"; "An exchange of Letters"; "The Coming Victory of Democracy"; "A Brother"; "What I Believe"; "This Peace"; "This War"; "Culture and Politics"; "The War and the Future"; "Thinking and Living"; "Address before the Emergency Rescue Committee"; "Niemöller."

Listen, Germany! Twenty-five Radio-Messages to the German People over B.B.C. New York: Knopf, 1943.

Germany and the Germans: An Address Delivered in the Coolidge Auditorium of the Library of Congress, May 29, 1945. Washington, D.C.: U. S. Government Printing Office, 1945.

Nietzsche's Philosophy in the Light of Contemporary Events: An Address Delivered in the Coolidge Auditorium of the Library of Congress, April 9, 1947. Washington, D.C.: U. S. Government Printing Office, 1947.

Essays of Three Decades. Translated by H. T. Lowe-Porter. London: Secker and Warburg, 1947. Contents: "Goethe's *Faust*"; "Goethe's Career as a Man of Letters"; "Goethe as a Representative of the Bourgeois Age"; "Anna Karenina"; "Lessing"; "Kleist's *Amphitryon*"; "Chamisso"; "Platen"; "Theodor Storm"; "The Old Fontane"; "Suffering and Greatness of Richard Wagner"; "Richard Wagner and the *Ring*"; "Schopenhauer"; "Freud and the Future"; "Voyage with Don Quixote."

BIBLIOGRAPHY 2:
BOOKS ON THOMAS MANN IN ENGLISH
AND GERMAN

The most complete bibliographies to date of secondary sources on Thomas Mann are:

1. Jonas, Klaus W. (ed.). *Fifty Years of Thomas Mann Studies.* Minneapolis: University of Minneapolis Press, 1955.
2. Jonas, Klaus W. and Ilsedore B. Jonas (eds.). *Thomas*

Mann Studies. Vol. 2. Philadelphia: University of Pennsylvania Press, 1967.

Altenberg, Paul. *Die Romane Thomas Manns: Versuch einer Deutung.* Bad Homburg: Gentner, 1961.

Andersch, Alfred. "Thomas Mann und die Politik," in Alfred Andersch, *Die Blindheit des Kunstwerks und andere Aufsätze.* Frankfurt am Main: Suhrkamp, 1966.

Baumgart, Reinhard. *Das Ironische und die Ironie in den Werken Thomas Manns.* Munich: Karl Hauser, 1964.

Bergsten, Gunilla. *Thomas Manns Doktor Faustus. Untersuchungen zu den Quellen und zur Struktur des Romans.* Stockholm: Bonnier, 1963.

Blume, Bernhard. *Thomas Mann und Goethe.* Berne: Francke Verlag, 1949.

Brennen, Joseph Gerard. *Three Philosophical Novelists: Joyce, Gide, Mann.* New York: Macmillan, 1964.

————. *Thomas Mann's World.* New York: Columbia University Press, 1942.

Eichner, Hans. *Thomas Mann: Eine Einführung in sein Werk.* Berne: Francke Verlag, 1953.

Eloesser, Arthur. *Thomas Mann: Sein Leben und sein Werk.* Berlin: Fischer, 1925.

Flinker, Martin. *Thomas Manns Politische Betrachtungen im Lichte der heutigen Zeit.* s-Grevenhage: Mouton, 1959.

Hamburger, Käte. *Thomas Manns Roman "Joseph und seine Brüder:" Eine Einführung.* Stockholm: Bermann-Fischer, 1945.

————. *Thomas Mann und die Romantik: Eine problemgeschichtliche Studie.* Berlin: Junker, 1932.

Hatfield, Henry. *Thomas Mann.* New York: New Directions, 1951.

————. *Thomas Mann: A Collection of Critical Essays.* Englewood Cliffs, N.J.: Prentice-Hall, 1964.

Heller, Erich. *The Ironic German: A Study of Thomas Mann.* Boston, Toronto: Little Brown, 1958.

Heller, Peter. *Dialectics and Nihilism: Essays on Lessing, Nietzsche, Mann and Kafka.* Amherst: University of Massachusetts Press, 1966.

Hofman, Alois. *Thomas Mann und die Welt der russischen Literatur.* Berlin: Akademie-Verlag, 1967.

Holthusen, Hans Egon. *Die Welt ohne Transzendenz: Eine Studie zu Thomas Manns Doktor Faustus und seinen Nebenschriften.* Hamburg: Ellerman, 1949.

Hommage de la France à Thomas Mann. Paris: Flinker, 1955.

Kaufmann, Fritz. *Thomas Mann: The World as Will and Representation.* Boston: Beacon Press, 1957.

Lehnert, Herbert. *Thomas Mann: Fiktion, Mythos, Religion.* Stuttgart: Kohlhammer Verlag, 1965.

Lesser, Jonas. *Thomas Mann in der Epoche seiner Vollendung.* Munich: Kurt Desch, 1952.

Lukács, Georg. *Thomas Mann.* Berlin: Aufbau, 1950.

Mann, Erika. *Das Letzte Jahr: Bericht über meinen Vater.* Berlin: Fischer, 1956.

Mann, Heinrich. "Mein Bruder," in Heinrich Mann, *Ein Zeitalter wird besichtigt.* Berlin: Aufbau, 1947.

Mann, Monika. *Vergangenes und Gegenwärtiges: Erinnerungen.* Munich: Kindler, 1956.

Mann, Victor. *Wir Waren Fünf: Bildnis der Familie Mann.* Constance: Südverlag, 1949.

Mayer, Hans. *Thomas Mann: Sein Leben und sein Werk.* Berlin: Volk und Welt, 1950.

Peacock, Ronald. *Das Leitmotiv bei Thomas Mann.* Bonn: Haupt, 1934.

Scherrer, Paul, and Hans Wysling. *Thomas Mann Studien.* Vol. 1: *Quellenkritische Studien zum Werk Thomas Manns.* Berne, Munich: Francke Verlag, 1967.

Schröter, Klaus. *Thomas Mann in Selbstzeugnissen und Bilddokumenten.* Reinbeck bei Hamburg: Rowohlt, 1964.

────── (ed.). *Thomas Mann im Urteil seiner Zeit.* Hamburg: Christian Wegener Verlag, 1969.

Venohr, Lilli. *Thomas Manns Verhältnis zur russischen Literatur: Frankfurter Abhandlungen zur Slawistik.* Vol. 1. Meisenheim: Hain, 1959.

Weigand, Hermann J. *Thomas Mann's Novel "Der Zauberberg": A Study.* New York: Appleton, 1933.

BIBLIOGRAPHY 3:
ESSAYS ON THOMAS MANN

The most complete listings of essays on Thomas Mann are:
1. Jonas, Klaus W. (ed.), *Fifty Years of Thomas Mann Studies*. Minneapolis: University of Minneapolis Press, 1955.
2. Jonas, Klaus W. and Ilsedore B. Jonas (eds.). *Thomas Mann Studies*. Vol. 2. Philadelphia: University of Pennsylvania Press, 1967.

Blume, Bernhard. "Aspects of Contradiction: On Recent Criticisms Of Thomas Mann," in H. Hatfield (ed.), *Thomas Mann: A Collection of Critical Essays*. Englewood Cliffs, N.J.: Prentice-Hall, 1964.

Beharriell, Frederick J. "Psychology in the Early Works of Thomas Mann," *Publications of the Modern Language Association*, Vol. 77 (March 1962).

Blackmur, Richard P. "Parody and Critique: Notes on Thomas Mann's *Doctor Faustus*," *Eleven Essays in the European Novel*. New York: Harcourt Brace & World, 1964.

Butler, E. M. "The Traditional Elements in Thomas Mann's *Doctor Faustus*," *Publications of the English Goethe Society*, Vol. 18 (February 1949).

Cassirer, Ernst. "Thomas Manns Goethebild: Eine Studie über *Lotte in Weimar*," *Germanic Review*, Vol. 20 (October 1945).

Daemmrich, Horst. "Friedrich Schiller und Thomas Mann: Parallels in Aesthetics," *Journal of Aesthetics and Art Criticism*, Vol. 24 (December 1965).

Gronicka, André von. "Thomas Mann and Russia," in Charles Neider (ed.), *The Stature of Thomas Mann*. New York: New Directions, 1947. Unabridged in *Germanic Review*, Vol. 20 (April 1945).

————. "Myth plus Psychology: A Style Analysis of Thomas Mann's *Death in Venice*," in H. Hatfield (ed.), *Thomas Mann: A Collection of Critical Essays*. Englewood Cliffs, N.J.: Prentice-Hall, 1964. Unabridged in *Germanic Review*, Vol. 31 (October 1956).

―――. "Thomas Manns *Doktor Faustus*. Prolegomena to an Interpretation," *Germanic Review*, Vol. 23 (October 1948).

―――. "Ein Symbolisches Formelwort in Thomas Manns *Zauberberg*," *Germanic Review*, Vol. 23 (April 1948).

Hatfield, Henry. "Thomas Mann's *Mario und der Zauberer*. An Introduction," in Charles Neider (ed.), *The Stature of Thomas Mann*. New York: New Directions, 1947. First appeared in *Germanic Review*, Vol. 21 (December 1946).

―――. "Religion in Thomas Mann's *Joseph and His Brothers*," *Graduate Journal of Boston University*, Vol. 15 (Fall 1967).

Heller, Peter. "Some Functions of the 'Leitmotiv' in Thomas Mann's *Joseph* Tetralogy," *Germanic Review*, Vol. 22 (April 1947).

Kahler, Erich. "The Devil Secularized: Thomas Mann's *Faust*," in H. Hatfield (ed.), *Thomas Mann: A Collection of Critical Essays*. Englewood Cliffs, N.J.: Prentice-Hall, 1964.

Mann, Erika and Klaus Mann. "Portrait of Our Father Thomas Mann," *Atlantic Monthly*, Vol. 163 (April 1939).

Mautner, Franz. "Die griechischen Anklänge in Thomas Manns *Der Tod in Venedig*," *Monatshefte*, Vol. 44 (January 1952).

Michael, Wolfgang. "Thomas Mann, Ludwig Derleth, Stefan George," *Modern Language Forum*, Vol. 35 (March–June 1950).

―――. "Thomas Mann auf dem Weg zu Freud," *Modern Language Notes*, Vol. 65 (March 1950).

Müller, Joachim. "Thomas Manns 'Doktor Faustus'. Grundthematik und Motivgefüge," *Euphorion*, Neue Folge, Vol. 54 (March 1960).

Politzer, Heinz. "Of Time and Doctor Faustus," *Monatshefte*, Vol. 51 (April–May 1959).

Seidlin, Oskar. "Picaresque Elements in Thomas Mann's Work," *Modern Language Quarterly*, Vol. 12 (June 1951).

Taubes, Jacob. "From Cult to Culture," *Partisan Review*, Vol. 21 (July 1954).

Van Doren, Mark. "Joseph and his Brethren. A Comedy in Four Parts," in H. Hatfield (ed.), *Thomas Mann: A Collection of Critical Essays*. Englewood Cliffs, N.J.: Prentice-Hall, 1964.

Venable, Vernon. "Poetic Reason in Thomas Mann," in Charles Neider (ed.), *The Stature of Thomas Mann*. New York: New Directions Press, 1947.

Walter, Bruno. "Thomas Mann," *Theme and Variations. An Autobiography.* New York: Knopf, 1946.

Weigand, Hermann J. "Thomas Mann's Gregorious," *Germanic Review,* Vol. 27 (February–May 1952).

————. "Thomas Mann's *Royal Highness* as Symbolic Autobiography," in H. Hatfield (ed.), *Thomas Mann: A Collection of Critical Essays,* Englewood Cliffs, N.J.: Prentice-Hall, 1964.

Wysling, Hans. "Die Technik der Montage: Zu Thomas Manns *Erwähltem," Euphorion,* Vol. 57 (January–February 1963).

INDEX

THE WORKS OF THOMAS MANN (English titles)

ABOUT THE AUTHOR

André von Gronicka is Professor and Chairman of the Department of Germanic Languages and Literature at the University of Pennyslvania where he has taught since 1962. He received his B.A. and his M.A. from the University of Rochester, where he was elected to Phi Beta Kappa, and his Ph.D. from Columbia University. Professor von Gronicka's area of specialization is Russo-German literary relations, the modern German drama, and Thomas Mann. He was granted, among others, the Fulbright, the Guggenheim, and the American Council of Learned Societies Fellowships. A frequent contributor to various journals such as *Germanic Review*, *German Quarterly*, *PMLA*, and *Comparative Literature*, he has also had articles accepted for the anthologies *The Stature of Thomas Mann*, edited by Charles Neider, and *Twentieth Century Views: Thomas Mann*, edited by Henry Hatfield. He is the author of *Henry von Heiseler: A Russo-German Writer*, *Essentials of Russian*, and *The Russian Image of Goethe*.